Nick Mauss
Dispersed Events.

Selected Writings

After 8 Books

Dispersed Events.
Selected Writings of Nick Mauss

Editors: Antonia Carrara and Benjamin Thorel
Design: Marco Caroti

Published by After 8 Books, Paris

With the support of:
303 Gallery, New York
Galerie Chantal Crousel, Paris
Shelley Fox Aarons and Philip Aarons

Distributed in Asia and the Americas
by ARTBOOK | D.A.P.
www.artbook.com

Distributed in the UK by Art Data
www.artdata.co.uk

Distributed in France and Belgium by Interart
www.interart.fr

Printed by Tallinn Book Printers (Estonia)
First printing

After 8 Books
7 rue Jarry, F–75010 Paris
www.after8books.com

Texts by Nick Mauss, Lynne Cooke
© The authors

ISBN 978-2-492650-09-3
Dépôt légal: Avril 2024

Nick Mauss
Dispersed Events.

Selected Writings

Foreword by
Lynne Cooke

Edited by
Antonia Carrara
Benjamin Thorel

After 8 Books

TABLE OF CONTENTS

TABLE OF CONTENTS

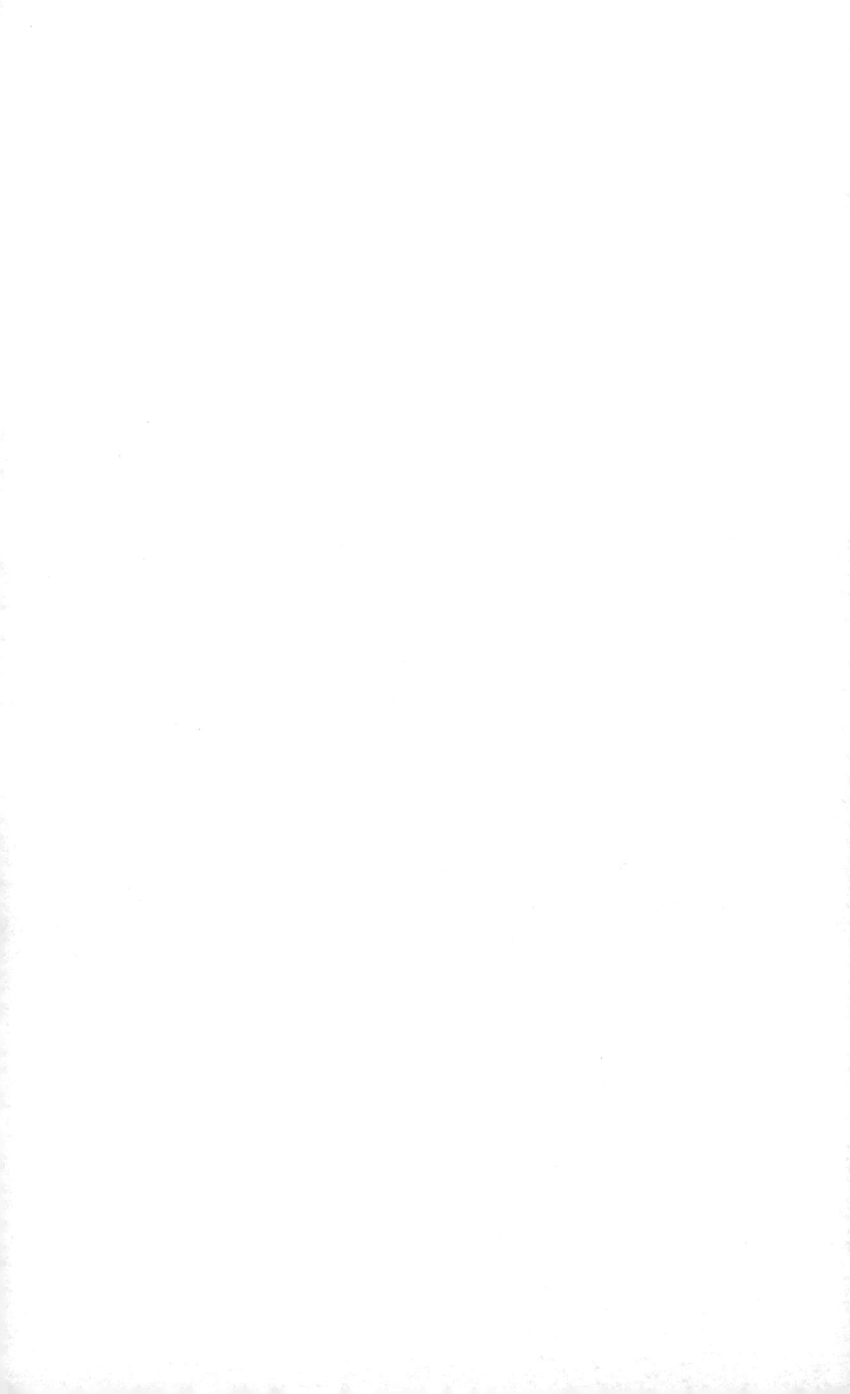

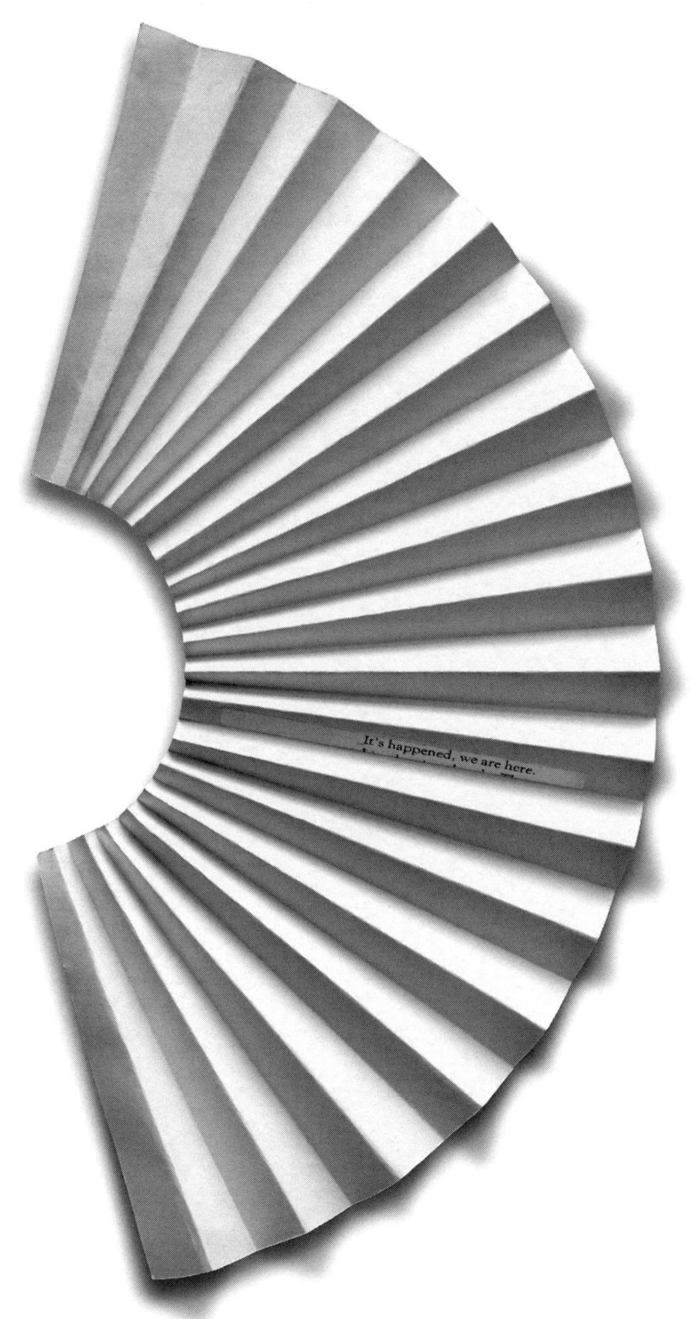
It's happened, we are here.

An Infectious Swarm
by Lynne Cooke

Couturiers, dramaturges, photographers, choreographers, art historians, filmmakers, and artists (past and present), are but some of *Dispersed Events'* many subjects. Among what might initially appear, following the author, "a wildly inscrutable web of lineages," the reader quickly perceives unexpected, unheralded, conjunctions: affiliations, alignments, and affinities. "I Always See Relationships," reads the telling header to one of the book's entries.

In "Gesturing Personae" Nick Mauss limns the formation of his vision: ". . . my interest in dance was kindled at about the same time [c. 2001] that I had begun to grow suspicious of a naturalized art-historical canon. The discrepancy between that canon and my own interests or possible artistic antecedents drove me to fashion a new frame of reference for myself."[1] That genealogy manifested not only in writing but in his art practice and in exhibition-making. "I began to pull at loose threads

---

1. "Gesturing Personae" was first published in the catalogue accompanying *Transmissions*, Mauss' 2018 exhibition at the Whitney Museum of American Art. See pages 289–90.

in the modernist narrative," he went on, "and these drew my attention to theater, couture, architecture, and decoration, as well as to practitioners who were seldom or no longer spoken of but who opened up worlds outside given categorical limits." Informed and shaped by parallel developments in the larger cultural arena, Mauss' trajectory involved foregrounding "performance, collaboration and intersecting media," and "casting about for gay antecedents who had not been prepackaged." Each text comprises a wealth of interwoven discoveries, analyses, and ideas whose goal is neither the recuperation of overlooked practitioners, nor the writing of "minor histories," but something more ambitious: a revisionist Modernist narrative. Essay by essay, he weaves a richly textured tapestry of mid-century American Modernism. In a bold inversion of the long-entrenched status quo among art-forms, Mauss places ballet at its apex. Newly conceived in a nativist idiom, it drew on the cross-disciplinary talents of a cadre of cosmopolitan evangelists who included luminaries Lincoln Kirstein and Florine Stettheimer, others like George Platt Lynes barely recognized today, and, not least, Christian "Bébé" Bérard, the virtuosic French designer/painter who once "bridged every world" including MoMA's inner circles.

A second constellation coalesces toward the century's end. Spurning "the logics of masculinity and homogeneity", their compass spans Nicholas Moufarrege's embroidered canvases, Jochen Klein's "paintings against the straight mind," Ian White's "pulverized" lecture-performances, Lorraine O'Grady's racialized artworks, and renegade designs by Susan Cianciolo. "The story goes," Mauss notes, that Cianciolo left the fashion system at the moment it claimed her, when her brand marketability was burgeoning." Adopting the art gallery as her stage, she deployed "fashion as an exploratory vehicle" in transgressive "re-imaginings of spectatorship, consumption and collaboration."

In ever-shifting ways, dialogic relations between authorship and receivership lie at the heart of Mauss's project. While he attends carefully to each creator's intentions, he nonetheless hews to the viewer's vantage, teasing out how the work is remade by its audiences, how publics are assembled. Enlivened by asides and anecdotes—references to Temple Grandin on animal behavior, Jonathan Crary on "impossible temporalities," and a cushion cover featuring Roy Lichtenstein's painting of a ball of twine, embroidered by "Mrs. Leo Castelli"—his lively texts keep the reader on their toes. As he defines "[his] own context within and against one that was already given," he speaks conversationally, companionably. Eschewing polemic, he brings his audiences along through vivid ekphrasis, granular close-reading and lucid argument.

The essays originate variously. Several subjects had, as Mauss puts it, "a way of "appearing unannounced": "Asleep in a footnote, pinned to the background, a name suddenly everywhere, until the din of recurrence reaches a frequency so startling I wake up to the fact of an unshakeable presence." Invitations and commissions also provided points of departure, not least for a masterly reading of Anne Teresa de Keersmaeker's *Work/Travail/Arbeid*. Exhibitions yet others. Indeed, some of his most impassioned writing was generated by an incomparable retrospective of the work of Madame Grès at the Musée Bourdelle, which profoundly marked him. "Beyond the shadow of a doubt, Madame Grès . . . was one of the most exceptional sculptors of the twentieth century, an age in which both couture and genius died," he asserts; "the depth of her influence is yet to be truly understood." Late in an illustrious decades-long career, Grès lost control of her maison. The loss, Mauss contends, was more than that of a genre-defying couturier, for hers was "a practice of unmatched profundity and rigor, beyond the realm of fashion." Like hers, his practice of learning by doing is self-directed and speculative. It generates a conviction that, in the best sense, is partisan. Singular, independent, illuminating. ◆

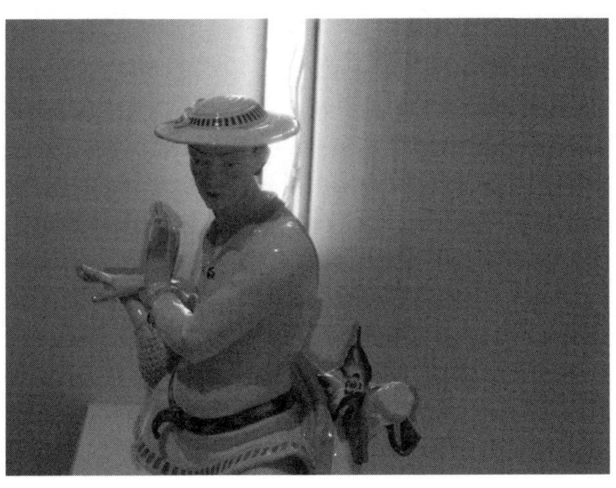

*This interview between Nick Mauss and the editors
of the book—Antonia Carrara and Benjamin Thorel—
was realized by email in fall 2023.*

The Indirection of Influence: A Conversation with Nick Mauss

— *First, very pragmatically: how did you come around to writing about other artists' work? Was there a defining moment in which you felt that it was necessary or relevant to engage in writing?*

— It was an invitation that really catalyzed my writing, and here I have to give full credit to Tim Griffin, who asked me to contribute a text to *Artforum* in 2008. My work at that point was very literary, but reticent, and I didn't identify as a writer; but I knew Tim as a poet and understood his gesture on those terms. In retrospect, his open invitation was decisive in that it forced me to decide how I wanted to participate—or intervene—in the magazine and, by extension, in the world of art it described. My response was to write what I needed, and that meant introducing other subjects, and a different approach, to assert something in this context that I wouldn't usually find there.

I wrote my first feature on Jochen Klein, whose work was already a crucial touchstone for me, but not well-known. When I saw the 2008 Klein survey at the Pinakothek der Moderne in Munich[1] the paintings almost dictated themselves to me, giving me license to explore art history, personal poetics, and queer politics on my own terms. To suddenly tap into a parallel process like that, and to reveal the intensity of my response to a body of work, was very energizing, and illuminated something about my own work. I was writing ekphrastically (before I even understood what that could mean), developing a referentially dissonant style through the experience of looking, feeling, and trying to understand the span of Klein's work, and ultimately, to invent a context for myself as a viewer and an artist. "Abandoned Painting" became my refusal of a dominant painting discourse, and a way for me to make sense of, and declare, my own stance.

My second feature, on Lorraine O'Grady, was written in response to the relative lack of attention accorded her work at the time, despite a renewed emphasis on performance in the early 2000s (by an art world still unwilling to address its tacit racism). This has been a continuous impulse: to write the texts that might otherwise not get written, in order to give weight to certain practices—which in turn becomes a way to understand my own priorities.

— *Several of the texts gathered in the present book were first published in magazines; however they often seem to be part of a conversation with the artist, or to be first and foremost driven by your own interest for a certain topic.*

1. The exhibition *Jochen Klein* at the Pinakothek der Moderne (March 6–June 8, 2008) was curated by Bernhart Schwenk in collaboration with Wolfgang Tillmans.

— My first essays coincided with the first exhibitions I organized, which brought together work by artists I respected with artists no longer living, or no longer known. You asked about necessity, and I think I turned to these two branching processes—writing and making exhibitions—as a way to elaborate the conditions of making beyond what I made alone in the studio, because it felt necessary and more accurate to present my work as indebted to, or enmeshed with others'. I longed to see exhibitions that were not bracketed generationally, secured by "themes," or limited by medium-specificity, but that reflected how art is actually made, and how people actually relate to artworks, or to one another, meaning: exhibitions structured by contingency, affection, caricature, ventriloquism, homage, critique, inversion, etc. Making exhibitions gave me a sense of agency, and writing was also a form of learning in public—as someone who did not go to graduate school, I found these other ways to continue to initiate dialogues, generate knowledge, and create a framework for myself.

Besides the texts I published in magazines or journals, I started writing for catalogs on artists who had already inflected my work, such as Florine Stettheimer, or Isa Genzken.[2] And in some instances, public talks I'd given on the occasion of monographic exhibitions or film screenings were turned into texts for publication in another context. For example, a screening of Werner Schroeter's *Eika Katappa* (1969) I'd introduced at Light Industry in 2021 then turned into a meditation on mis-alignment in Schroeter's work published in *October* a year later. I'm no good at writing on assignment, even (or especially)

2. Along with other artists, Nick Mauss contributed to the monograph *Isa Genzken* (Bolzano: Museion & Milano: Mousse Publishing, 2010).

if someone has tried to find a good subject "for" me. In that sense, the writing has always been very close to how I arrive at my work. I need to go through the first-hand experience of encountering an artist, a practice, an irritation, an exhibition, or finding a dropped stitch in the fabric of history; then I start worrying over it, and other associations come into play, and eventually this may grow into a piece of writing. It doesn't happen the other way around. Of course every once in a while, a specific prompt can also coax something unexpected. When Caroline Busta invited me to contribute to a *Texte zur Kunst* issue on the theme of "The Canon," I tried to think of a contemporary practice that simultaneously addressed and resisted processes of canonization, and I recalled a trilogy of performances by the late—and uncategorizable—Ian White that had made a very deep impression on me, and in that same recollection I first articulated my skepticism towards the fashion for belated canonization of certain queer artists.

— *Is writing something that you do on a regular basis, or is it connected to specific encounters or stages in your work? Do you keep notes, like a journal?*

— I write in waves, but I also make my work in waves, and sometimes they overlap. I keep a dispassionate journal—so the writing in this collection is strangely more personal. I take notes, write skeletons of texts; by now I have many beginnings of things that may never be finished, or could collapse into something else in the future—it's not systematic, always multiple things running in the back of my mind. In a lot of these texts you'll notice an individual artist becoming a portmanteau for others. I've always been interested in locating nodes, points of contact, jumping-off points, multiplying linkages, and seeing how these might create a structure. There are cameo appearances and walk-ons, such as Tina Chow in the text on Madame Grès, or Brigid Berlin in the text on Ian White. A feedback loop emerges between my writing and my work. Recurring strains of thought around fashion, theatricality, representation, painting, performance, decoration, cinema, after-image, and historical transmission—but oftentimes I won't know how a text relates to my work until much later, these things can be very indirect. In the 2010 review I wrote about two concurrent transatlantic exhibitions centered on textiles I first came across the (false) category "bizarre silks" which ultimately erupted into one of my own exhibitions almost a decade later.[3] The writing has taught me something about incubation, durations and delays in my own process.

— *What's at stake in your writing is to propose new approaches to the history of art: you suggest alternative narratives, shedding a new light on scenes and artists to create a different picture.*

— Who can take history for granted? That was never an option for me. There were just too many oversights, absences, and cover-ups, so I felt compelled early on to piece my own histories together. I remember in art school I was only reading outdated art magazines, going back as far as the 1920s—marveling at their language, stumbling over names in advertisements, and asking myself: What *is* this? Why don't I *know* this?

---

3. *Bizarre Silks, Private Imaginings and Narrative Facts, etc.*, presented at Kunsthalle Basel (February 7–September 20, 2020) included works by Gretchen Bender, Felix Bernstein and Gabe Rubin, William S. Burroughs and Brion Gysin, James Ensor, Hannah Höch, Ray Johnson, Ketty La Rocca, Rosemery Mayer, Nick Mauss, Robert Morris, Ken Okiishi, Edward Owens, Anton Perich, Georgia Sagri, Bea Schlingelhoff, Megan Francis Sullivan, and further anonymous works. See "In Anticipation of a Body," pages 289–90.

— A prominent question in your thinking is also to acknowledge and unearth the role of queerness in the history of art practices.

— I went looking for queer subjects out of desperation, trying to find the queer art history behind the blockade of straight art history, and I found what in German are called *Schlüsselfiguren* ("key figures," or "figures of unlocking"), who give the lie to narratives of historical coherence. And I noticed that a focus on such figures demands that everything around them shuffles into a new order, and that became a crucial dynamic in my work: reconfiguration, and the dizzying realization that history can be turned inside-out. I often return to the temporal juncture just before a language around queerness emerges—what José Esteban Muñoz refers to as "a kind of queer potentiality that existed before the stultifying effects of some identitarian narratives installed after the modern gay movement took hold."[4] Because it is so rich with unnameable behaviors that don't align with our clichés about liberation, and emphasizes queerness as historically specific and fluctuating, in need of constant reinvention. My task is not so much to find queerness in art history, but to tell art history as queer history, which sometimes can mean writing against the way queer histories are narrativized. (I would argue, for example, that there is no such thing as "queer modernism," but that there can be no modernism that is not queer.)

— Today, artists like you are more engaged in doing this work than art historians . . . How, or why (!) can an artist do it differently than an academic?

4. José Esteban Muñoz, *Cruising Utopia: The Then and There of Queer Futurity* (New York: New York University Press, 2009), 86.

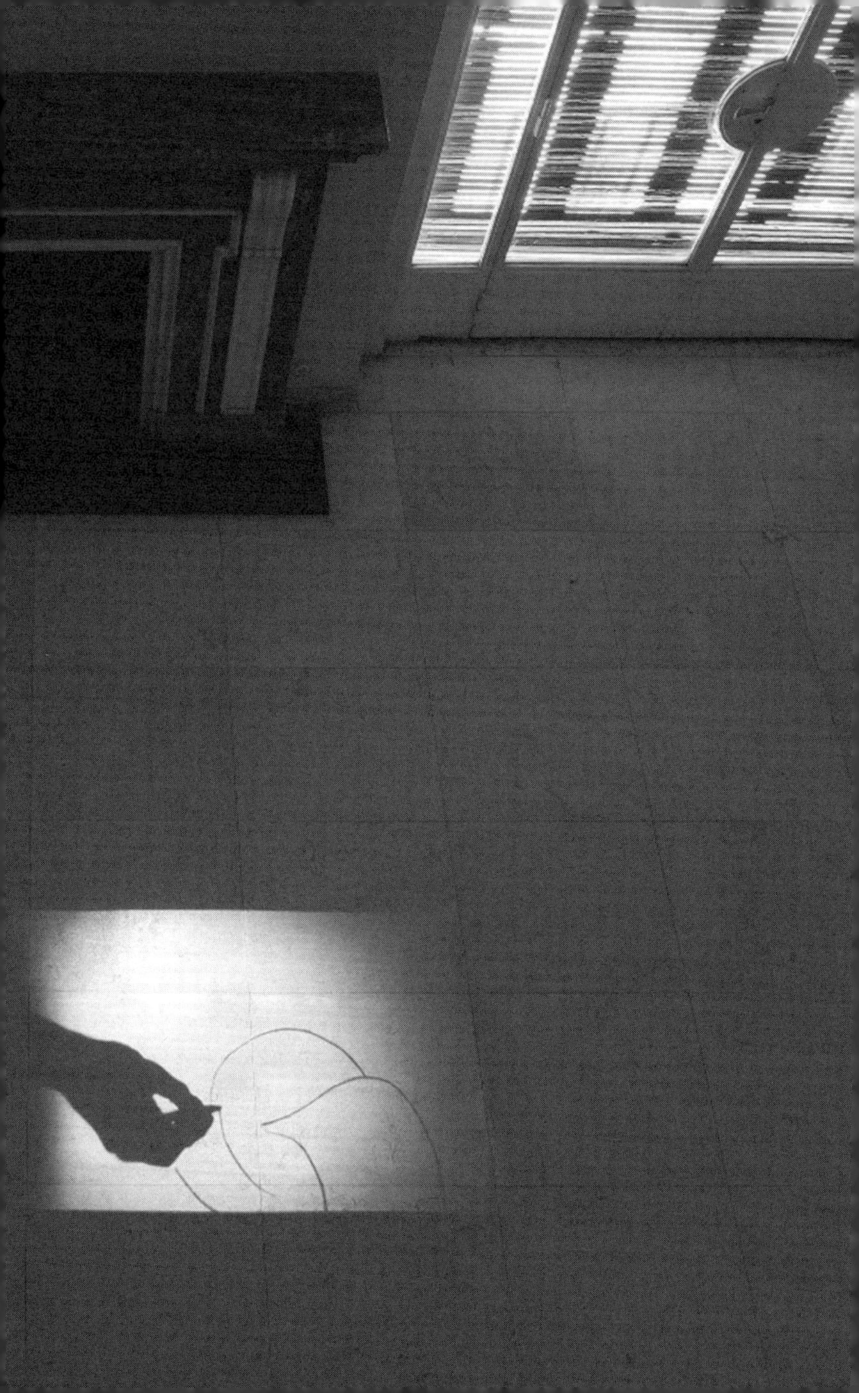

— I know how things are made in a very innate way—that's perhaps the main difference—I can embody the process. At the same time I like not being an expert—I trust in the knowledges and curiosities I bring to a subject that is unfamiliar. But I've also tried to develop a particular rigor—in part because I give weight to subjects that have been overlooked or dismissed, without wanting to accept the notion of "minor histories." I went from writing as a form of "close reading" to working in archives with conservators, conducting oral histories as well as material research and finding other approaches that help me see the subject, how it has been put in a limiting frame, and how we might see it again, against our misconceptions. But I resist linking this way of working to what has come to be known as "research-based-practice" in art, a mode that often falls back on normative methodologies to achieve a false authority dressed up as art. There's a strong intuitive dimension to how I move through someone else's work. I sense their influences and follow those traces in multiple directions. I think about this as "the indirection of influence," in reference to these irregular and oblique pathways, and to the ways in which works of art tend to reflect compounded influences refracted by images, text, performance, after-images, but also gossip, incident, misunderstanding, memory and false memory.

— *The notion of "research-based" work has become a genre by itself, that seems less connected to the determination of one's work and practice, than it is connected to grant systems and the necessity for institutions to find legitimacy through the language of academia! The connection you make between research, intuition, and influence, suggests of course a different dynamics. Maybe it is worth discussing a bit more this notion of "practice"?*

— What most people call research feels to me like being lost. The pleasure lies in working with uncertainty, inventing ways of doing, constructing new archives, but not necessarily arriving. To paraphrase Tirza T. Latimer, every subject demands its own unorthodox methods.[5] These are processes that, like making, can be unending and don't lead to answers, but generate more questions. So I deny the closure connoted by "research" as a self-legitimizing function. I'm trying to find attitudes that are unfamiliar, that may lead me very far away from where I am.

If you scan the list of subjects in this collection, they appear very different from one another, but in the course of reading, they begin to interrelate, and I think those new forms of interrelation are an important cumulative effect that I only see now as I read across them. The text on Stettheimer, for example, folds in Bernadette Mayer anachronically, and it is Bernadette who would lead me, years later, towards her sister Rosemary Mayer. Similarly, the essay on Jochen Klein already calls out Moufarrege and Christian Bérard, but it would take a few years for me to understand how to involve Bérard in my work, or, as I said before, how to write about Nicolas Moufarrege. I think of writing and many of the exhibitions I've made as proposing genealogies rather than "alternative narratives"—genealogies that help me make sense of certain interrelationships beyond linear history or direct causality, towards other forms of relating. The introduction I gave to Thomas Beard's 2016 screening of Jean Cocteau, Kenneth Anger, and Jean Genet's "pre-queer" films at Lincoln Center enacts a type of genealogical mapping by treating the films as interconnected spaces. Similarly, the texts I

5. See Tirza T. Latimer, *Eccentric Modernisms: Making Differences in the History of American Art* (Berkeley & Los Angeles: University of California Press, 2016), 1.

wrote in 2022 on drawings by Jean Cocteau, Andy Warhol, and Ray Johnson function as vignettes that are stitched together, intimating a type of discourse between the works. In a text accompanying my 2010 exhibition *Bloodflames III*, I described this as an impetus to "[lash] together works which previously had no reason to be related, but which by now had no other possible way of making sense."[6]

I make things with my hands, with other artists, musicians, performers, curators, and historians; I draw, invent supports, think with distinct materials, create spaces, movement scores, books, and exhibitions. But writing has been an important way to investigate practices that nourished me, that I gravitated towards because they served as models or resonated with questions I had about my own work. That is how I arrived at a sense of an expanded practice, opening up a space beyond stable self-definition as an artist, towards a form of engagement foregrounding history, dialogue, collaboration, influence, perhaps a kind of loss of contour of single authorship, by pointing to processes that take place outside the work, but are intrinsic to it.

— *You insist that your curatorial work and your writing aren't separate endeavors, but an integral part of your artist's work, of your practice—implying that one's practice determines itself without necessary relying on a medium, on the studio, or a unique method. It's so interesting to see that this concern is already present in that first text you wrote about Jochen Klein: you insist on the cogency of his work as a determined whole, in spite of (or thanks to) its contradictions. You sum up this notion*

6. Press release for the exhibition *Bloodflames III*, presented at Alex Zachary, New York (October 9–November 6, 2010).

in a very precise phrase: "Art as a space for interpersonal artic- ulations of politics and love: a plea." This notion of the "inter- personal" seems very accurate: Would you say that writing has proved to be an important "tool" to activate or expand such ar- ticulations/connections? To examine or acknowledge the role of "influences"?

— Rather than conveniently compartmentalizing, it's precise- ly this questioning of practice—how practice is defined, or de- stabilized—that I am interested in. As you can see in this book, I'm drawn to artists who span disciplines and multiply roles: Stettheimer, working in painting, poetry, designs for the stage and for her home/studio; Moufarrege, the artist, critic, and cu- rator; Schroeter fusing of opera, cinema, and literature; Mayer collapsing translation, illuminated writing, drawing, architec- ture, textiles and painting.

Emmelyn Butterfield-Rosen has written that, in relation to my work, "the word 'influence' should be interpreted in a his- trionic and etymological sense: it carries the connotations of liquid movement, contagion, influenza, emanations from the stars, even possession, a *Beinflussungsapparat*."[7] I love the sense she conveys of influence as uncontainable, and omnidi- rectional, and yes, I think that the interpersonal can have this kind of dimensionality as well. In my experience, writing has often led to encounters that would otherwise have been fore- closed, and set off certain reactions: for example, my 2009

7. Emmelyn Butterfield-Rosen, "Fanfare. Merry Christmas!," in *Nick Mauss: Ges- chenkpapiere*, ed. kunstzeitraum (London: Koenig Books, 2010), 135. The *Beinflussung- sapparat*—or "Influencing Machine"—was described by Austrian psychoanalyst Victor Tausk in 1918, as an imaginary, remotely controlled technical apparatus, that some pa- tients suffering from schizophrenia accused to be in control of their thoughts and bodies, influencing their behaviors.

essay on Lorraine O'Grady grew out of her participation in my 2006 exhibition *Between the Lines*,[8] and continued to spiral into conversations (once, O'Grady made the significant observation that my work is generated by rupture, such as the moment at which the European avant-garde exiles to the United States). When I began looking at performance archives I suddenly became aware of a tension that's been constantly at play in my work between the intimate and the social. The challenge of queer archival work and its ephemeral histories, how they are remembered, cared for, and how they might be described or exhibited opened up another dimension of sensitivity, and a kind of interpersonal relationship with people I can never know. In writing, as in making exhibitions, the subjects and objects will tell you how to treat them, there is an ethical dimension to exposition and display that I consider as much part of my "practice" as anything I have made. ◆

8. *Between the Lines* was presented at Daniel Reich Temporary, the Chelsea Hotel, New York (March 4–April 8, 2006).

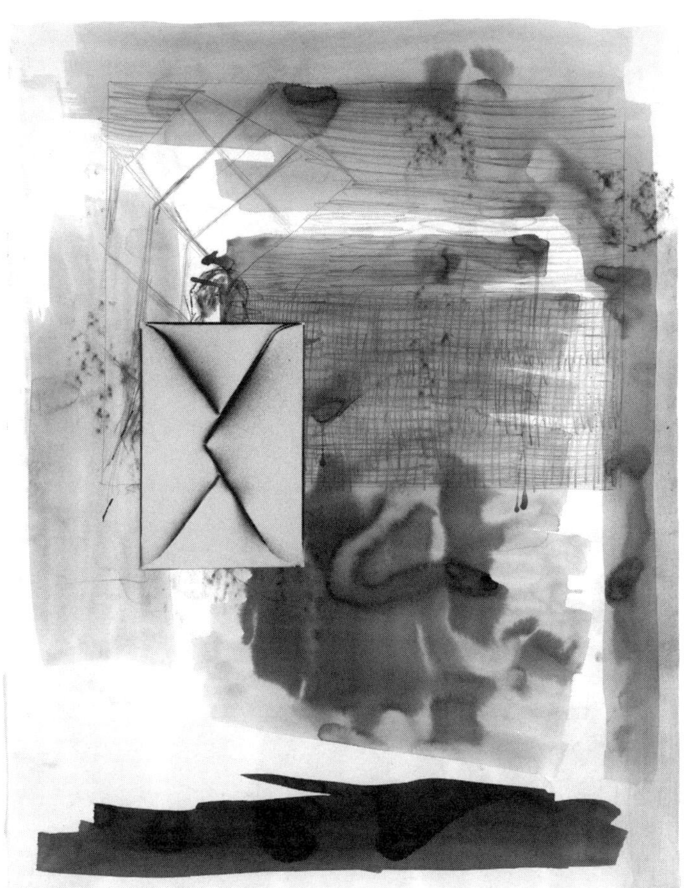

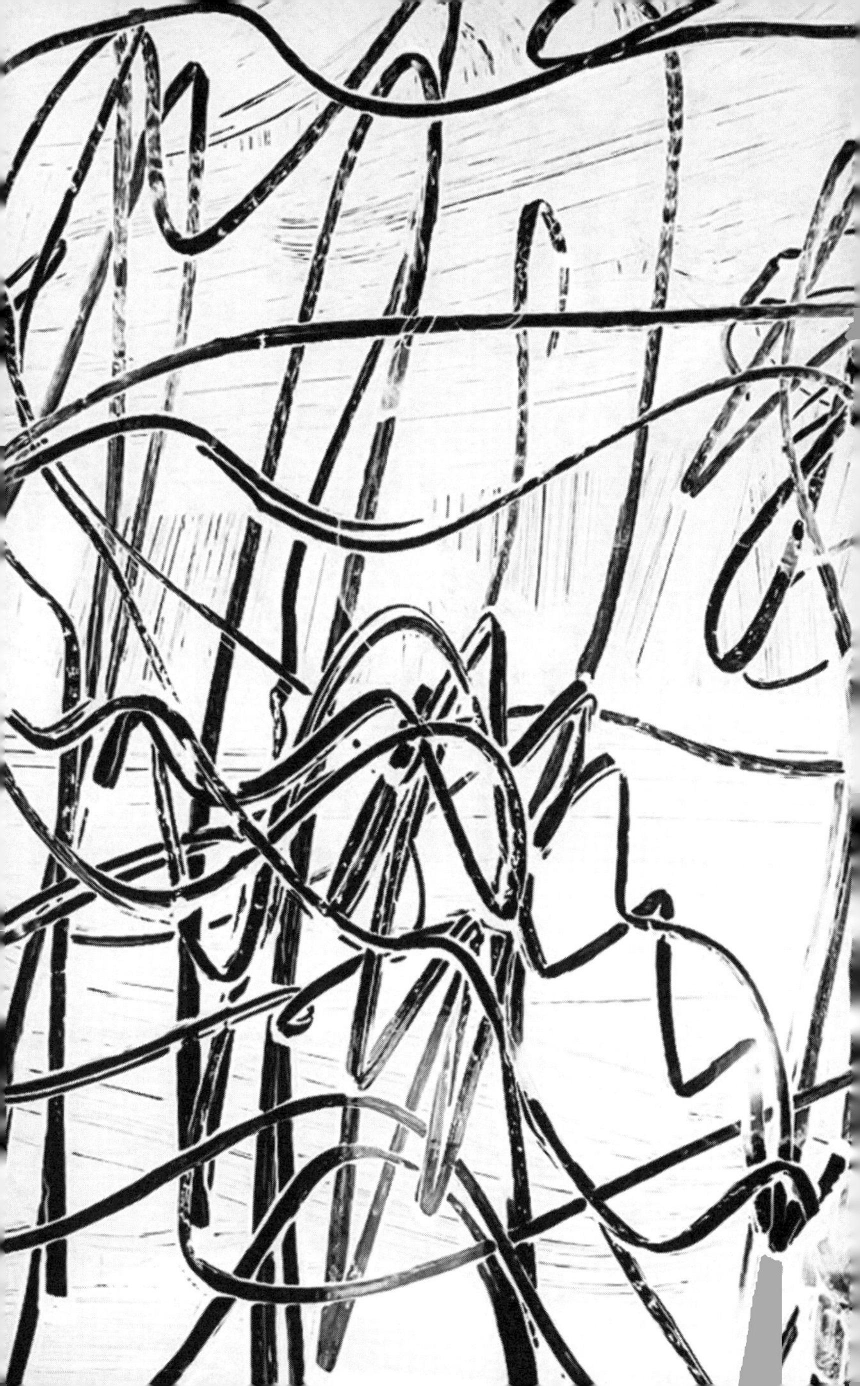

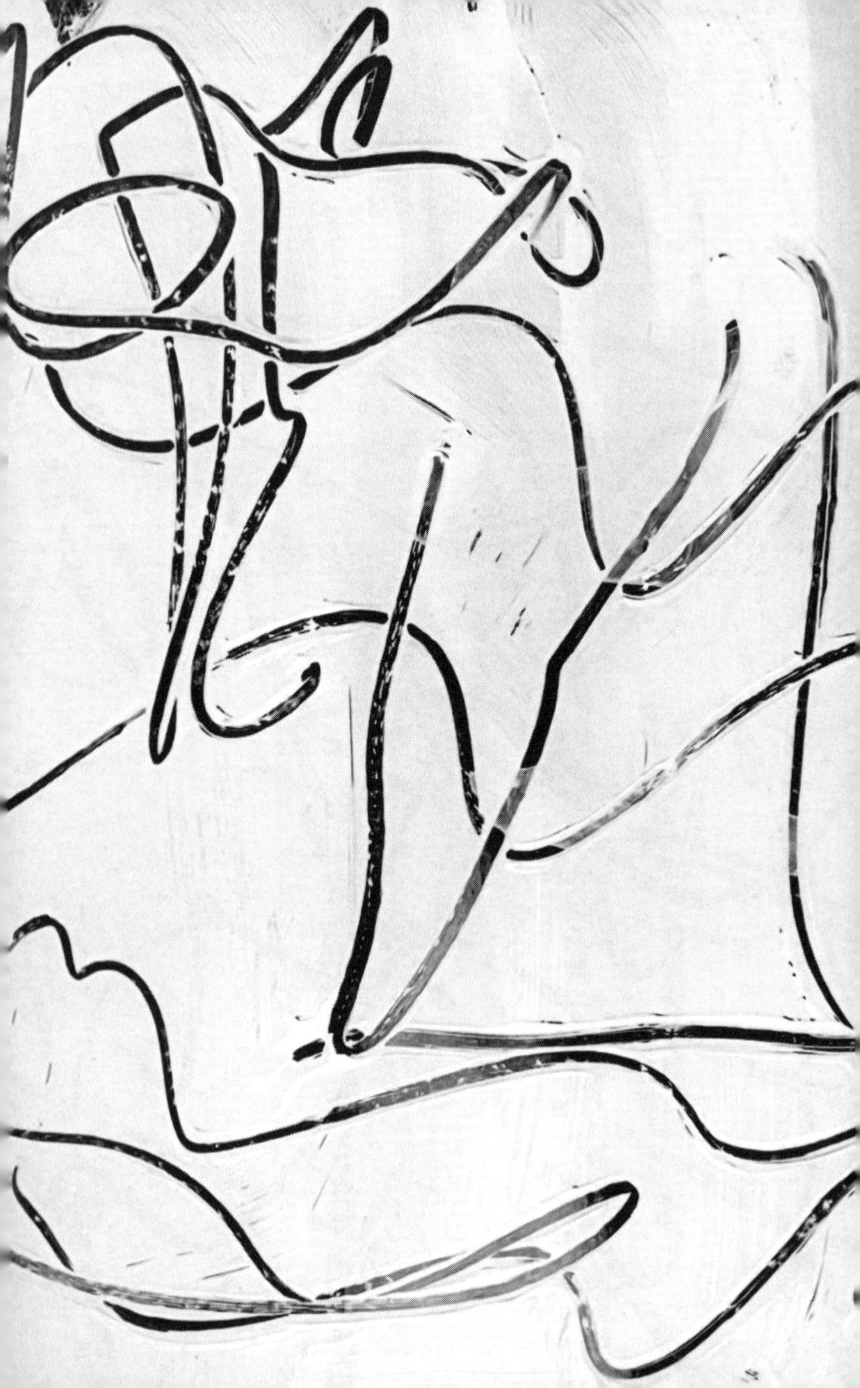

*This essay was originally published in
Artforum 47, no. 2 (October 2008).*

Abandoned Painting.
On Jochen Klein

What is that lovely thread of water running through this soft land?
It is so shy.
It hides under the ground.
Is it a smile from the landscape?
Is it an anonymous gift of Nature?
Is it an exquisite tear, wrung from the rocks?
I do not think so: it is the main sewer.
—ERIK SATIE[1]

Even if the small reproductions of Jochen Klein's paintings that I saw many years ago (in a catalogue loaned to me by a friend), nestled themselves obstinately in my mind, I am always surprised by these inimitably weird and touching works when I see them in person. They do not age, and to stand in front of them brings back an unmistakable quiver of shrill sweetness. The paintings have such a lightness that it's easy to miss their significance. But it is in contempt of the artistic taxonomies on which such judgments are founded that Klein's paintings evince a self-conscious use of the medium against itself, infiltrating painting with alien implications. They are landscapes without genealogy, heterotopias, that insist on the freedom to call into reality something that has not yet existed, which cannot exist. Revealing themselves in layers that are not pure and that keep dissolving or tearing away at one another, they have the particular quality of a blurry sensation turned into an image. When a cobbled-together fantasy coalesces as a distinct vision,

1. Erik Satie, "Piping" (1914), in *A Mammal's Notebook: Collected Writings of Erik Satie*, ed. Ornella Volta, trans. Antony Melville (London: Atlas Press, 1996), 23.

as it does in Klein's paintings, it follows the logic of the fragment that dreams itself whole. Children, young men, or women (sometimes in the company of domesticated animals)—cut from popular printed material such as calendars, posters, or hetero "soft" porn—are collaged onto canvas and elaborated, given a setting by their painted surround of trees, clearings, patches of flowers, and the streaks, daubs, and drips of paint that also count as flowers, pleasure, delight. Filigree shorthand, vermicular strokes, and halos of light hang together in the conviction that ornament is a code for the chaotic relatedness of incidents. When the figures are not glued, but painted with Watteau-like delicacy, they remain foreign to the landscape that has been dreamed up around them—or which they themselves are dreaming, in wilder, experimental strokes. Where is this place, between art history and any afternoon, lying in the sun in a public park? Is it the surrealism of childhood? Academic painting, parlor painting, Sunday painting, the hysterical dream kitsch of antihistamine commercials? People appear, isolated in brief instances of rest, privacy, reflection, amid passages of flamboyant color, as though I were passing them on a bicycle. A peculiar interiority is heightened by the draining of narrative—the paintings are moments of quiet, pauses drawn out to a complete stillness in which I find myself. I am reminded by these works of the potential for paintings to embarrass: I am never sure how to behave around them; they seem to know my foibles. Some flirt, or correspond to a recent mood, like the ballerina wearing a concerned look as, above, a squall of viscous varnish threatens to overcome her. Or like the young man in a pale blue summer shirt, in another painting, who looks out at me with great benevolence, emanating such sweet-toothed empathy that everything around him falls out of focus: distortions of vision induced by great happiness, silliness, sadness, love. The shirtless boy in blue jeans, huddled on a blanket in the grass, his hands comfortingly close to his face, dreams with his eyes open and I can't stand to look for very long. It is, as Michel Leiris wrote of the theatricality of death:

A dream objectified, a dream that we look at, that touches us though we are not in it—What can this be, then, if not a set of actions that are proposed to us and that we consider with a passionate interest, as we would if, extracted from our lives but remaining lucid, we could be detached from our own history and see it played out before us, transformed by the perspective inherent in our new status?[2]

While a student at the Munich Academy of Fine Arts in the early 1990s, Klein actually abandoned painting, perhaps with no intention of ever returning to the tradition into which he had been educated. This suspension of painting, shared also by Klein's friends and fellow students Thomas Eggerer, Amelie von Wulffen, and Josef Kramhöller, stressed the conclusion that to paint is to embellish power, or to stagger under the weight of an unwanted inheritance. For some time Klein devoted himself to producing socially critical texts and projects, in collaboration with Eggerer (from '93 to '96) and as a member, along with Eggerer, Julie Ault, and Doug Ashford, of Group Material (from '94 to '96), before his return to painting in wild profusion from 1996 to 1997—the year of his sudden

2. Michel Leiris, *Scraps*, trans. Lydia Davis (Baltimore: Johns Hopkins University Press, 1997), 41.

death, at age thirty, from AIDS. Klein's interest in individual self-determination, as well as in the possibility of articulating public spaces against their normative inscription, forms links among all his projects of the '90s. In his catalogue contributions for *Die Utopie des Designs*—the 1994 exhibition at the Kunstverein München conceived by artists as part of a seminar led by Helmut Draxler—Klein presented an arrangement of historical data that draws out the streamlining of utopian ideals within corporate identities. He zeroed in on, among others, Otl Aicher, whose philosophy privileged design as the only creative form equipped to address the broad social and cultural challenges posed by the *Neuaufbau* (Germany's postwar reconstruction), yet who is now known for the universal legibility of the logos he designed for Braun and Lufthansa and his pictograms for the Olympics.[3] In *Ikea*, a collaborative installation with Eggerer made for the windows of New York's Printed Matter in 1996, playful and precise juxtapositions of quotes and archival material take on the absorption of radical politics into "lifestyle" marketing; the slick rendering of bland universality is made terrifying. "I was fed up. In place of revolution, reforms became sufficient. We bought ourselves new beds. You are right, the others [old beds] were impossible," reads a line from Bernward Vesper's 1977 novel *Die Reise*,[4] printed on a poster-size enlargement of a page from a '70s IKEA catalogue in which female models in stocking feet loll about, indisputably

3. See *Die Utopie des Designs*, ed. Helmut Draxler, Holger Weh, et al., exh. cat. (Munich: Kunstverein München, 1994).

4. *Die Reise* [The Voyage], an unfinished autobiography "essay-novel" written by Vesper between 1969 and 1971, is an essential text on the 1968 generation in Germany. (It hasn't been translated into English.) Bernward Vesper committed suicide in 1971; he was the partner of Gudrun Ensslin, who cofounded the Rote Armee Fraktion. [Editors' note]

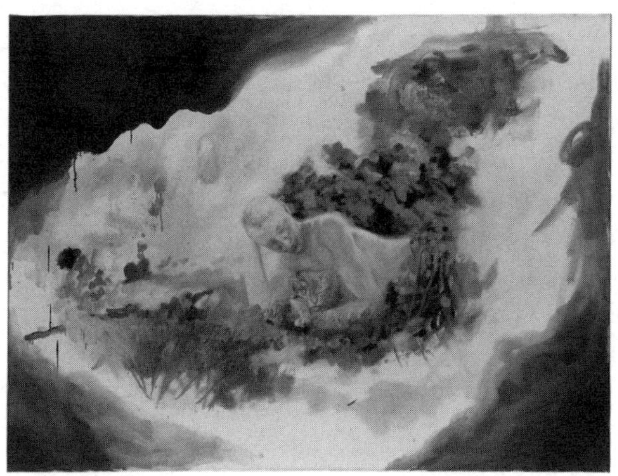

Jochen Klein, *Untitled*, 1997.

boredom. "The English Garden in Munich," an unpublished[5] 1994 manuscript by Eggerer and Klein, presents the park as a palimpsest upon which the eighteenth-century lifeworld collides with the park's illicit repurposing as a cruising area, while in "Virtually Queer—Gay Politics in the Clinton Era," which appeared in 1996 in *Texte zur Kunst*,[6] the artists unravel the leveling of gay activism and resistance. It is interesting to go from the paintings to the documents and back again; there is a refusal to make a closed loop. The sense of continual reconsideration and incorporation of past concerns into the present, of keeping the object of contemplation turning in constant crisis, poses a problem for the airtight packaging of "practice" so eagerly

5. The text has since been published as a book: Thomas Eggerer and Jochen Klein, *The English Garden in Munich* (Vienna: sax publishers, 2017). [Editors' note]

6. Thomas Eggerer and Jochen Klein, "Virtually Queer—Gay Politics in der Clinton-Ära," *Texte zur Kunst*, no. 22 (May 1996).

assimilated by many artists today. What is clearly not a contradiction in Klein's work—the critical framework versus the pleasure of painting—exposes a formulation of art as a space for interpersonal articulations of politics and love: a plea. In the blurring of paint that approximates the soft focus of commercial kitsch photography, there is a confusion between the concrete and the contrived; this is the threshold between the complacent gloss of *le bonheur* and that which I can barely acknowledge that I want. Figures are lifted from the continuum of empty image-production and placed in a scene over which a banner seems to be unfurling: it could also be different. To look is to enter into a pact with the subject, the object, and the whole vanishingly rapturous scaffolding of the picture. The fragility of this proposition is cruelly underlined by Klein's deliberately bawdy "failure" to adhere to the delicate tropes of sentimentality. I am reminded of Martha Rosler's film of industrial flower farming. I am also reminded of Walter Benjamin's hermetic definitions of flower types in *One-Way Street*:

> *Geranium.—Two people who are in love are attached above all else to their names.*
> *Carthusian pink.—To the lover the loved one appears always as solitary.*
> *Asphodel.—Behind someone who is loved, the abyss of sexuality closes like that of the family.*
> *Cactus bloom.—The truly loving person delights in finding the beloved, arguing, in the wrong.*
> *Forget-me-not.—Memory always sees the loved one smaller.*[7]

7. Walter Benjamin, "Loggia," in *One-Way Street and Other Writings*, trans. Edmund Jephcott and Kinsley Shorter (London: New Left Books, 1979), 77.

In the painting of a naked man lying in the grass, his head propped up on his hand over a dozing kitten, both engulfed in a bath of yellow light, a flimsy attempt has been made to paint flowers over his crotch. The attempt goes beautifully wrong in its muddiness, trails into a fragment of out-of-focus something, and on to a soliloquy of confused brushwork. Shit-brown sludge encroaches upon the scene from all sides, rendering completely hysterical what might have otherwise been a splendid paradise. It is as if you are peering into the scene through an asshole, becoming wedged between complete frustration, devotion, fits of laughter, perfection, irreverence, and lack of care. The "straight mind," Monique Wittig writes, "cannot conceive of a culture, a society where heterosexuality would not order not only all human relationships but also its very production of concepts and all the processes which escape consciousness, as well."[8] Yet Klein's throbbing hieroglyphs turn away in passive contempt from logics of masculinity and hegemony: to unfold themselves in the company of paintings like Chuck Nanney's monochrome canvases stretched over tree branches, Jutta Koether's *Apfelsinenfrau*, Christian Bérard's *On the Beach (Double Self-Portrait)*, the embroidered canvases of Nicolas Moufarrege, and Michaela Eichwald's *Animals at War Memorial*—all paintings against the straight mind. ◆

8. Monique Wittig, "The Straight Mind," in *The Straight Mind and Other Essays* (Boston: Beacon Press, 1992), 28.

*This essay was originally published in
Artforum 47, no. 9 (May 2009).*

The Poem Will Resemble You. On Lorraine O'Grady

I have never seen a performance by Lorraine O'Grady. Yet even their documentation communicates a moment in time that was and still is a severe interruption. I can't claim to fully understand what I'm looking at. The continual internal refraction in O'Grady's art forbids its assimilation within a framework that is already known, but this struggle to come to terms with her work's implications strikes at the core of her major artistic contribution.

O'Grady, who first gained visibility in the art world in the early 1980s through her invasions of openings at venues such as the then-new New Museum and the black avant-garde gallery Just Above Midtown, insisted that there could be a complex subjectivity outside "whiteness" and "blackness." In *Mlle Bourgeoise Noire* (1980–83), O'Grady embodied her alter ego, a debutante from Cayenne, French Guiana, dressed in a cape and gown made from 180 pairs of debutante's white gloves. She carried a cat-o'-nine-tails spiked with chrysanthemums and whipped herself while shouting vituperative poems. At Just Above Midtown, she railed:

THAT'S ENOUGH!
No more boot-licking . . .
No more ass-kissing . . .
No more buttering-up . . .
No more pos . . . turing
of super-ass . . . imilates . . .
BLACK ART MUST TAKE MORE RISKS!!!

And at the New Museum, she jeered:

WAIT
wait in your alternate/alternate spaces spitted on fish hooks
of hope [. . .]
THAT'S ENOUGH don't you know sleeping beauty needs
more than a kiss to awake
now is the time for an INVASION![1]

Within the safe zones of these restricted communities, "Miss Black Middle Class" inserted hybridity and disagreement into social situations that were meant to protect and encourage the production of consensus. By now, this performance is justifiably iconic and has become O'Grady's best-known artwork. It is also her most aggressive, but its subtleties and symbolic opulence can easily be drowned out by overemphasizing O'Grady's badass attitude. While the work appeared to have emerged out of nowhere, it has a long but decidedly *not* art-historical genesis.

1. Lorraine O'Grady, "Mlle Bourgeoise Noire 1955" (1981), in *Writing in Space, 1973–2019*, ed. Aruna D'Souza (Durham: Duke University Press, 2020), 10.

O'Grady's peripatetic biography and uncommonly varied occupations leading up to her artistic debut included studying economics and Spanish literature at Wellesley and a stint at the Writers' Workshop at the University of Iowa, jobs at the US Bureau of Labor Statistics and the State Department in Washington, an attempt at writing a novel, a successful career as a rock critic for the *Village Voice* and *Rolling Stone*, and extended teaching at New York's School of Visual Arts on subjects ranging from Dada to Catullus. But it was at the end of a hospital stay in 1977 that O'Grady began shifting from conventional aspirations as a writer to constructing poems that make spacious, looping fields of words out of phrases clipped from the Sunday *New York Times*. Headlines and ad copy glued in spare, dynamic arrangements on blank sheets of paper look less like ransom notes than like Mallarmé's experimental typography. "At the time, two things had happened simultaneously," she recalls. "I began to think that psychoanalysis might not be a bad idea; and I had to have a biopsy on my right breast. I took some books by André Breton to the hospital to help take my mind off it. *Nadja* and the *Manifestos* may have got mixed up with coming out of the general anesthetic."[2]

Transforming Faces
THE WOMAN AS ARTIST
COSMETIC LIB FOR MEN
Years Ago it Was a
LANDSCAPE OF THE BODY

2. O'Grady, "Re *Cutting Out the New York Times, 1977*," binder statement for the exhibition *Between the Lines*, held at Daniel Reich Temporary, the Chelsea Hotel, New York (March 4–April 8 2006); reproduced in *Writing in Space, op. cit.*, 6–7.

An Escorted Tour
Around Chicago
Birthplace of the Skyscraper[3]

"The poem will resemble you," Tristan Tzara warns in his step-by-step instructions for creating a Dada poem. But unlike similar experiments in making the familiar strange, O'Grady's poems make the familiar deeply personal, refusing the generation of accidental meaning and the thrill of nonsense that are the prerogative and legacy of the white male avant-garde. These poems know that to mean something is difficult enough. Though the disunity of the poems' parts is camouflaged by the congenial tone of the newspaper from which they are cut, the cloak of language quivers against what it is being made to say. Turning the technique in on itself, O'Grady finds herself everywhere and re-collects herself in a process meant to generate randomness. Predating by three years *Mlle Bourgeoise Noire*, these poems crystallize an aesthetic that demands critique be both concussive and elegant.

'The modern artist,
finding himself with
no shared
foundation, has
begun to build on
Reckless Storytelling
STAR WORDS

3. O'Grady, *The Renaissance Man Is Back in Business* (1977), parts 7 and 8 of 11; from the series, *Cutting Out the New York Times* (1977). See reproductions of the original collages of these two parts on the following spread.

and
The Deluxe Almost-Everything-Included
WORK OF ART

This could be
The Permanent
Rebellion
that lasts a lifetime.
Calling a Halt
To the Universe
BECAUSE LIFE DOESN'T WAIT
THE SAVAGE IS LOOSE
where we are.[4]

"Calling a halt to the universe"—this is what O'Grady did as Mlle Bourgeoise Noire. But when she was later actually invited to perform, O'Grady found that the agitprop effect of these appearances was highly contingent. This realization led to the creation of deeply personal, staged reflections, more like making "narratives in space as well as in time."[5]

Rivers, First Draft (1982), which O'Grady considers to be her most autobiographical and feminist piece, can be seen as a multilevel *Trauerspiel* allegorizing the subjectivity of the artist, represented by the character of the Woman in Red. It was performed only once, on August 18, 1982, in the wooded Loch section at the north end of Central Park. In documentation, the piece has the sense of a surrealist dream transposed

4. *Ibid.*, parts 4 to 6 of 11.
5. O'Grady, "Nefertiti/Devonia Evangeline," *Art Journal* 56, no. 4 (Winter 1997), 64.

'The modern artist,
finding himself with
no shared
foundation, has
begun to build on

Reckless Storytelling

STAR WORDS

and

The Deluxe Almost-Everything-Included

WORK OF ART

onto reality, though in reality it was probably more like several dreams occurring side by side. A multitude of characters, reminiscent of New Wave cinema or religious paintings, describe in tableaux vivants the arc of O'Grady's becoming-an-artist as the simultaneous and incompatible experiences that actually constitute a life coming into focus.

The Woman in the White Kitchen, reduced by the deep synthesis of O'Grady's memory to her most evocative characteristics, sits within a schematic "house" erected among the parks' boulders and shrubs. Described in the script as "a brown-skinned woman wearing a white halter dress and white wedgies, with a '40s hair style," she has been grating coconut at her white table for so long that the floor of the house is already a carpet of shavings.[6] The sounds of a West Indian radio broadcast and the cartoon of a palm tree beside the house indicate the faraway zone that she mentally inhabits—though in the setting of an urban park, everyone is out of context. A gray door standing amid the trees marks the entrance to the club of the Black Male Artists in Yellow, who are endlessly absorbed in their work and their admiration and support for one another. Alongside these persistent archetypes, the drama of a tryst unfolds between the Girl in Magenta and the Young Man in Green (played by a young Fred Wilson). Some of the "still images" speak, like the Young Girl in White who is "memorizing lessons" through a megaphone while sitting on a rock, dressed in her Sunday best. Her idealism is symbolized by a sun hat re-fashioned into the helmet of Pallas Athena, goddess of wis-

6. All stage descriptions and quotations from *Rivers, First Draft* can be found on O'Grady's website in "Rivers, First Draft. Working Script, Cast List, Production Credits" (1982), at https://lorraineogrady.com/art/rivers-first-draft (last accessed March 8, 2024).

dom. Further up the hill, two Art Snobs in motorcycle goggles engage in circular rants, striking dismissive, cool poses and making the Woman in Red "feel out of it." Figures of exclusion, the characters in this landscape are consumed with themselves and their own realities. Only the coterie of the Debauchees offers the Woman in Red a temporary feeling of participation, of moving between worlds. Their dancing sound track—Tom Tom Club's "Wordy Rappinghood" and John Foxx's "Metal Beat"— adds to the confounding mesh of sounds and voices, resulting in the counterpoint of a *poème simultané*. When the young girl has finished her dutiful memorization, she recites the following poem:

Back home deep in the woods of Vermont,
I dropped the first atomic bomb
[. . .]
Come to our place for Thanksgiving.
We'll serve you the Carribbean with all the
trimmings.

Come to Jamaica—all we have to offer is
three days on an island
where dance is a way of life
Isn't it time you took a vacation?

It's no coincidence that when people speak in O'Grady's performances, they speak symbolically, in poems or supersaturated streams of language. While the artist herself has said that *Rivers, First Draft* is among her most overdetermined works, its perplexity is a result of O'Grady's desire to say what she has to say completely, touching on every level of meaning. Even the refined economy that characterizes her aesthetic can't rein in the sense of urgency that so often makes her work seem to be bursting, overloaded, or going beyond the limits of what can be expected of an audience. "I'm not interested in meaning or significance, or importance," says the naked man who emerges from a stream onto a bridge made from a bed on which the Woman in Red lies dreaming or watching television. "And what about the Bomb?" ask the production assistants. "Will anything last?"

One turbulent climax of *Rivers, First Draft* comes when the Woman in Red is rejected by the Male Artists in their studio, is jostled and assaulted by the Debauchees, and, leaving them all behind, makes her way to the "castle kitchen," where she creates her first artwork by spraying a stove with red spray paint. Ultimately, though, it is the reunion with her former selves, the Girl in White and the Girl in Magenta, that draws her out of the oppressive cacophony, "the stuff that goes on constantly as we lead our private, inner lives." For O'Grady, *Rivers, First Draft* explores a new psychological terrain in which political agency bravely includes the right to expose vulnerability in public: "I confess [that] in my work I keep trying to yoke together my underlying concerns as a member of the human species with my concerns as a woman and black in America. It's hard, and sometimes the work splits in two-within a single piece, or between pieces. But I keep trying, because I don't see how history can be divorced from ontogeny and still produce meaningful political solutions."[7]

7. O'Grady, "Thoughts about Myself, When Seen as a Political Performance Artist" (1981), in *Writing in Space, op. cit.*, 38.

This splitting finds its most poignant realization in the sixteen-part photo installation *Miscegenated Family Album* (1980/1994), a piece that actually traces its origins to an earlier performance. One month after Mlle Bourgeoise Noire's invasion of Just Above Midtown, O'Grady was invited by the gallery's founder-director, Linda Goode Bryant, to participate in a performance showcase called *Dialogues*. O'Grady's contribution, *Nefertiti/Devonia Evangeline* (1980), juxtaposed the story of her relationship to her estranged sister, Devonia, with a chronicle of Nefertiti's relationship to her younger sister, Mutnedjmet. The first part of the performance consisted of side-by-side projections of slides of Nefertiti and Devonia and their families, set to a sound track that narrated the stories of the women's lives, one from a historical point of view, the other from the point of view of the little sister (O'Grady). The progression of slide pairings activated a flickering of resemblance and dissemblance, thanks to the often uncanny similitude between the projected faces or the noble poses and the contrast or correlation between the trajectories of the title characters' lives. "They die at the ages of thirty-seven and thirty-eight respectively," O'Grady later explained, "Nefertiti in 1344 BC after a banishment of six years, and Devonia in 1962 from the complications of an illegal abortion. The screens contain sarcophagi with lifted lids."[8]

In the second part of the performance, O'Grady herself came onstage wearing a red caftan and attempted to enact the narrator's directions for the ancient-Egyptian Opening of the Mouth ceremony, the last ritual before burial, whose function was to

8. O'Grady in conversation with the author, January 2009.

free the deceased for a full afterlife. O'Grady's demonstrative struggle and failure to fulfill the commands of the tape-recorded voice pronounced the hope for and ultimate ineffectuality of reconciliation through art. As images of the two "sisters" reappeared on the screen, O'Grady approached the projected faces and struck their mouths with an adze as the tape proclaimed, "Hail, Osiris! I have opened your mouth for you. I have opened your two eyes for you." If, as O'Grady recounts, many members of the audience perceived the juxtaposition of her own middle-class family with ancient-Egyptian royalty as arrogant, their verdict missed the greater provocation of her conceptual linking. In an interview with Linda Montano, O'Grady states, "Putting a picture of Nefertiti beside my sister was a political action."[9] *Nefertiti/Devonia Evangeline* enacted legitimate pain in a complicated work of mourning, triangulating between the present and two irretrievable pasts. In the installation of photographic diptychs that developed fourteen years after the performance, O'Grady gave form to the concept of a "miscegenated family album" by framing a selection of the double images she had first projected as slides. The counterintuitive pairing of interdynastic "siblings" creates a third temporal image, a bridge that is neither visual nor textual, a space of not knowing. While *Nefertiti/Devonia Evangeline* articulated the struggle to mend loss and division, the juxtaposed images that constitute *Miscegenated Family Album* brilliantly illuminate one another, creating what O'Grady calls "a novel in space."[10] Nefertiti, by her proximity to Devonia, is lifted into the present, and her own

9. O'Grady, "Interview with Linda Montano" (1986), in *Writing in Space, op. cit.*, 82.
10. O'Grady in conversation with the author, January 2009.

idealized bearing restores something like dignity to Devonia. With the diptych, "it isn't either/or. There's no implied before and after, no being saved," O'Grady writes. "[It's] always both/ and, at the same time. And with no resolution, you just have to stand there and deal."[11]

In September 1983, O'Grady initiated yet another invasion in the form of a float for Harlem's African-American Day Parade. Conceived as an artwork expressly not for the art world, the float featured an enormous empty golden frame; its message was its title, spelled out in large block letters on the float's base: ART IS . . . Framing the bright afternoon, building facades, spectators, street signs, birds, and balloons as it traveled the parade route, the float also carried a festive squad of men and women dressed in airy white, each carrying a golden frame of his or her own. Gamboling from the float into the street and toward the spectators, the performers danced through the crowd, holding up frames to mothers, gestures, policemen, accidental groupings, fleeting poses, children, exclamations, and clusters of friends, "framing" in close-up what the float itself only registered as the "big picture." An intricate crisscross of art and activism, *Art Is . . .* spectacularizes O'Grady's ongoing condition of being both part of and not part of, inside and outside, a society that relies on coeternal binary opposition. Simultaneously proposing to answer and question what avant-garde art has to do with lived experience, *Art Is . . .* frames life as a time-based medium. As in all of O'Grady's work, the "political" is approached as a question of visibility and sensation. As Jacques Rancière has said of art: "It is political insofar as it frames not

11. O'Grady, "The Diptych vs. the Triptych" (1998), in *Writing in Space, op. cit.,* 140.

only works or monuments, but also a specific space-time sensorium, as this sensorium defines ways of being together or being apart, of being inside or outside, in front of or in the middle of, etc. It is political as its own practices shape forms of visibility that reframe the way in which practices, manners of being and modes of feeling and saying are interwoven."[12]

O'Grady's work denies the impoverishment of art as a delimited zone, maintaining instead that it is contiguous with the real world. There is no escape. Certainly, such honesty risks neglect by those who are invested in the maintenance of the illusion that the art world is "the best of all possible worlds." As a friend recently wondered about "our" current petit bourgeois iteration of the New Museum, "Imagine what would happen if Mlle Bourgeoise Noire were to invade one of those overstuffed openings. Would it be something, or would it be nothing?"

You're the artist
Have we found the
beginning of existence—
or the end of it?[13]

◆

12. Jacques Rancière, "The Politics of Aesthetics," (c. 2004); available online at www.metamute.org/editorial/articles/politics-aesthetics (last accessed March 8, 2024).

13. O'Grady, *The Renaissance Man Is Back in Business, op. cit.*, part 11 of 11.

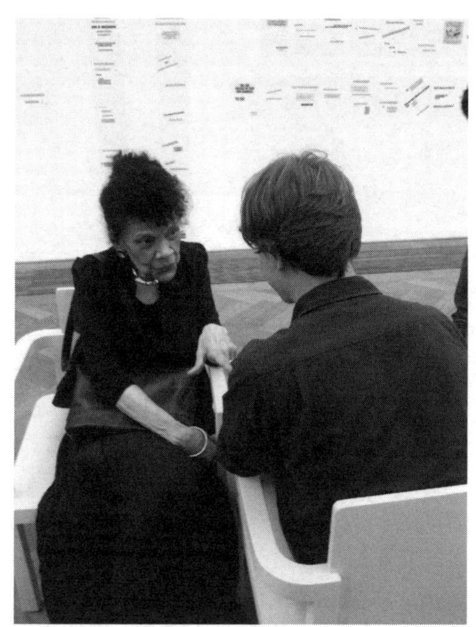

*"By strange coincidence, the c. 1920's carpet by Evelyn Wyld
I had included in* Bloodflames III *(after discovering it in the
basement of an antiques dealers on Astor Place) traveled to Paris
for an exhibition at the Musée d'Art Moderne de la Ville de Paris
some three years later, making a cameo in* Decorum: Carpets
and Tapestries by Artists, *curated by Anne Dressen. I reviewed*
Decorum *together with a parallel exhibition in New York,*
Interwoven Globe, *curated by Amelia Peck at the Metropolitan
Museum of Art, as a way to think through contemporary
questions of currency, quotation, imitation, translation,
rehabilitation, and exchange—something akin to an early form
of shanzhai—but more specifically, about how it is that mis-
categorized, or uncategorizable classes of objects coax new forms
of knowledge, value, research, display, and collaboration."*

This joint review of Decorum: Carpets and Tapestries by
Artists, *at the Musée d'Art Moderne de la Ville de Paris
(October 11, 2013–February 9, 2014) and of* Interwoven
Globe: The Worldwide Textile Trade 1500–1800, *at the
Metropolitan Museum of Art, New York (September 16,
2013–January 5, 2014) was published in MAY, no. 12 (2012).*

Interwoven Globe:
The Worldwide Textile Trade
1500–1800 and *Decorum: Carpets*
and Tapestries by Artists

More readily than other art forms, textiles offer an oblique entry into social histories of art that can open up and reconfigure neglected narratives. The currency of textiles in contemporary art as artifacts and as carriers always already imbued with content exudes from the materiality of textiles as objects created through processes of translation, synthesis, and encoding. Or, in the words of Ann Bergren, the woven thing "bears the ability to enable a resurfacing of something that has laid hidden, that has been repressed."[1] The recent coinciding of two of the most important exhibitions of textiles in many years raises some questions with regard to the current receptivity towards textiles as a form of cultural production that has been hiding in plain sight.

In her catalogue essay for *Interwoven Globe*, Amelia Peck recounts how this 300-year survey of trade textiles was triggered by the request to identify a piece of blue-resist fabric that

1. Ann Bergren, "Language and the Female in Early Greek Thought," , quoted in Jennifer Bloomer, *Architecture and the Text: The S(crypts) of Joyce and Piranesi* (New Haven, CT & London: Yale University Press, 1993), 10.

reappears in several Matisse paintings. The eighteenth-century fabric in question—found by Matisse in a Parisian flea-market—is the only fabric of its kind to have been located in France. Patterned with generic European-style floral motifs, but dyed in a method first perfected in India and East Asia, this type of fabric was long thought to be the first American-made fabric, though it was later mistakenly attributed to British production. Discovering that the earliest of these Indian fabrics were "distributed" by the Dutch East India Company set off questions about the interrelationship between these textiles, India, Europe, and America that led Peck to embark on a project "following the roots (and the routes) of textiles during the early modern era."[2]

The vast scope of this exhibition called for the collaboration of nine museum departments because textiles are collected and categorized according to their cultural context, whereas these particular textiles, traded for spices, gems, bodies, and influence, require double (and often multiple) attribution: where the textile was made, and for which market(s) it was intended. Falling "in-between" cultures, these textiles span and document the process of shuttling back and forth "in-between," and dizzyingly throw into question the notion of cultural context and origin.

An enormous embroidered tapestry depicting the abduction of Helen of Troy dates from the first half of the seventeenth century and was produced in China for the Portuguese market. While the writhing figures in battle and the stylized border of floral scroll-work and medallions appear approximately

---

2. *Interwoven Globe: The Worldwide Textile Trade, 1500–1800*, ed. Amelia Peck; exh. cat. (New York: The Metropolitan Museum of Art, 2013), 3–4.

Western at first glance, the overall visual field seems pumped up, or dilated, with a different notion of pictorial coherence, and certain unknown gaps become areas of invention where the unknown is fused with the makers' more fluent decorative vocabulary. Phoenixes live in the Renaissance border ornamentation and lychee fruit tumbles from the edge of the rocking boat into waters roiling with stylized waves in the graphic *degradé* of Chinese landscape painting. This wall-hanging is a work of projection and blind anticipation, a site where one type of language breaks up as it meshes with the piece-meal incorporation of another. In *Interwoven Globe* successive carpets, quilts, and garments are more densely nested and overloaded in their graphic and inter-textual messages as well as in their multiple uses and global trajectories, to the point that the textiles are no longer simply artifacts, but mobile, communicating documents, literature, mythology, money, and art at the same time.

Bizarre silk—a "type" of fabric born out of the free mobility of motifs engendered by the trade in textiles—are in themselves a kind of ornamental feedback loop, a faux synthesis of various styles and "origins," distorted beyond recognition but resolved in a distinctly European iteration. Memories plucked from rococo, *chinoiserie*, and the stylization and scale-shifts of Japanese graphics collide in bizarre silks to produce illogical flaming architectonic zips that anticipate, almost hallucinate, Art Nouveau. One example on view is actually a Chinese re-assimilation of the European melange, a bizarre silk made in the European "taste," possibly "in a conscious attempt to fool European customs officials or consumers, or both, in the wake of bans on the importation of Asian silk fabrics that were passed in England and France at the turn of the eighteenth century."

The undeniably "virtual" reality of moving through the textile interfaces and cultural travesties amassed in *Interwoven Globe* made it seem perfectly timed with much of the anxious parroting, blogging, and art production around "the network" and "the market." Reading, or grazing the results of more love hours than can ever be repaid, and getting lost in the density of each work—as it spun a cloud-like web that became like a flying buttress to the flamboyant mental/global superstructure—burned up any received notions of authenticity, purity, and originality before my very eyes, while prodding me about the craving for these very qualities in today's markets. As an exhibition with political implications, *Interwoven Globe* brings to light the persistence of an operative cultural hybridism in its tracery of influence and taste in their fullest senses, as the total imbrication of political, social, economic, and aesthetic forces. In this morphing mind-frame of influence through arcs of exchange, projection, miscegenation and interpretation I have to ask: what is the contemporary form of the trade textile?

Decorum: Carpets and Tapestries by Artists, curated by Anne Dressen, both refutes and flaunts the notion of weaving as a "minor literature" with countless masterpieces by anonymous, celebrated, and no longer known artists, architects, weavers, and activists of the 20th and 21st centuries. Indeed, it is surprising to see how many familiar names are gathered in this exhibition alongside the un-named, those who may have had no other aspirations (or choice) than to be devoted to the material of their work. In an essay included in the *Decorum* catalogue, K.L.H. Wells recounts how weavers at the Ateliers Tabard refused to execute tapestries based on Josef Albers' *Homage to the*

Square, because they were too mechanical and lacking in interest for their talents as weavers.[3] This tension between artists and the weavers whose skills they depended on in the translation of their original designs has a precedent in the shifting value relationships of European paintings to tapestries, a co-dependent relationship that began to dissolve by the eighteenth century, when "limiting concepts," such as the "preoccupation with the autograph work of the individual artist," took hold, and in becoming "intrinsic to connoisseurship . . . continued to color our perspective of the tapestry medium to the present day."[4] Yet, in the nineteenth century, it was in the state-controlled Gobelin tapestry workshops that Chevreuil developed his theory of contrast of colors and optical mixing by studying the color effects achieved by placing different colored yarns next to one another, exploding a new way of seeing that would cast a long shadow of influence, from Delacroix, to the Neo-Impressionists and even to the paintings of Josef Albers that the weavers refused to weave. To follow another of the avenues in this garden of forking paths leads to the relegation of women to the weaving workshops of the Bauhaus, where some of the most complex visual objects of the twentieth century were produced.

Guided by the material traces of these and many other historical processes, *Decorum* celebrates weaving as a vast osmotic terrain edged and interpenetrated by painting, sculpture, installation, and theatricality, while fantasizing, in its cacaphonous display, about a different type of museum model than is

---

3. See K. L. H. Wells, "Artistes contre liciers: la renaissance de la tapisserie française," in *Decorum: tapis et tapisseries d'artistes*, ed. Anne Dressen, exh. cat. (Paris: Skira/Flammarion, 2013), 55–59.

4. Thomas Campbell, *Threads of Splendour: Tapestry in the Baroque* (New Haven, CT & London: Yale University Press, 2007), 325.

currently in use. By no means exhaustive, but with a thrilling sense of everything-ness, the exhibition is intent on flinging open as many doors as possible to the continued study, interpretation, exhibition, and re-contextualization of fiber-based works. There is a sense of audacity in the headlong plunge into a modernism that was more decorative and playful than many people currently acknowledge, and the galleries are alive with astonishing examples of weaving that will probably not be seen again for a long time (for example, a runner by Gunta Stölzl and a carpet by the brilliant designer Ivan da Silva Bruhns, a wall-hanging depicting swarming dovecotes produced in the Ateliers Wissa Wassef, and a small square wall-hanging by Giacomo Balla)—at least not until their full incorporation into the museums of the future.

While the works in this exhibitions are frequently displayed as "pictures" or "image-fields," the sense that carpets and tapestries were once silent witnesses to the clutter and clamor of (bourgeois) life is evoked by guest artistic director Marc Camille Chaimowicz' poignant interventions: select pieces of furniture hinting at ensembles, a small, repeated cropping of the bare foot in a Boucher painting, and runners printed with an abstract emblem accompanied by the dithering footprints of a little dog, who has already run ahead. *A Partial Vocabulary*, one of the artist's works in the exhibition, presents the carpet as a zone of recent anguish, strewn with throw pillows and a rotary telephone, evoking the sobbed monologue of *La Voix Humaine*.

The decision to juxtapose twentieth century works in textile with more recent works that play into a "return to craft" brings up the question of what happens when these two rather different impulses of creation meet. For one, any contemporary artwork can be shown "with" a textile, and profits from the juxtaposition, because textiles are so densely loaded with historical and affective signification. *Decorum* raises the question of what is at stake in distinguishing between major and minor works when there is so much to be gained, and several contemporary works puncture the expectation of what both art and a carpet can be. Albert Oehlen's tufted rug is a total home-wrecker. The deployment of textiles by Mike Kelley and Rosemarie Trockel confuses and undermines feminist and minimalist tropes to volatile and different effect. Pae White's gargantuan plume of smoke is rendered immaculate by a digital loom, putting the woven thing to use as a storage device of the evanescent. Magdalena Abakanowicz' *Abakan Rouge*, last seen in *WACK! Art and the Feminist Revolution*,[5] is shown here in a less emphatic context. But, it also needs to be said that a weaving put on stretcher bars or hung on a wall does not necessarily make an interesting artwork—it too often banks on a certain atmosphere of history and craft as the work of "the other" and the attendant aura of "realness." Carpets are not to blame for the fact that contemporary painting in particular has become an arena of sanctioned amnesia. But one of the symptoms of this amnesia is the reliance on a "straight" or "straightening" flavor of modernism, a certain coolness derived from a smoothed interpretation of modernist aesthetics that gives permission to "practices" intent on simply rearranging coordinates like craft, utopia, modernism, and feminism into a desultory package.

5. *WACK! Art and the Feminist Revolution*, curated by Connie Butler, first presented at the Museum of Contemporary Art, Los Angeles (March 4–July 16, 2007).

Compared to the living tissue of *Interwoven Globe* or the silent witnesses of *Decorum*, many artworks that currently crowd the booths of art fairs register as muted "found" artifacts of a real, lost, or dreaded culture. It is interesting to realize in exhibitions brave enough to embrace decorative textiles that teeter near, or completely give in to what is mistakenly derided as kitsch, that the more recent products intended to circulate solely as "artworks"—*not* the trippy carpets of the 30s, 40s, or 70s (*Decorum*), not the thirteen-year-old's embroidery sampler featuring a Turkish harem (*Interwoven Globe*)—look and feel, by comparison, quite hollow. ♦

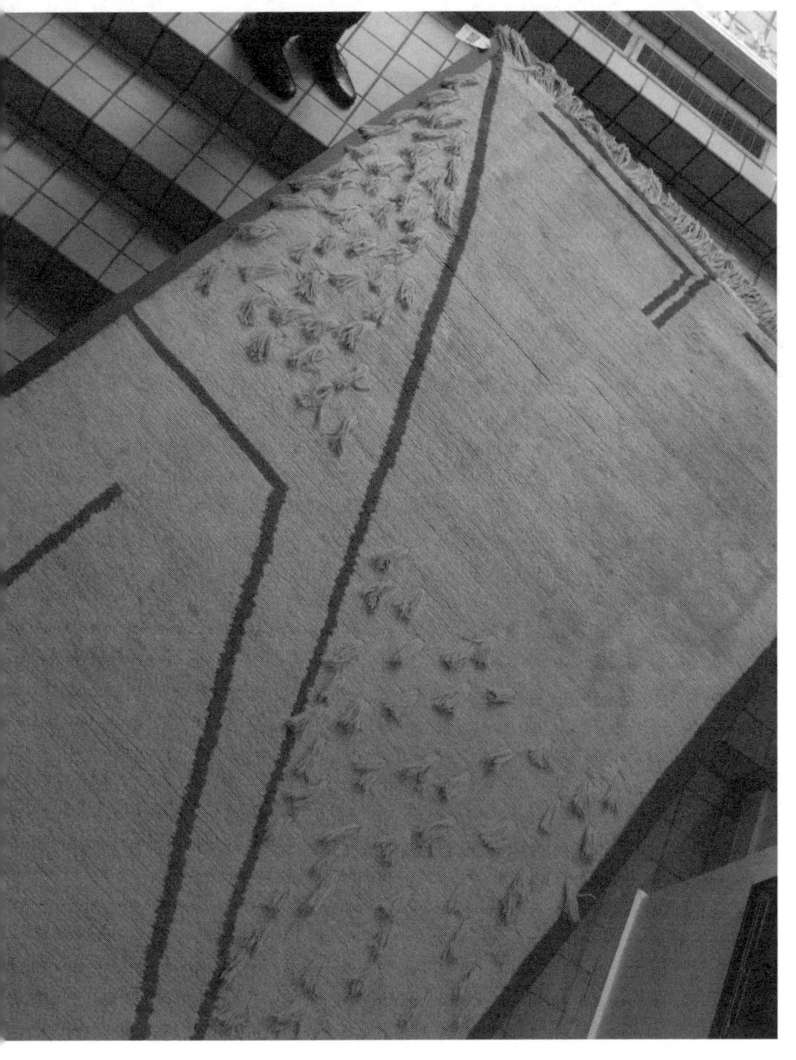

Madame Grès
at the Musée Bourdelle

Each garment is an exact formulation. The inner logic of the clothes—made visible on their surfaces in asymmetrical puckers, bandaging, floral detail, lashings, exhalations, interpenetrations, knife pleats, bulbous involutions, starbursts of folds, slashes, rhythmic poufs, pleated rolls, and impossibilities—dissolves, or anticipates the dissolution of, inside and outside. The textile operations are themselves a poetic syntax: *robes poèmes*. A black viscose jersey dress from winter 1942 is ruched along a virtual line over the sternum, so that the millimetric pleating emits an irrational frequency—strictly concentrated at the center but slackening as it radiates out toward the shoulders, from which, in turn, other kinds of tucks create vertical folds that drop and lose themselves in their denouement down the sleeve. Over the abdomen, pleats alter direction dramatically at the invisible waistline, creating a decisive counter-tensile "X" of pleats at the pelvis, intercepted by a symmetrical alien medallion entirely engorged with semilunar, almost intestinal, folds. None of this interrupts the gravitational rush of the imbricated pleats that constitute the skirt. And somehow everything seems to be held together without seams and instead by internalized threads, ethical underpinnings, self-possession. No decoration, only structure, or a flickering between the two.

Beyond a shadow of a doubt, Madame Grès (aka Germaine Krebs, 1903–1993) was one of the most exceptional sculptors of the twentieth century, an age in which both couture and the concept of genius died. While the depth of her influence is yet to be truly understood, curator Olivier Saillard's decision to insert the exhibition *Madame Grès: Couture at Work* into the Musée Bourdelle in Paris broke the conventional frame through which Grès' contribution has been previously regarded. The exhibition opened the door to understanding a practice of unmatched profundity and rigor, beyond the realm of fashion. Placed among sculptor Antoine Bourdelle's heroic subjects, Grès' dresses, capes, and coats read both as artifacts of history and as hard-edged, monochrome, volumetric certainties. In contrast to the rough bodies (often gargantuan, sometimes draped) housed in Bourdelle's turn-of-the-century atelier-museum, the high precision of Grès' gowns established a tension that caused visitors to whisper in the face of this solemn drama. The rooms of the museum teemed with gasping fashion students, *amateurs*, and elderly women, whose grave study and recognition of the clothes differed significantly from my own novice enthusiasm. While in the gardens, modernist Byzantine equestrian statues coexisted with unkempt rose bushes, trans goths, and young fathers with baby strollers, a presentation with all the pandemonium of a Paul Cadmus painting.

The dynamism of this show was in no small part contingent on this very cacophony. Here, Mme Grès' empty dresses could be not just viewed but *experienced*, so that, even without a body—as artifacts divested of ritual—they seemed to have so much to say, causing us to wonder: What is the origin of the pleat? Does it conjure a narrative, like the acanthus leaf, or a gesture, like the fist used to print the first paisley pattern? And jersey: What accounts for its particular gravity and supplication? Sportswear comes to mind, the summer whites in the final scene of Giorgio Bassani's *The Garden of the Finzi-Continis* (1970), in which Micòl and Alberto play slow-motion tennis with an invisible ball under a lamentation (sung in Hebrew) for the dead of Treblinka and Auschwitz. There is Halston, and the island of Jersey in the English Channel, where Claude Cahun and Marcel Moore

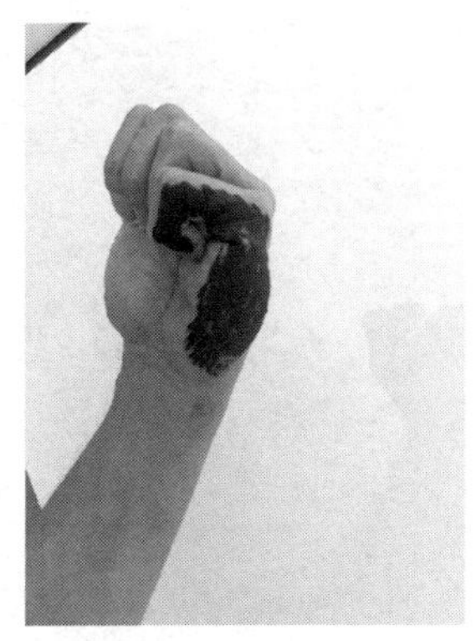

(née Suzanne Malherbe) were imprisoned for their active resistance to the Nazi occupation, and where they lie buried today. Jersey, originally a wool knit, comes from this same island and was first used in high-end fashion by Chanel. Madame Grès demanded so much silk jersey, even when fabric restrictions were imposed during World War II, that weavers joked she "used enough . . . to surround the world."[1] It's difficult to fathom the massive yardage that goes into her dresses—fabric that comes close enough to the body that we might be able to describe its interior, the "folds of the soul."

Having a body. The inspired overlay of Grès and Bourdelle is hard to characterize: The effect it produces trumps the value of any historical link between the two artists—it profits from a light touch, an irreverent choice. Placing dresses next to

1. Arlene Cooper, "How Madame Grès Sculpts with Fabric," *Threads Magazine*, no. 10 (April/May 1987), 32.

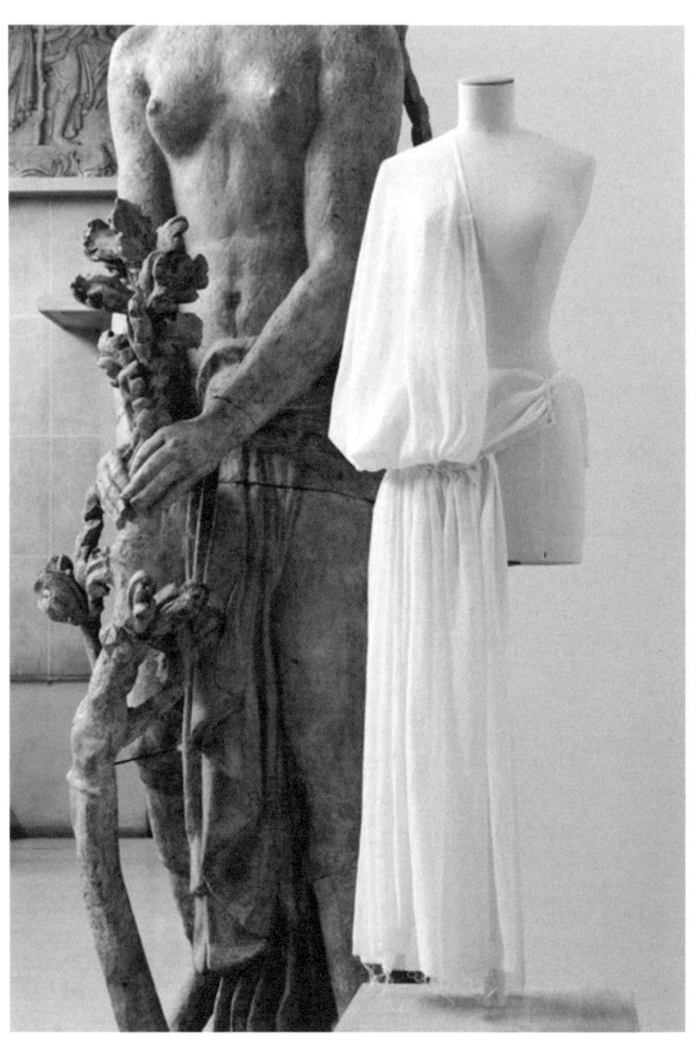

Installation view of *Madame Grès: Couture at Work*, Musée Bourdelle, 2011.

statues, among humans. It helps you to think about how long it takes to make something, about the afterlife of art objects, hard and soft. The exaggerated visual rhythms of flowing hair and moving fabric in Bourdelle's work, a frenzy inspired by the dynamism of Nijinsky and Duncan, against the unshakable self-assurance emanating from Mme Grès' creations. As I call to mind the first dress, I think of an anecdote once told to me by Benjamin Liu (aka Ming Vase) about how Tina Chow used to keep an Issey Miyake dress crumpled in her purse to slip on after work when she wanted to go dancing at Studio 54.

The argument that Grès' output constitutes a total oeuvre, as opposed to a succession of collections, was sustained by a display of garments spanning a fifty-five-year arc that begins in 1933 and is unified by both perfectionist consistency and the absence of periodizing details (even the clothes from the '60s and '70s seem, somehow, higher than haute couture, above style). It has often been said that what set Grès apart from other couturiers was her "authorial" approach to a self-taught and self-invented métier. But the designer's significance was not simply artistic: a communiqué issued by the Chambre Syndicale de la Haute Couture in 1944 tries to account for the material necessity of high fashion to the French nation by weighing its evanescent products against the products of industry: "The figures show that before the war, export of a single dress made by a leading couturier enabled us [the French] to buy ten tons of coal; a liter of perfume was worth two tons of petrol; a bottle of champagne, three kilos of copper." In this context, the famous Cecil Beaton photograph (titled *Fashion Is Indestructible*) of a model posed in front of a bombed-out London temple in 1941 is not just a surrealist collision but earnest propaganda. The ideological and economic role that fashion would go on to play in postwar France has been something of a trade-off, as Serge Guilbaut has suggested—a forfeiting of art for fashion. Indeed, the immediate postwar years saw the great success of designers such as Christian Dior and Mme Grès, among others. The expansion of Grès's atelier and the introduction of her wildly popular perfume Cabochard (meaning "stubborn," and still in production after more than fifty years) made her internationally famous, her market success—and silhouette of material abundance—eclipsing that of any comparable Parisian painter struggling under the Marshall Plan. Though Grès' life story is long, strange, and as ambiguous as her invented name— everyone seems to have a different projection—she herself tried to undercut frivolous speculation, for she cared only for her work, the process of draping fabric on living bodies. "I have nothing to say and everything to show. I don't do anything but work, work, work. When I am not sleeping, I cut. That's my life."[2]

The intricacies and pitfalls of licensing necessary to the maintenance of a fashion house led to the dissolution of Grès' practice. Earlier this year, the Parfums Grès website still narrated the heartbreaking story of the house's liquidation: "Three stories emptied in one day. A shattered life." According to Anne Grès, Mme Grès' daughter: "They broke the furniture and the wood dress forms with axes. The fabrics and dresses were taken away in garbage bags. The place was completely sacked."[3] On the same site, subsequent events were also rattled off: "The

---

2. Madame Grès quoted in Laurence Benaïm, *Grès* (Paris: Éditions Assouline, 1999).
3. Anne Grès quoted in *ibid.*

company 'Parfums Grès' was taken over by the distribution company Lamotte Taurelle and later sold to FMF (Financière des Manufactures de France), a subsidiary of Altus Finance. The Escada Group bought the licenses later on and sold it to Silvio Denz in 2001. Parfums Grès SA is currently based in Cham, Switzerland. In 2003, the new fragrance 'CABARET' was first presented to the public and in 2004, the men's line 'CABARET HOMME' and 'CALINE' were launched." But that was several months ago. Now the website just says: "Coming Soon." ◆

This essay was originally published in
Texte Zur Kunst, *no. 100 (December 2015),*
the theme of which was "The Canon."

Ian White

I only had the chance to see three of Ian White's performances: *Ibiza, Black Flags,* and *Democracy,* performed as a trilogy at the DAAD Galerie in Berlin in July of 2010. The demands made by this event—or rather, this succession of three distinct events—are still hard to resolve. My initial expectation of a lecture-performance (an invention of the 1960s that has seen a smug resurgence in the last 10 or so years) rapidly shattered into a vertiginous force-field that exposed the audience, leaving everyone raw in the face of a piece of queer theater of stunning economy, performed by a single body amid a suspension of "found" textual artifacts. Ranging from a list of "dislikes" culled from dating apps Gaydar and Manhunt, to Tony Conrad's 1965 film *The Flicker,* to an awkwardly reenacted fragment of a Pina Bausch piece, to images of Elizabethan formal gardens, White's conjunctive layers worked up to an extreme tension of reception that tended to dissolve, quite dazzlingly, even achingly, into nothing. Any attempt to "keep it together," was baffled by a hellbent drive towards deflating narrative, or by the always different, but insistent gesture of the rug being pulled out from under certain justifiably venerated classics of the avant-garde. It's as if, by using his body as a vulnerable filter—through which, for example, Yvonne Rainer's so-called

"No Manifesto"[1] could be stuttered together with the litany of contemporary self-loathing: ". . . no camp or fem, non-camp, non-effem, no effems, no fems please, no effeminate fellas . . . sorry,"—White corrupted mental frames, pulverizing them until there was nothing left to hold on to. In these performances, resonant forms, actions, and speech-acts were made into oscillating devices, made to mean things they never would have otherwise said or done. And while each performance crisped into peaks of ecstasy and threat, gestures of liberation were often fantastically performed as dispossession.

White's form of address would not resolve into a clearly legible political position, though it couldn't be called ambivalent. At one point, his jeans were around his knees as he stood, interminably, on one leg, pointing towards an imaginary distance, before vacating the space as the Powerpoint still looped, and then finally shut itself down. He never returned. As I waited awkwardly in the audience for some kind of directive, I thought of the stories I'd heard of Brigid Berlin's 1968 performance *Brigid Polk Strikes! Her Satanic Majesty in Person*, during which she called her mother from an amplified telephone in front of an audience to ask her for money for an abortion, and after her mother refused, called a friend who was willing to give it, and left the theater, hailed a cab, and drove uptown to pick up the money.

In his analysis of the social repercussions of the deletion of Times Square, beginning in 1985, Samuel Delany offers up two

---

1. See Yvonne Rainer, "Some Retrospective Notes on a Dance for 10 People and 12 Mattresses Called 'Parts of Some Sextet Some Sextets,' Performed at the Wadsworth Atheneum, Hartford, Connecticut, and Judson Memorial Church, New York, in March, 1965," *Tulane Drama Review*, vol. 10, no. 2 (Winter 1965).

modes of social net practice that he designates as "contact" and "networking." "Like all social practices," he writes, "they make/generate/create/sediment discourses, even as discourses create, individuate, and inform with value the material and social objects that facilitate and form the institutions that both support and contour these practices."[2] Admittedly, this is a crude gloss, but Delany contends that the forms of inter-class and -race "contact" that were possible in Times Square before its "renovation" were annihilated in favor of erecting spaces to facilitate "networking." What is so poignant about Delany's study is that it assails the gentrification of public spaces and histories at the same time. He goes on to say, "Considered as information dispersal processes, nets are far more efficient than chains. Not all nets are, however, the same."[3] In *Times Square Red, Times Square Blue*, Delany articulates critique that cannot be untethered from subjective experience, much as White was able to level his engagement as a curator with his performative interventions. In the years since I saw his three performances, I've thought about the trilogy again and again, and perhaps again more recently in light of a certain orthodoxy in the streamlining (and mainstreaming) of queer discourses as they are historicized and made viable, and dutiful, within the art world—a zeroing in on an ever smaller cast of canonized queer saints and "techniques" that can be pushed and pulled arbitrarily through different (homosocial) value matrices. Five years later, this is the memory of the urgent aftertaste White's performances left me with. ◆

2. Samuel R. Delany, *Times Square Red, Times Square Blue* (New York and London: New York University Press, 1999), 123.

3. *Ibid.*, 122.

BOOK TITLES

TITLES	PHOTOS
KAREN	24
PETER BEARD	14
TRASH	16
WHEN THE SUN GOES DOWN	16
THEY COME IN PAIRS	16
GOOD ENOUGH TO...	14
GARBEIGE	12
THE FLOWERS AGAIN	16
ZOX	14
TOUCH - ME	10
SPEED CITY	16
SILLY STRING	24
WILL THE REAL DAVID WHITNEY PLEASE...	12
EVEN IN THE TUB	10
THE HEAVIEST	16
THE BIG PRICK	18
BRIGID POLK RETROSPECTIVE THE WHITNEY MUSEUM 1970	28
MINI TOPICAL BIBLE	12
SWEET LAY LON KNEE	12
CURVATURE OF THE SPINE	12
BLACK ON BLONDE	14
BEAVERS	12
EN ROUTE ...	14
SARATOGA	12
ANDY WARHOL - ALICE NEEL	16
NEW YORK - COLOGNE	18
BB	12
REVENOL	10
BOUTIQUE	12
SARA SURPRISE	16
CHELSEA GIRLS	12
SUNDAY LUNCH	22
DANCE JOURNAL	16

This text originally appeared in Florine Stettheimer, *ed. Karin Althaus, Susanne Böller, and Matthias Mühling, exh. cat. (Munich: Hirmer Verlag, 2014), published in conjunction with the exhibition presented at the Lenbachhaus Kunstbau, Munich (September 27, 2014–January 4, 2015). Several works by Nick Mauss were part of the show, including the audio piece,* Crystal Flowers, *which he had conceived in 2011–12, inviting various artists and writers to transpose Stettheimer's poems into songs or spoken interpretations. Mauss' writing about Crystal Flowers was first published in* Triple Canopy *in 2011 as part of its "Immaterial Literature" project (see https://canopycanopycanopy. com/contents/etudes, last accessed March 8, 2024).*

Quivers in Time and Place. On Florine Stettheimer

The thing that is important is the way that portraits of men and women and children are written, by written I mean made. And by made I mean felt. Portraits of men and women and children are differently felt in every generation and by generation one means any period of time. One does mean any period of time by a generation. A generation can be anywhere from two years to a hundred years.
—GERTRUDE STEIN, *PORTRAITS AND REPETITION* [1]

Flipping through issues of Charles Henri Ford's *View* magazine in the Cooper Union library when I was a student there (c. 1999), I came upon Virgil Thomson's 1943 *Portrait of Florine Stettheimer*, a musical composition as portrait, printed as notes on a staff in the issue called "Americana Fantastica." [2] *View* was a utopia on subscription that could host various forms in American-inflected surrealist incompatibility. As a prospective reader (in the magazine's distant future), I was invited to peruse the collage of contributions, shift registers, and then prop the issue on a piano to read and play the *Portrait*. Stettheimer, in my mind, was a rumor I had yet to confirm. And the process of confirmation led, in a sense, nowhere and everywhere.

1. Gertrude Stein, "Portraits and Repetition," in *Lectures in America* (New York: Random House, Inc., 1935; reprinted by Boston: Beacon Press, 1957), 165.
2. *View*, series II, no. 4, "Americana Fantastica Issue" (January 1943), 49–52.

Stettheimer's work poisons the canon, it fits no category, and something in it seemed to bristle against my initial rush of adoration—somewhere there is a hole. I did not wish to be a part of the scenes Stettheimer painted, I did not feel I had come too late, but when I read her poems, I heard Frank O'Hara— and even Bernadette Mayer—as an echo.

What appealed to me: looking to the margins to see if they can be braided to split the center (like a French braid). The chains of associations and relationships. The elevation of individuals and moments. The ornate frames and gestures of commemoration around certain events. (The conversations sparked by her work continue to this day in semi-private, among a few friends, in a parallel discourse, since Stettheimer's work still lives outside consensus.)

Like Gertrude Stein's written portraits, Marius de Zayas' ink caricatures, Charles Demuth's painted "poster-portraits," Apollinaire's *calligrammes*, Sonia Delaunay's *robes poèmes*, Thomson's *Portrait* of Stettheimer—composed after a "sitting" with the subject—is a hybrid form in a new genre of sliding languages: portrait = autograph/caricature/poem/painting/text/ song/collage/sign/diagram/dress. Florine Stettheimer's own poems—published posthumously in the lavish volume *Crystal Flowers* (printed and distributed by her sister Ettie "for Florine's friends and the friends of her paintings")[3]—emerge in the flow of this milieu, and, read with or "through" her paintings, attest to her interest in the reconsideration of the portrait as a modern emblem or prism. As made among friends, the

3. Florine Stettheimer, *Crystal Flowers* (New York: Banyan Press, 1949); *Crystal Flowers: Poems and a Libretto*, ed. Irene Gammel and Suzanne Zelazo (Toronto: Book-Thug, 2010).

warped portrait, or one perceived in a new way (or in the transposed idiom), constituted a new form of exchange and critical commentary in American and European artistic circles during the early half of the twentieth century.

I got to know Florine, and "Florine's friends and the friends of her paintings" through the various portraits they made and held up to one another, as much as through the portraits and self-portraits Florine painted and wrote: lists and associative chains, networks, fretworks, and trellises spiked with affection, flirtation and lustre. The hyper-attenuated architecture of grotesque ornament is the scaffolding on which Stettheimer suspends her "multiple" perception of her world, propped up and held together by hyperbole, chants, billboards, tendrils, gauzes, rays. Including satirical portraits of humanoid animals, portraits of personal possessions, enumerations, passages written "As 'Tho From a Diary," "Notes to Friends," homages, reminiscences, reflections, descriptions of travel, and time-travel (in the sense of autobiography), *Crystal Flowers* poses "as 'tho" spontaneous, but reveals a direct reciprocity between the intensely deliberate composition of a poem and the arrangement of flowers in a vase, or in the cartographic precision of a seating-arrangement around a dinner table, or the disposition of ornaments in formation as its center-piece. Everything is emblem: paintings as visual poems; poetic notes as boutonnieres; bouquets as self-portraits, as group portraits; moments as costumes; parties and days as paintings.

While Stettheimer's poems and paintings entwine in attitude and even in shimmering effect, to read these arch forms of writing, speaking, and swanning is perhaps a more inward experience than being glamored by her paintings. Dazzles of vulnerability and pain show through cracks in the dominant voice, reminiscent of the complex narration of Charlotte Salomon's graphic paintings in the cycle *Life? or Theater?* (1940–42). The Watteau-like commemoration of "Our Parties" takes turns with more critical verses, such as "Art is Spelled with a Capital A," and "The Unloved Painting," in which the selling of art, artists, and women is served on ice.

> *I was pure white*
> *You made a painted show-thing of me*
> *You called me the real-thing*
> *Your creation*
> *No setting was too good for me*
> *Silver – even gold*
> *I needed gorgeous surroundings*
> *You then sold me to another man*[4]

Another poem begins with a manifesto-like pronouncement, "My attitude is one of love," only to float away in a defiantly distracted, vapid irony. An attitude of true ambivalence that imbues her portraits, transliterations, and syntheses transmits more depth and blind moments of entangled feeling than any historical account could convey of these figures and their lives together. ◆

4. Stettheimer, "The Unloved Painting," in *Crystal Flowers: Poems and a Libretto*, op. cit., 69.

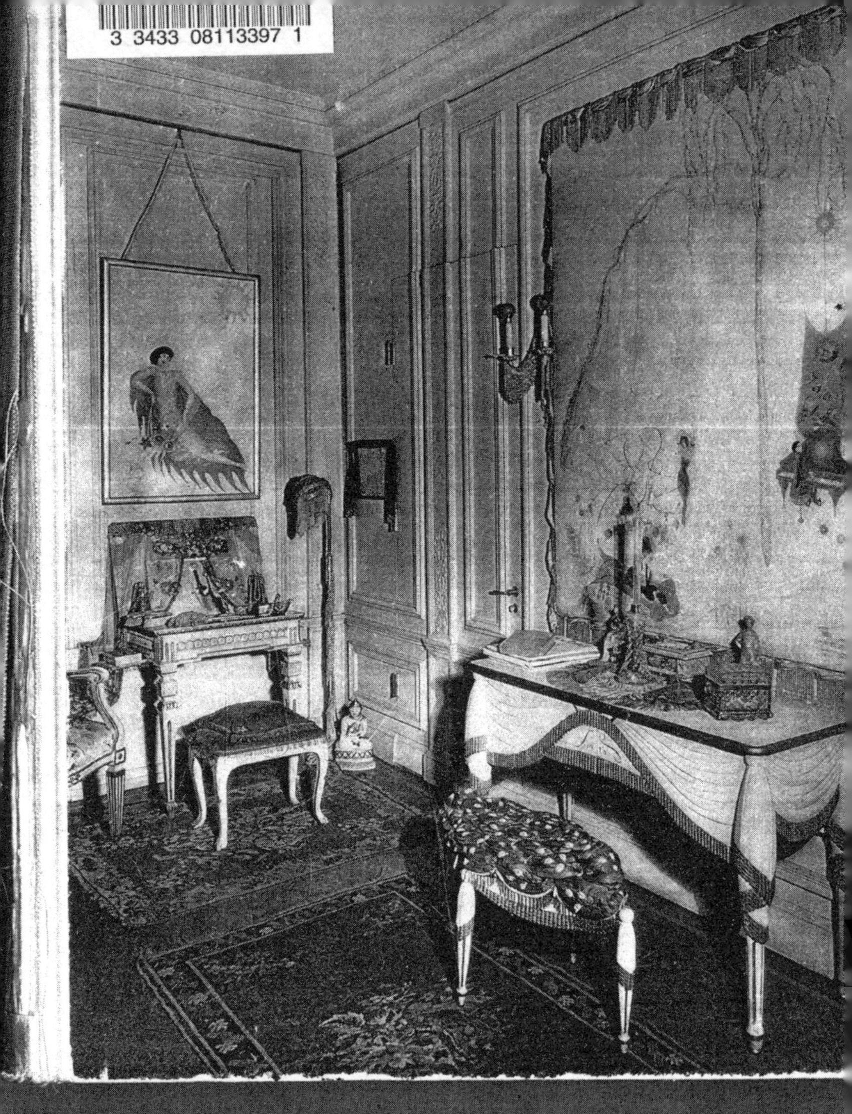

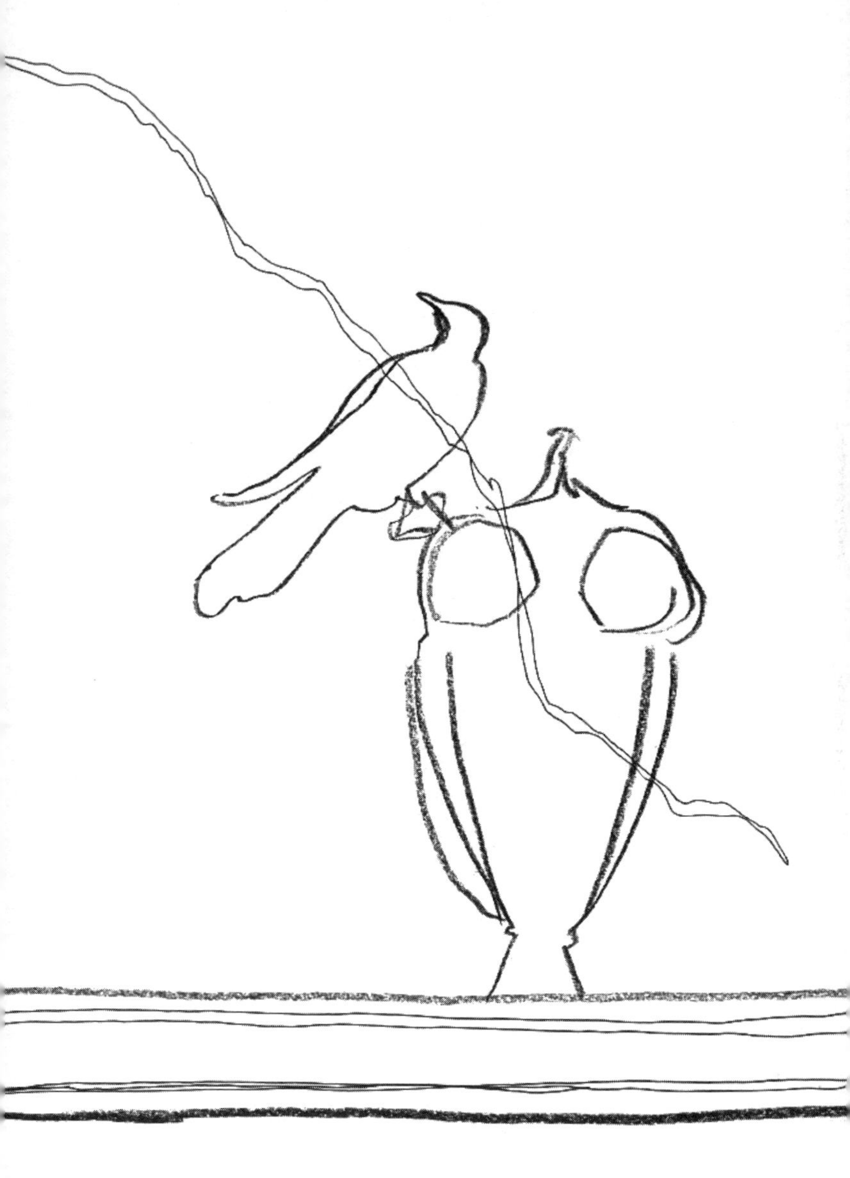

The Beauty Possible
Under These Conditions.
On Reza Abdoh's
Father Was a Peculiar Man

In the summer of 1990, Reza Abdoh made his recklessly ambitious New York debut with a three-hour-long, roving, intermission-less *détournement* of *The Brothers Karamazov*, using a stretch of Little West 12th Street as its readymade set. *Father Was a Peculiar Man* recast Fyodor Dostoevsky's existential family drama as an ahistorical pageant, shot through with repressed fantasies, agitprop theater, American myths, and cameos by stars of television and the silver screen, presented to "patrons of the streets of the notorious meatpacking district by the Hudson river . . . normally frequented only, during the hours of performance, by prostitutes and their customers."[1] As with much of Abdoh's work, the play was so congested with text and media, image and action, that it proved impossible to take in as a totality, an aspect further stressed by the work's spatialization across four city blocks—including

1. "All the World's a Stage: The Open Theater Experience of En Garde Arts," *J-Club*, vol. 2, no. 1 (1991), 36-38, here 37.

vacant lots and a disused slaughterhouse—in gleeful disregard of proscenium conventions. While reviews of the production go to great lengths to make sense of this "charivari"[2] performed by sixty actors, invoking the Karamazovs, the Kennedys, a transvestite baby chased by a chainsaw-wielding suburban TV dad, Buster Keaton, the *Leave it to Beaver* clan,[3] Miss Arizona, Marlon Brando, Marilyn Monroe, Richard Nixon, and Christ (all accompanied by a marching band), few mention the sensual dimension of the thick stench of coagulated blood and rancid fat in the uncleanable crevasses of the cobblestone streets that served as stage, frame, and spatiotemporal context for this "colorful gallery of allegorical eccentrics."[4] All my memories of the Meatpacking District in the 90s are embedded in the visceral recall of that wall of smell, provoked even now as I walk through the tidied neighborhood of art and commerce whose stage-like textures have been stripped of everything but patina.

Commissioned by the nonprofit En Garde Arts, known for staging works of "site-specific theater" throughout New York, *Father* remains a singular example of that fin-de-siècle genre, which grew out of the hybrid legacies of avant-garde theater and site-specific art of the 1960s and 1970s, anticipating the demand for interactivity and immersion in our current attention economy. Abdoh had seen an En Garde Arts production in Central Park during a trip to New York the previous summer, accompanied by the writer Mira-Lani Oglesby, his collaborator

2. Jerry Tallmer, "'Peculiar' Pastiche," *New York Post*, July 16, 1990.

3. Originally broadcast between 1957 and 1963, *Leave It to Beaver* was a popular US sitcom centred on a suburban boy, Theodore "Beaver" Cleaver, and his family. It had reruns throughout the 1980s; a revival series was produced and aired in 1985–89. [Editors' note]

4. Stephen Holden, "A Carnival of Satire and Savagery, with Karamazov as Ringmaster," *New York Times*, July 11, 1990.

on a number of plays back in Los Angeles, including *Peep Show* (1988), a site-specific work set in six rooms of a sleazy Hollywood hotel.[5] In the program notes to *Father*, Ann Hamburger, founder of En Garde Arts, explains: "I spend an inordinate amount of time walking around the city looking for interesting sites—interesting by virtue of their architectural history or by virtue of the populations that frequent or inhabit a particular neighborhood. I then match artists with sites—artistic ideas with cultural iconography. We talk about our impressions of the site—the artistic and the production process begins—a project is born."[6] *Father* developed out of her conversations with Abdoh and Oglesby while they walked the Meatpacking District for several days. Neither of the writers went into detail about the precise nature of their attraction to the Meatpacking District and its "populations,"[7] beyond vague endorsements of this place where "various segments of society with different energies converge . . . and yet they maintain a strange balance."[8] But I would venture that it was more than the evocative nineteenth-century literary setting that attracted Abdoh to "this rather grim area, then unfamiliar even to most New Yorkers."[9]

Reviewers struggled to situate *Father* within an historical or contemporary context. The production elicited comparisons ranging from Hieronymous Bosch to *Satyricon* to *Springtime*

5. *Peep Show* was described as a "fun, exhausting, and intimate . . . non-linear hodgepodge of scenes." See Jeffrey Goldman, "An Absurd, Exhausting Peep Show Makes Voyeurs of the Audience," *Village View*, April 22–28, 1988.

6. Anne Hamburger, "Note From the Producer," program notes for *Father Was A Peculiar Man*, En Garde Arts, June 1990.

7. *Id.*

8. Gerard Raymond, "Theater Takes to the Streets," *New York Times*, June 24, 1990.

9. Marvin Carlson, *10,000 Nights: Highlights from 50 Years of Theatre-Going* (Ann Arbor, MI: The University of Michigan Press, 2017), 160.

for Hitler, as well as *Tamara, Tony 'n' Tina's Wedding*, and the Bread and Puppet Theater.[10] The *New York Post* called it "a moveable theatrical feast with roots all the way back in the 'happenings' of the 1950s, and boy, does it happen."[11] Yet there are other artistic precedents of uses and misuses of the urban environment among which *Father* could be more productively situated. Both Trisha Brown's *Roof Piece* (1971), a semaphoric dance executed by multiple dancers stationed on SoHo rooftops, and Joan Jonas' *Song Delay* (1973), filmed in an empty field near the river on the Lower West Side, activated performance as a kind of irrational demonstration in and against the spaces and vacancies of the city. The demolished tenements of San Juan Hill—a predominantly African-American neighborhood razed to make way for Lincoln Center—feature in Jack Smith's film *Scotch Tape* (1963) and in the opening scene of *West Side Story* (1961)—the violence of "slum clearance" put to picturesque gain. Central Park served as setting and fixed reference point for William Greaves' film *Symbiopsychotaxiplasm* (1968), neither documentary nor fiction, yet both. Mierle Laderman Ukeles' *The Social Mirror* (1983) deployed a mirrored sanitation truck in the first New York Art Parade—reflecting the city streets filled with spectators and allowing "citizens to see themselves linked with the handlers of

10. *Springtime for Hitler* is the musical that the main characters in Mel Brooks' *The Producers* (1968) intend to produce as a programmed failure. *Tamara*, written by John Krizanc, first performed in Toronto in 1981 and staged at the Park Avenue Armory in New York in 1987, and *Tony n' Tina's Wedding*, written by the Artificial Intelligence comedy troupe and premiered in New York in 1985, are examples of experiments in immersive theatre. Founded by Elka and Peter Schumann in 1963, the Bread and Puppet Theater championed a form of radical, politically engaged street theatre. [Editors' note]

11. Jerry Tallmer, "'Peculiar' Pastiche," *New York Post*, July 16, 1990.

Father Was A

their waste."[12] Finally, Charles Atlas' *Butcher's Vogue* (1990) was a defiant reclamation of the art form Madonna had appropriated for her chart-topping song earlier that year. Atlas' insouciant answer-video tracked a pair of legendary queens as they vogued along the streets of the Meatpacking District—around the corner, in time and space, from Abdoh's play—and into its chicest restaurant, Florent (whose advertisement graced the back cover of *Father*'s program).

Mira-Lani Oglesby described the aleatory process that generated the text—a technique that reads, in her telling, as a kind of surrealist divination ritual:

I wrote the Left Handed Notebook / The Moose of Poetry section with my left hand. It was an exercise. It opened another part of my brain. I wrote it at the same time I was writing the Revised Draft section. There were 360 parts. A circle. Once the circle was created, I performed an alchemical sifting, a right handed sifting. 0, 30, 60, 90, etc., 1, 31, 61, 91, etc., 29, 59, 89, 119, etc. The results were exhilarating to me—Fathers and their Children, Women as a Species, Gold-Mines in Siberia."[13]

Oglesby's "initial premise" was to map the village in Dostoevsky's novel onto the "village" of the Meatpacking District, and "then using sort of vaudeville ideas."[14] (*Father* took its title from an old vaudeville sketch that began, "Father was a peculiar man,

12. The Freshkills Park Alliance, "Mierle Laderman Ukeles and Maintenance Art at Freshkills Park," www.freshkillspark.org/blog/mierle-laderman-ukeles-and-maintenance-art-at-freshkills-park (last accessed March 8, 2024).

13. Production notes by Mira-Lani Oglesby, dated June 26, 1990.

14. Quoted in Allan Wallach, "Cobblestones for a Stage," *Newsday*, June 24, 1990.

he was always getting into trouble.")[15] She had remained in Los Angeles while Abdoh workshopped the play in New York, sending portions of the script in installments, and was surprised to see what had happened to her text when she arrived for rehearsals in June. "I'm the writer and I don't know which scenes are coming where," she said. "That's site-specific theater."[16] Oglesby saw her role as generating raw material, "a well of text from which Reza could draw the play according to the Meatpacking District sites being used and the company of performers he assembled."[17] *Father*'s "vaudeville structure" allowed the ostensible narrative to be interspersed with seemingly unrelated acts or events, performed in wildly disparate genres. Abdoh later described the overriding motif as "the family as a degenerating unit. We were dealing with things I'm obsessed with, like the killing of authority, in several different stages."[18]

Actors in the production describe *Father* as a collective improvisation, in which Abdoh encouraged them to insert material of their own devising—often generated in the heat of the moment—into the armature of a script that was sprawling and prone to fracture. "My technique is to open the text up and shatter it to bits, then bring it back together again," Abdoh once said, of the classics he renovated through bricolage.[19] *Father*'s

15. From Jack Murphy's monolog in *The Log Cabin Varieties* (1877), reprinted in Douglas Gilbert, *American Vaudeville: Its Life and Times* (New York, Whittlesey House, 1940), 25.

16. Quoted in Wallach, "Cobblestones for a Stage," *art. cit.*

17. *Id.*

18. Quoted in Thomas Leabhart, "Excerpts from 'Reza Abdoh,' an Interview" (1991), in *Reza Abdoh*, ed. Daniel Mufson (Baltimore & London: The Johns Hopkins University Press, 1999), 42.

19. Glenn Collins, "Street Theater Audience Chooses What to Watch," *New York Times*, July 19, 1990.

bits were particularly difficult to reassemble—after so many transpositions and disarticulations, *Karamazov* appears less as a primary text than as the abandoned remains of a stolen car that has been stripped and sold for parts. One reviewer, after attempting to keep track of all the competing characters and plot lines, described feeling "exhausted and perplexed about what actually happened in these lower Manhattan streets."[20]

Over the course of twenty evenings, *Father* unraveled in the manner of a passion play along a number of "stations," beginning at a battered white sedan parked at the corner of Little West 12th Street and 9th Avenue—the ticket office. *Village Voice* critic Erika Munk described her initial impressions of the play: "*Father* starts with an open coffin dragged over the cobblestones and couples dancing, some dressed like Russians of 150 years ago, others as if they came from the East Village. Drunks, idiots, beggars. Around the corner, in the middle of the street, a little frame house with a little white picket fence is set up on Astroturf. Very '50s-TV, with Mrs. Beaver holding a pan of brownies."[21] The view down the street toward the West Side Highway offered hints of things to come: a scattering of living room furniture, a video monitor, salon dryer chairs, a body dangling from the edge of a building, a toilet, and gravestones sprouting from the cobbled streets. According to Marvin Carlson, "almost all of the play shared this same general shape—a more or less guided procession to a new location, defined by a number of theatrical set pieces, this location serving as a central

20. Lauren Sanders, "Father Was a Peculiar Man," *Show Business*, July 11, 1990.
21. Erika Munk, "Meaty Metaphors," *The Village Voice*, July 18–24, 1990.

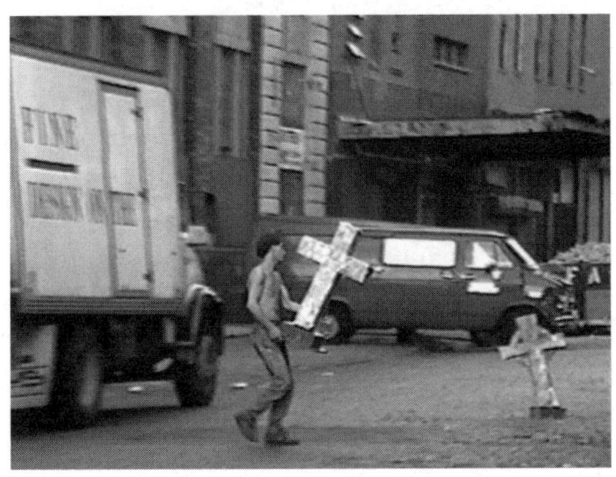

gathering spot for a variety of images, events, and speeches (but with tangential activity spreading away in various directions, and sometimes flowing in and out of the central location) and the sequence terminated by a larger 'production number,' involving most of the company in song and dance."[22] The protagonists of Dostoevsky's family drama, dysfunctionally conflated with all manner of American icons, soliloquized on such subjects as Madonna (Ciccone) and Christ, the weather in Siberia, and the proposition that "every guy is like Donald Trump for at least part of his life." At any moment the audience's attention might be derailed by a massive song and dance routine, choreographed by Maggie Rush and Ken Roht, to insufferably upbeat numbers like Perry Como's "Hot Diggity (Dog Ziggity Boom)." Convulsive shifts in sentiment and dramatic thrust created effects similar to the cognitive dissonance of hard cuts in video or the addled plenitude of channel surfing. As I watched countless

22. Marvin Carlson, *10,000 Nights, ibid.*

hours of Miestorm Serpent's grainy, lovingly observed footage of the play, its environment, and its audience, Abdoh's meditation on the inescapable fallout unleashed by every father somehow evoked a mental image of Friedrich Engels' *Origin of the Family, Private Property, and the State* (1884) made into a movie musical by Jacques Demy.

"We're a pretty sick family, I guess. But we all love each other" explains the Alyosha character (played by Roht), speaking as much for the All-American Family as for the characters in Dostoevsky's novel—and for Abdoh's own family, for that matter. Daniel Mufson recounts an episode from Abdoh's epically tragic family history that could have been a page from *Father* itself, wherein Regina, Ali Abdoh's daughter from his first marriage, informs her father that her half-brother Reza is gay—showing him pornographic magazines taken from Reza's apartment as proof. "Reza nearly strangled Regina, stopping only when bystanders pulled him away from her neck," Mufson writes. "Two weeks after this incident, Ali Abdoh was dead."[23] Abdoh's take on *The Brothers Karamazov* explores the fantasy of patricide, spun into a concatenation of fathers whose relentless humiliations structure the very fabric of lived experience.

Father's centerpiece—a sardonic exaggeration of dinner theater as endurance art—arranged the audience around a banquet table nearly half a city block in length, covered in a "spotless white tablecloth" that served as a stage on and around which a panoply of characters converged, lit by chandeliers hung from the corrugated metal meatpacker's awning, and menaced by a giant pendulum swinging over the center of the

23. Daniel Mufson, "Notes on a Life Imagined and Lived," www.danielmufson.com/the-abdoh-files/notes-on-a-life-imagined-and-lived (last accessed March 8, 2024).

table. Guests took their places along the street-length table to watch Miss Arizona deliver her acceptance speech and Ophelia give birth to twin chicks, while waiters took orders ("We're having a 'special' on chicken today."[24]) and a disembodied head erupted at intervals to shout "I want to FUCK you!" Night after night, Fyodor Pavlovich Karamazov raped one of his sons on the dinner table while a handsome medieval bard blew smoke-filled soap bubbles over the heads of the assembled. Somebody on the sidelines screamed, "I can't think straight!"

Abdoh talked about the importance of "incorporat[ing] the life of a neighborhood into a piece of work so that the piece does not fight it."[25] An elderly man who happened upon the rehearsals asked how he could participate and was instructed to show up every night at the same time and eat his dinner at the endless table and make conversation. At dusk, transvestite prostitutes came out and cars began to circle just outside the play's perimeter. The sex workers accepted their temporary displacement; Julia Brothers, who played Miss Arizona, remembers them fixing her makeup on occasion. Jim Ortenzio of Long Island Beef, a Shakespeare-quoting meat magnate and de facto boss of the district, gave his blessing to the project, and (perhaps least comprehensible, three decades on) the local community board approved a nighttime blockade of four city blocks for an entire month. For audiences, the blurring boundaries of the "odd alfresco play"[26] could induce a sense of alienation from reality: "While watching the play, I kept noticing things in the

24. David Kaufman, "Take It to the Streets," *Downtown*, July 18, 1990.

25. Quoted in Renfreu Neff, "Taking It to the Streets," *Contemporanea*, no. 21 (October 1990), 85.

26. Thomas Connors, "Theater, Setting in New Embrace," *International Herald Tribune*, July 25, 1990.

neighborhood—cars driving by trying to figure out what was going on, a prostitute trying to watch the street and the play at the same time, and diners in a nearby restaurant. While I could conjecture that these were 'real' as opposed to theatrical events, I could not be certain."[27] The effect was heightened by local residents (actually actors) hurling trash and invective from windows and rooftops as "dumb-founded, bewildered"[28] onlookers were swept up in the momentum of *Father*'s proceedings, as speakers in wheelbarrows rolled from station to station to be hooked up to car battery-powered amps. Adding to the confusion, actors might play multiple roles, which often included changing genders. There was a sense that no matter where one stood, one was always missing something. In Adam Soch's documentary film on Abdoh, Tom Fitzpatrick, who played Fyodor Karamazov, recalls a particularly frenzied scene change:

You had to run to get from one position to the other. And I had done the scene on the table with the friggin' shot gun and I had to run—book!—way to the other end of Little West 12th Street for my next scene. And I'm running and I'm running and I run into Reza and he grabs me and says, "What happens next? What happens next?! You have to help me. You have to help me!" I'll always remember that. And I said, "I don't know! All I know is that I have a fuckin' entrance and that I'm late. Let go of me!"[29]

27. Thomas Mygatt, "Father Was a Peculiar Man," *Backstage*, August 3, 1990.

28. Carlo Pizzati, "Che macello quel teatro," *Il Venerdì di Repubblica*, September 1, 1990.

29. *Reza Abdoh: Theater Visionary*, dir. Adam Soch (documentary, USA, 104 min, 2015).

Abdoh had devised a play that proved nearly impossible to direct.

On the cusp of gentrification, the Meatpacking District of 1990 oscillates between backdrop and subject of Abdoh's multimedia intertextual pandemonium. Not only a business district and "a home for discos, sex clubs, restaurants, drug dealers, and prostitutes,"[30] this "no-man's-land" had been one of the most popular sites for gay public sex in New York City until the advent of the AIDS crisis. The district was bounded to the south by the Westbeth, perhaps the only affordable artists' housing in New York, and crossed diagonally by elevated rail tracks that had served the defunct West Side Freight Line (later redeveloped into the High Line tourist promenade); to the west, the Hudson River and its crumbling piers, as well as a zone formerly known as "the trucks," where transport vans, cabs, and trucks parked overnight, their open flatbeds playing host to a cultural activity most vividly described in Samuel Delany's 1988 memoir *The Motion of Light in Water*:

> *To step between the waist-high tires and make your way between the smooth or ribbed walls was to invade a space at a libidinal saturation impossible to describe to someone who has not known it. . . . [W]ithin those van-walled alleys, now between the trucks, now in the back of the open loaders, cock passed from mouth to mouth to hand to ass to mouth without ever breaking contact with other flesh for more than seconds; mouth, hand, ass passed over whatever you held out to*

---

30. Mygatt, "Father Was a Peculiar Man," *art. cit.*

them, sans interstice; when one cock left, finding a replacement—mouth, rectum, another cock—required moving only the head, the hip, the hand no more than an inch, three inches.[31]

And yet despite its literal superimposition onto these sites, references to AIDS were few and reticent in reviews of *Father*, as though the play were too irreverent or cacophonous to contend with the terrifying reality of the subject. Perhaps it didn't need to be spelled out. In the year 1990 alone, over 6,000 New Yorkers died of AIDS-related causes. The only real mention of the epidemic appeared in a negative review in *Downtown*, which charged *Father* with not "having anything much to do with the specific site for which it was written,"[32] except for a section:

Near the end, described in the program as "Ivan's Nightmare." Those members of the audience who actually had tickets were ushered inside for this sequence, to the second floor of a building off Washington Street. If this space was not itself The Mine Shaft, the most notorious of a number of gay sex clubs in the area that flourished for a decade prior to the onset of AIDS, it certainly evoked it. A couple could be seen fucking (simulated, of course) in an elevator shaft at the top of the stairs where you entered the space. In the main room, a number of naked men were washing themselves,

31. Samuel R. Delany, *The Motion of Light in Water* (New York: Arbor House, 1988), 150. Here Delany recalls "the trucks" in the early 1960s. [Editors' note]

32. Kaufman, "Take It to the Streets," *art. cit.* While abundantly supportive of Abdoh and his vision, Anne Hamburger later noted that one "thing I'm interested in, which hadn't happened as much as I'd have liked with *Father* . . . is creating a piece out of the fabric of a neighborhood." Quoted in "All the World's a Stage," *art. cit.*, 38.

He was absolutely an unfit father.
IVAN
He'd have done the same for anybody.
FYODOR
How bout some brandy for Balaam's Ass?
Ivan, give him--
SMERDYAKOV
Smerdyakov
FYODOR
some brandy.

I'm having some very mixed feelings at this point, but I'm glad I moved my desk to a better position in the room.

A model walking on long skinny legs down the hallway and out the front door.

Old photographs descend from a hundred apartment windows. Remember our dead with us. Remember our dead.

Oh God! More AIDS Literature.

DMITRI
You're line was busy. I felt like making an emergency breakthrough.
I am a passionate man Katya. Katya, forgive me. Forgive me for being a Karamazov.
KATYA
I want a Karamazov.
MRS. H
Ivan is the Karamazov for you. Don't you see?
KATYA
Ivan? I thought Ivan was a homosexual.

being washed, or involved in a variety of S&M activities. One was hanging upside down and being whipped by another. Still another was sprawled naked and tied to a bed where clothespins were applied over different portions of his body.[33]

Abdoh had told one interviewer that "it was Ivan's nightmare that really hooked me on the tenor and history of Dostoevsky's novel, and thinking about it in this environment."[34] In the script, the scene is introduced with an explanatory note: "THIS PART AND EVERYTHING THAT FOLLOWS SHOWS THAT YOU END UP BEING YOUR FATHER WHETHER YOU WANT TO OR NOT. NO MATTER HOW HARD YOU TRY, YOU END UP BEING YOUR FATHER."

The countless images of *Father* that come down to us in news clippings and photographs, inscribed in viewers' memories or recorded on videotape, often have the quality of a requiem crossed with a Dionysian rite. Yet what they reveal is ultimately a social document. Kyle Chapuis' sets and props, installed along Little West 12th Street, magnify the strangeness of seeing that New York, long since eradicated, in which this spectacle could have taken place. Viewed in retrospect, *Father*'s improbable pageantry calls to mind, and meshes with, images of actual protests in the streets of New York at that time. The massing of bodies in procession or parade, the jumble of effigies, signs, and detritus are nearly indistinguishable from

33. Kaufman, "Take It to the Streets," *art. cit.*
34. Neff, "Taking It to the Streets," *art. cit.*, 85.

the scrambled signifiers of public demonstrations and the anti-logic of riots. "We went back where the little house had been; it was just an outline, in flames."[35] A small American flag conceals a box of Entenmann's donuts on the lawn of the Cleavers' fenced-in home; Mrs. Cleaver plucks the house's "For Sale" sign up from the lawn and brandishes it as an ambivalent protest sign. A strong reciprocity emerges between many of *Father*'s images—of bodies and their surrogates scattered on the cobblestones, crucified, copulating, or hanged from the highway overpass—and the "die-ins" and "kiss-ins" staged by ACT UP at the time. One journalist who had been involved with the group recalled that "ACT UP protests tended to be staged with the panache and precision of a Broadway play, designed with visible props and performed in acts that followed one after another."[36]

If, in the words of Marvin Carlson, the kind of anti-traditional theater practiced by Abdoh marked a "shift in the role of the audience member from passive observer to a figure in some manner actively involved in the production,"[37] *Father* in particular resonates with Louis Marin's reflection on "festive perambulatory events," which proposes "a general structure of theatricality or spectacularity" linking:

35. Munk, "Meaty Metaphors," *art. cit.*

36. Garance Franke Ruta, "History Will Recall, George Bush Did Nothing at All," *The Cut*, December 3, 2018, www.thecut.com/2018/12/george-h-w-bush-aids-protest-act-up.html (last accessed March 8, 2024). Photographer James Estrin, who covered the AIDS crisis for the *New York Times* as a young freelancer, remembered the "die-ins" as "extraordinary. . . . So many people involved in ACT UP were involved in theater or the arts. The types of protests they did were completely different. It had dramatic structure. It was fascinating to photograph. They were, by far, the best protests." Quoted in "Loss, Bravery, and a Deadly Disease," *New York Times*, December 3, 2018.

37. Carlson, *10,000 Nights, op. cit.*, 158.

*Corteges, parades, processions, and demonstrations [which]
all unfold (and the term itself is highly significant) in a preexisting space already articulated in characteristic sites,
which are named or marked: thus, in cities, we find streets,
squares, intersections, bridges, religious or public buildings,
historical monuments, neighborhoods, boundaries, and
frontiers. . . . The parade extracts its setting and its backdrop from this space: because some places are selected and
others are not, because some buildings or monuments will
be visited and others will be bypassed, [it] manipulates the
preexisting space and sites. It gives this space a highly telling structure in which the places selected by the itinerary
articulate the "sentences" of a spatial discourse whose lin-
guistic equivalents (varying according to the situation—
nominal sentences, narrative sequences, and so on) would
be interesting to study. In this discourse, to be sure, the places rejected or avoided by the itinerary proffer a sort of count-
er-discourse, a negative discourse, even a denied or repressed
discourse, that constitutes the background for the chosen
itinerary and on the basis of which this itinerary takes on
supplementary meaning.*[38]

Given the regimentation of sexualities and language during the
AIDS crisis and the culture wars, and amid the mobilization of
bodies in mass acts of civil disobedience—of protest as group
improvisation—Abdoh articulated a baroque vision of corpo-
reality. *Father* generated an excess of dramatic activity, vying

38. Louis Marin, "Establishing a Signification for Social Space: Demonstration, Cortege, Parade, Procession (Semiotic Notes)," in *On Representation*, tr. Catherine Porter
(Stanford, CA: Stanford University Press, 2001), 41–42.

for and with spectator's bodies and attentions. Perhaps an afterimage from their childhood in Tehran recounted by Abdoh's brother Salar provides a cornerstone for *Father*: seeing the city transformed by Ashura, an Islamic martyr's commemoration that for an entire day transforms the streets into a stage for mourning rituals, passion plays, and self-flagellation. Abdoh himself cited "old-fashioned musicals" as an inspiration, because they "really understood how to create realities that were multilayered. . . . That sense of abandon to me, is very liberating, very moving, especially if the culture is really repressive."[39]

The theater historian Stefan Brecht—son to a particular father—noted in his treatise on *Queer Theater* that "the queer artist, having no justification for it, cannot allow himself the disfigurement of care, his art is entirely dependent on energy. But since his energy is entirely dependent on an exuberance of rage, his art, an active rebellion, is prone to degenerate into good-humored comedy and unthinking repetition, and to fall apart."[40] For Abdoh, an artist whose output escalated—after his HIV diagnosis—to what *Der Spiegel* called "a killing-spree against death,"[41] the massed energies, cultural contradictions, and repressions of the Meatpacking District proved crucial to his *Trauerspiel*, in the desire to make "a tapestry that involves some historical context, but is not a history lesson."[42] ◆

39. John Bell, "To Reach Divinity through the Act of Performance: An Interview with Reza Abdoh," *The Drama Review*, vol. 39, no. 4 (T148) (Winter 1995), 50.

40. Stefan Brecht, *Queer Theatre* (Frankfurt am Main: Suhrkamp Verlag, 1978), 9.

41. "Gestorben: Reza Abdoh," *Der Spiegel*, May 1995.

42. John Bell, "To Reach Divinity through the Act of Performance," *art. cit.*, 53.

This text is adapted from an introduction given by Nick Mauss on April 22, 2016, on the occasion of the opening night of Thomas Beard's film series, An Early Clue to the New Direction: Queer Cinema Before Stonewall, *at Lincoln Center in New York.*

"I'm sure I hadn't watched any of these three 'classics' since I rented them on VHS from Kim's video at least 15 years earlier, but as I watched them again, I was surprised by how radical they felt, and how much I still had to learn from them. I remember that I was very nervous giving this introduction, and that I nearly fell off the stage when I finished."

Opening Night of
An Early Clue to the New Direction: Queer Cinema Before Stonewall

The three elaborate fantasies we are about to see—Kenneth Anger's *Fireworks* (1947), Jean Genet's *Un chant d'amour* (1950), and Jean Cocteau's *Blood of a Poet* (1932)—are perhaps best described in Cocteau's words, as "realistic documentaries of unreal events."[1]

By now we can regard the set of conventions that runs through these films much as we would look at red-figure vase painting, or Dutch still-lives. By which I mean we can't really see them at all.

I like how distant the films seem, and I envy the gorgeous megalomania that all three of these artists share.

In the epilogue to *Blood of a Poet*, Cocteau writes that "poems are like coats of arms." Like emblems, one must learn to read them, their parts, together. And in a way this can be said for all three of the films. Cocteau and Genet were celebrity poets who ventured into film—*Un chant d'amour* would be Genet's only realized film—and while Anger is a child of Hollywood, he also speaks of his short films as "film poems."

---

1. This is how Cocteau defined his own film, *Blood of a Poet*. [Editors' note]

Each one demonstrates, flagrantly, the art of fixation, of magnifying something as insignificant as a US Navy matchbook, or the curious pleasure of scraping out the thick dirt from under a toenail—the things close at hand—into a sign or a craving of monumental implications. This is what Genet calls, in *Funeral Rites*: "Poetry . . . or the art of using leftovers. Of using shit and making you eat it."[2]

Is it impossible to see anything today as if for the first time? I can only pose the question in relation to these films: what conditions and ways of being together produce fantasies and language such as these, and how does the viewer stand in relation to them?

Of course, certain things hooked me right away: Jean Desbordes' bakelite hair in *Blood of a Poet*, the poignant lighting of schoolyard cigarettes and the ensuing snow-ball fight where it looks as though the boys are hurling powdered sugar at each other. Lee Miller as an armless classical statue, the defiant masturbation dance by the black prisoner in *Un chant d'amour*, flowers as foreskin and testicles and rosaries, also in *Un chant d'amour*. The buttoning of brand new jeans in *Fireworks*, and the great relief of cum—no—milk washing all over Kenneth Anger's battered face and body, the flaming faggot the sailor uses to light Anger's cigarette, not to mention the most elegant blowjob I've ever seen, imagined, or experienced, for that matter, in *Un chant d'amour*.

While we celebrate these works as among the earliest examples of homosexual film, none of the authors necessarily had

2. Jean Genet, *Pompes funèbres* (1947; Paris: Gallimard, 1993), 683.

this in mind. Genet's film was deemed obscene by the US Supreme Court in 1966 and was banned until 1975 due to its homosexual content. *Fireworks*, made by the seventeen-year-old Kenneth Anger at his parent's house one weekend while they were away, was also tried on obscenity charges. In 1942 a law was passed that condemned homosexuality in France for the first time since 1791, and would remain active until 1982.[3] And we know that sodomy laws in the US were upheld in some states until as recently as 2003.

It is telling how, in an interview with Genet from 1976, when the novelist Hubert Fichte insists that "there isn't a homosexual anywhere in the world now who hasn't been influenced, directly, or indirectly, by your work" (and of course the same could be said of Cocteau), Genet responds by saying:

This risks giving me an importance that in my opinion I don't have. Second, I think you're mistaken, too; what I wrote did not bring about the liberation you're talking about, it's the other way around: it was liberation that came first and that coincided more or less with Germany's occupation of France and the liberation and peace after the war. It was that kind of liberation and freeing up of minds that allowed me to write my books.[4]

---

3. The 1942 discriminative law increased the age of consent for homosexual relations to the age of legal majority (then 21; lowered to 18 in 1974) while it was 15 for heterosexual ones. [Editors' note]

4. Jean Genet, "Interview with Hubert Fichte," tr. Jeff Fort, in *The Declared Enemy: Texts and Interviews*, ed. Albert Dichy (Stanford, CA: Stanford University Press, 2004), 124.

When you watch all three films in succession, even anti-chronologically—as we will tonight—you can see how they are like doors opening up from one to another: they really seem spatially and atmospherically contiguous as a kind of echo-chamber, though *Blood of a Poet* is separated from *Un chant d'amour* and *Fireworks* by a World War. They are part of the same flamboyant architecture of corridors, walls, peepholes, doors, windows, and mirrors. It is possible to trace the influence of Cocteau's vision seeping through to Genet and Anger. But you can also trace other arcs and reciprocities: Cocteau to Genet and back; Anger to Cocteau; Genet to Fassbinder; Cocteau and Genet to Warhol, and it doesn't stop there. In fact, Cocteau seems to have been heavily involved in the aesthetics of *Un chant d'amour*. The title frame alone, styled to look like graffiti on a prison wall, recalls the tattooed walls Cocteau executed in chapels in the South of France and in London. The sailors that populate both Genet's and Cocteau's imaginary become a hot threat in Anger's *Fireworks*, which Cocteau greatly admired.

But if you do away with linear influence, and just let the films wash over you, they begin to refract all over one another, the elements of this elastic vocabulary of chains, doublings, liquids, masks, violence, of the reflected and distorted self, anti-gravity . . . If anything, I wish that as a coda to tonight's screening, we could walk across Lincoln Center Plaza and see a performance of Genet's only ballet, *Adame Miroir*, from 1949, which features US Navy sailors, with one of them dancing in front of mirrors, and suddenly his reflections come to life and the dance is coupled off between self and reflection. Folding Anger together with Cocteau into Genet.

In 1962, the year before he died, Cocteau made a final film called *Jean Cocteau s'adresse à l'an 2000*. In this film he reflects on the role of the poet in society, and on the future public's receptivity to art. He says about his own time:

We remain apprentice robots. I certainly hope that you have not become robots. But on the contrary, that you have become very humanized, that is my hope.

He goes on:

I have been made a character that I am not. A legendary character who is not at all like me, but who protects me in some way . . . I am not that self; I am him, without being him: which means that from our birth to our death we are a stream of others. We are always others . . .

It's possible that this house has disappeared, and, even if the means of transmission no longer exist and my image can't be projected anymore, in any case, I hope to be before you as a ghost even though I don't believe in death. I don't believe in death since it is merely one of the forms of life and I consider that St. Augustine wasn't wrong when he said that a man who believes in antipodes was an utter fool. He was a great saint and thus he couldn't be all wrong.

It is quite clear that we're living according to conventional norms like the calendar or the watch and its likely that we have misled ourselves.

And perhaps that you are still misleading yourselves.

It is possible that what we call progress could prove to be the development of an error. ◆

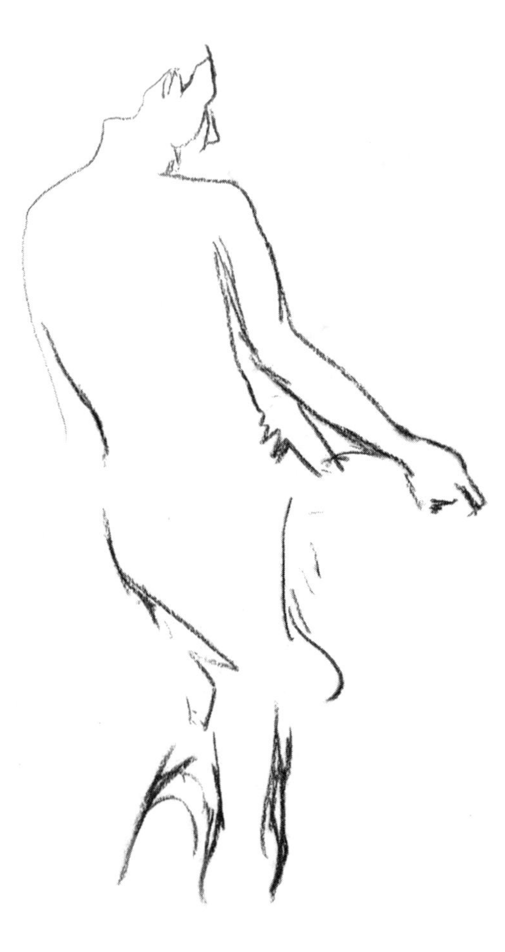

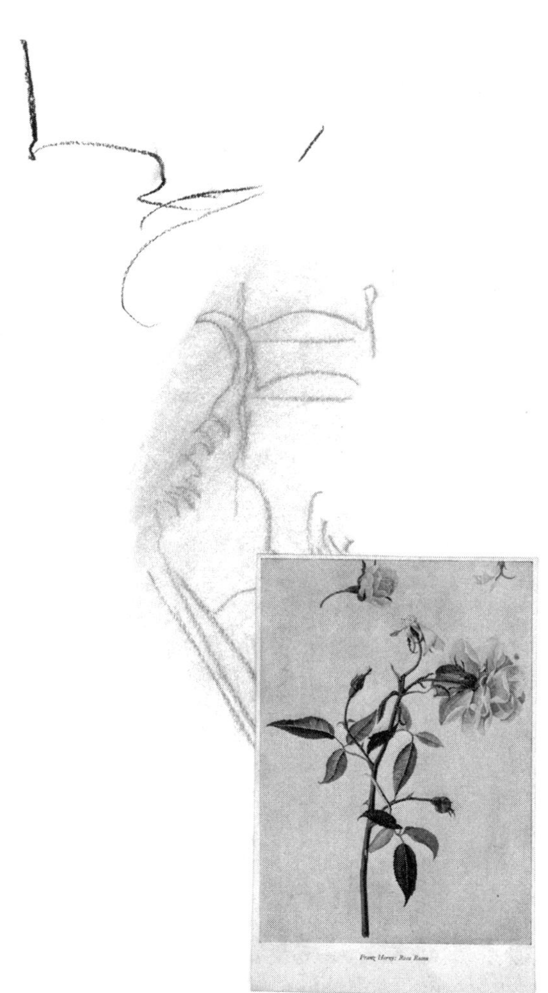

Franz Horny: Rosa Rosa

This essay was originally published in Transmissions, *ed. Nick Mauss, Karen Kelly and Barbara Schroeder, exh. cat. (New York: Whitney Museum of American Art & Dancing Foxes Press, 2020). The book followed the eponymous exhibition by Nick Mauss at the Whitney Museum of American Art, New York (March 16–May 14, 2018).*

Gesturing Personae

I came to ballet late and in reverse—I didn't grow up with it. My first exposure to live dance was through the 2001 White Oak restagings of Judson dances,[1] which made me a devotee of Judson Dance Theater and post-Judson dance. Ballet seemed reactionary, far away, and of no use to me. But my interest in dance was kindled at about the same time I had begun to grow suspicious of a naturalized art-historical canon. The discrepancy between that canon and my own interests or possible artistic antecedents drove me to fashion a new frame of reference for myself. I began to pull at loose threads in the modernist narrative, and these drew my attention to theater, couture, architecture, and decoration, as well as to practitioners who were seldom or no longer spoken of but who opened up worlds outside of given categorical limits. It was in reconsidering standard histories of modernist painting that I encountered Natalia Goncharova's

1. Formed in 1990 by dancers and choreographers Mikhail Baryshnikov and Mark Morris, The White Oak Dance Project aimed at recreating experimental dance pieces of the 1960s and '70s. Their project Past Forward, that gathered works by Trisha Brown, Simone Forti, and Yvonne Rainer, amongst others, was presented at the Brooklyn Academy of Music in New York in June 2021. [Editors' note]

and Marie Laurencin's designs for the Ballets Russes, which taught me that the unassailable version of modernism I had learned could be destabilized when seen from a different point of view where the relation to performance, collaboration, and intersecting media was made primary. Through a succession of different overlays of genealogies, I eventually arrived at the flamboyant intersection of modernist ballet and art in New York in the 1930s through the 1950s. I was surprised to find that this nexus not only articulated an overtly queer erotics long before the emergence of a public language around "queerness" but also engendered experimental cross-media collaborations and dialogues that presaged many of the techniques that are commonly assumed to have emerged in the 1960s. Indeed, as Gerald Murphy, the expatriate American artist who had designed sets for the Cole Porter jazz ballet *Within the Quota* (1923), remarked, "ballet was the focal center of the whole modern movement in the arts."[2]

If ballet really had been "the focal center," I wondered, then why was ballet only mentioned as an aside in histories of modern art? When had the centrality of ballet to the avant-garde been occluded from the historical narrative, and to whose benefit? By looking elsewhere—to the peculiar images and words sparked by ballet—I found what I had been looking for: traces of a wholly different conception of the reciprocity between visual art, dance, and life than the one I had been taught. It is a story that is not often told—one that poses as many questions about how history is constructed as about how it is disfigured and, of course, about how we occupy our own time.

2. Gerald Murphy, quoted in Calvin Tomkins, "Living Well Is the Best Revenge," *New Yorker*, July 28, 1962.

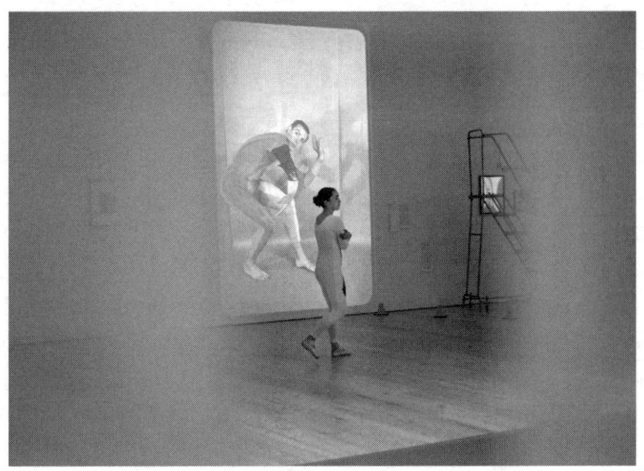

I wondered how the jarring effect of reading accounts, such as the following *Theatre Arts* article from 1951, could be made visible in the form of an exhibition:

List the artists who have been responsible for the settings and costumes of modern ballet and you have a Who's Who of modern art. Picasso, Matisse, Dalí, Rouault, Chagall, Leger, Braque, Dufy, Utrillo, Juan Gris, and Marie Laurencin, all would be included. It is no accident that the rise of the one art form coincides with the rise of the other. It is in large part due to the glamor, color, and excitement with which modern art invested it, that ballet, which traditionally had been the private amusement of aristocrats, became during the past two or three decades the delight of millions. It is also true that modern art won new converts for itself when an audience which normally would have little or no personal contact with the new art to be seen then mostly in small galleries, came under the spell of its brilliant fantasy and dazzling color at public ballet performances.[3]

Like modern art, ballet was not endemic to the United States and would have to be imported, its audience invented. The early twentieth century had produced a new paradigm for ballet in Europe, most notably in the production model of Serge Diaghilev, who invited avant-garde composers and painters to collaborate on ballets whose choreography borrowed as much from Greek vases, cinema, the machine age, and tennis as from the classical vocabulary handed down from the Imperial Russian Ballet. Ballet and painting, both art forms of the royal courts, subverted their classical conventions in tandem through the frame of the proscenium. The future proselytizer of an American ballet idiom, Lincoln Kirstein, wrote in 1937 about Diaghilev's catalytic genius: "Revolutionary cubism hit the ballet with its ton of bricks and horrified the old guard ballet-ballet lovers, which was Diaghilev's earnest intention. Social satire, American jazz, the everyday continental vacation and boulevard life of the nineteen-twenties; dada, neo-classicism, the falsely naïve, the falsely archaic, and decorative folklore . . . were all exposed to the caprice of Diaghilev's ingenious combinations."[4] A panoply of alternate designations for ballet stagings of the early twentieth century attests to the rigorous disarrangements to which this traditional form was subjected, as well as to the various attempts to think dance through its kinship dynamics with

3. Emily Genauer, "Modern Art and the Ballet: The Trend Is toward Separation," *Theatre Arts* 35, no. 10 (October 1951), 16.

4. Lincoln Kirstein, *Blast at Ballet: A Corrective for the American Audience* (New York: Marstin Press, 1938), 15.

other media: choreographic poem, burlesque scenes, danced legend in six pictures, choreographic picture, choreographic fantasy, romantic reverie, the first paranoiac performance, sculptural poses in three tableaux, entertainment, danced poem, mythological poem, pantomime in ten pictures, games and dances, rehearsal without décor, scenic work, a ballet document in one act.[5]

Prone to capitalize on public scandal, modernist ballet also inflamed controversies along ideological lines, such as the one that arose on the opening night of *Romeo and Juliet* in 1926, when André Breton and Louis Aragon, while chanting, "Long live the Soviets, long live the Russian Revolution!" scattered protest leaflets from the balcony over the ballet audience, accusing their former peers Max Ernst and Joan Miró of selling out Surrealism by collaborating with Diaghilev for the sake of entertainment.

PROTEST

It is inadmissible that ideas should be at the behest of money. Not a year goes by but that someone whom one thought to be unshakeable submits to forces to which he was opposed until then. Those individuals who capitulate to the point of disregarding social distinctions are of no importance, for the ideal to which they paid allegiance before their abdication survives without them. That is why the participation of the painters Max Ernst and Joan Miró in the forthcoming

5. The descriptors enumerated here are appended to the titles of the following ballets: *The Afternoon of a Faun* (1912); *Petrushka* (1911); *Nobilissima Visione* (1938); *Le Spectre de la rose* (1911); *Les Sylphides* (1909); *Bacchanale* (1931); *Mercure* (1924); *Le Bal* (1929); *Scheherazade* (1910); *Jeux* (1913); *Narcisse* (1911); *The Triumph of Neptune* (1927); *Midnight Sun* (1915); *Romeo and Juliet* (1938); *Le Train Bleu* (1924).

production of the Russian Ballet can never imply that although they have abandoned their class the surrealist ideal has done likewise. It is essentially a subversive ideal which cannot come to terms with such enterprises, whose goal has always been to tame the dreams and rebellions of physical and intellectual hunger for the profit of the international aristocracy.

It may have seemed to Ernst and Miró that their collaboration with M. de Diaghilev, legitimised by the example of Picasso, would not have serious consequences. However, it puts us under the obligation—we who have all the worry of maintaining slave-ships of every kind of advanced thought out of reach—of denouncing, without consideration of the people involved, an attitude which arms the worst partisans with questionable ethics.

We know that we are only making out a very relative case for our artistic relationship with such and such. Give us the honor of believing that in May 1926 we are more than ever incapable of sacrificing our sense of real revolution.[6]

I looked to American magazines of the 1930s and 1940s as carriers for multiple dissonant messages, their covers often featuring works by the same artists who intervened on transatlantic ballet stages, as well as in museums and galleries. The pages of fashion magazines, in particular, provided both a conduit for the popularization of vanguard European aesthetics, as

6. André Breton and Louis Aragon, translated in Alexander Schouvaloff, *The Art of Ballet Russes: The Serge Lifar Collection of Theater Designs, Costumes, and Paintings at Wadsworth Atheneum, Hartford, Connecticut* (New Haven, CT & London: Yale University Press, 1997), 196.

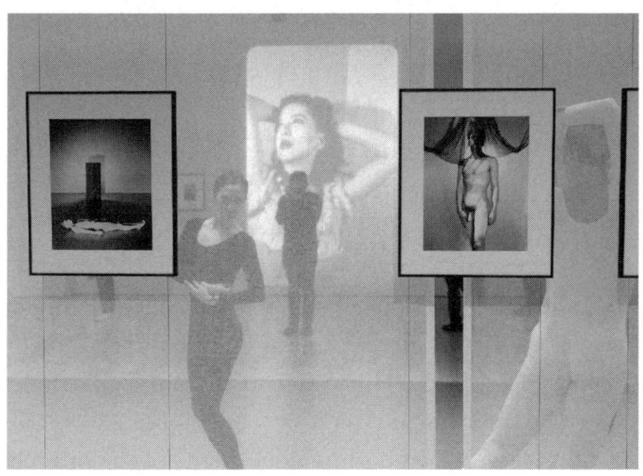

well as a stage for certain kinds of performance, in which the frozen pose of the model had clearly been lifted from a repertoire of danced gestures, as in a spread devoted to jewelry modeled by the Ballet Theatre dancer Sono Osato photographed by George Platt Lynes. In another instance, an invocation of ballet's recent past appears in an advertisement for American Enka brand rayon (transformed by the Hollywood costume designer Adrian into a "Greek-style" dress), via a cameo appearance by the dancer Leon Danielian costumed in the title role of Vaslav Nijinsky's iconic *Afternoon of a Faun.*[7] The interplay of glamour, vanguard art, ballet, and stylized history made a

7. I invoke the concept of the "recent past" as it is analyzed in Walter Benjamin's *Arcades Project*: "This unrelenting confrontation of the recent past with the present moment is something new, historically. Other contiguous links in the chain of generations have existed within the collective consciousness, but they were hardly distinguished from one another within the collective. The present, however, already stands to the recent past as the awakening stands to the dream." Walter Benjamin, *The Arcades Project*, trans. Howard Eiland and Kevin McLaughlin (Cambridge, MA & London: Belknap Press of Harvard University Press, 2002), 898.

potent cocktail, most poignantly blended by Lynes, for transmitting aesthetic innovation, coded desire, and commerce. During the course of his lifetime, Lynes created a vast body of studio photographs of ballet dancers in poses excerpted from their dances and of models in fashion tableaux or other allegories of war, mythology, and eros. Lynes' artistic output describes a double life of sorts, encompassing works made for public and commercial dissemination as well as private works made for friends or for a distant future. Often Lynes' models—including visual artists, lovers, and cultural icons—spanned both dimensions. Despite their high artifice, or maybe because of it, Lynes' photographs serve as crystalline documents of the interchange between him and his subjects, archiving tensions between intimacy and distance.

The Kinsey Institute for Sex Research houses one of the largest collections of Lynes' prints and negatives, a testament to its judicious founder, Alfred Kinsey, who understood the reciprocity between aesthetics and human sexuality as much as the need to preserve for future study all manner of images that produced or documented pleasure. Thus, Lynes' work, in which erotics and aesthetics are tuned to the same pitch, was saved from destruction by censorship laws that would have deemed it pornographic, housed in a heterogenous collection that would expand to include photographs of Nijinsky; dancers from the Denishawn School of Dancing and Related Arts; charts of tattoos; Japanese woodblock prints; scientific films of onanism, fellatio, sodomy (and more); as well as avant-garde films such as Jack Smith's *Flaming Creatures* (1963) and Kenneth Anger's *Kustom Kar Kommando* (1970). In looking through thousands of Lynes' images, I began to read them like a telephone book of artists, patrons, writers, models, impresarios, and dancers, and a highly enlivened view of New York's explicitly sexual cultural scenes emerged.

The dance critic, novelist, and cultural advocate Carl Van Vechten produced his own intimate archive of ballet in New York, photographing dancers, choreographers, lighting designers, and costumers in his apartment. Unlike Lynes, whose photographs' overt sexual content is intensified by their studio gloss, Van Vechten was an amateur in Roland Barthes' sense of "one who loves and loves again";[8] the photographer often privately circulated his images as self-made postcards or presented them to visiting friends as slideshows.[9] In these highly staged "photographic séances," Van Vechten's evident delight in set dressing and costuming—in selecting fabrics of an intense opticality as backdrops and evocative props to suit a subject's innate or performed character—heightens the sense of a playful rapport between the photographer and his subjects that led to digressions from balletic description into mutual fantasies of identity (de)construction. His subjects include the costume designer Barbara Karinska, prima ballerina Janet Collins, Alicia Markova's legendary hands isolated in classic ballet gestures, the young Arthur Mitchell flanked by Swedish Christmas angels, Hugh Laing posing in improvised costumes, and Nora Kaye as the ax murderer Lizzie Borden in Agnes de Mille's *Fall*

8. Roland Barthes, *Roland Barthes by Roland Barthes*, trans. Richard Howard (Berkeley & Los Angeles: University of California Press, 1994), 52.

9. See Paul Padgette, introduction to *The Dance Photography of Carl Van Vechten* (New York: Schirmer Books, 1981), 14. *Transmissions* was the first instance in which Van Vechten's slides of dances were publicly presented, and I am grateful to the Jerome Robbins Dance Division of the New York Public Library for the Performing Arts, Peter Kayafas, and Edward Burns of the Van Vechten Trust, for preserving them so beautifully and making it possible to share them with a greater public.

River Legend (1948). The artists portrayed in Van Vechten's slides range from some of the most famous in twentieth-century ballet to people who are all but forgotten. Many re-create for the camera instances from ballets that are still performed today, though with costumes that were shed from the repertoire long ago. As a repository of outmoded styles and lost languages of gesture and camp, Van Vechten's slides constitute an archive of singular importance.[10] It is fitting that Van Vechten's efforts to immortalize dancers and their dramatic roles lives on in immaterial form, as a succession of projections. The undeniable presence of these images shivers between the camera, the subject's gaze, and the contemporary viewer, who sees these larger-than-life slide-projection figures as if they are performing live. The brilliant color of the Kodachromes nearly shocks. Studying the backlit images through a loupe in the dance division of the New York Public Library, I couldn't help but dialectically conjure, like some kind of catechism, Yvonne Rainer's "No Manifesto" of 1965, to laugh at the glorious defiance of each of its provocations, which I and so many other inheritors of 1960s art and performance history had mistakenly internalized as unassailable tenets: "NO to spectacle no to virtuosity no to transformations and magic and make-believe no to the glamour and transcendency of the star image no to the heroic no to the anti-heroic no to trash imagery no to involvement of performer or spectator no to style no to camp no to seduction of spectator

10. The fact that some of Van Vechten's images of performing artists date from the early 1960s verifies the persistence of those languages and their overlap with not only modern but early postmodern dance aesthetics. One of Andy Warhol's assistants from the later years, Benjamin Liu (aka Ming Vase), remembers that Van Vechten was discussed in an early issue of Warhol's *Interview*, a context in which he registered no longer as a mainstream cultural commentator but as a kind of subcultural curio. Liu, conversation with the author, April 2018.

by the wiles of the performer no to eccentricity no to moving or being moved."[11]

But I was moved by these performances for the camera.[12] I had been looking for antecedents for recent queer, experimental, collaborative, transdisciplinary practices, and I had been looking for a certain New York—one that I didn't have any evidence of and that nobody ever spoke about. It is no accident that this search fixated on a historical blind spot, somewhere between Van Vechten, Judson, and Stonewall, though it also kept shifting depending on where I placed emphasis. I wanted to know what an art history of pre-Stonewall New York would look like, and both Van Vechten's intimate images and Lynes' tableaux offered visual evidence of sensibilities, complex interrelationships, modes of exchange, and ways of being that did not conform to the streamlined narratives of art or its progress through the twentieth century as we have internalized them.

11. Yvonne Rainer, "Some Retrospective Notes on a Dance for 10 People and 12 Mattresses Called 'Parts of Some Sextets,' Performed at the Wadsworth Atheneum, Hartford, Connecticut, and Judson Memorial Church, New York, in March, 1965," *Tulane Drama Review* 10, no. 2 (Winter 1965), 178.

12. I do not intend here to enforce an opposition between Rainer's work and the images of a lost aesthetic captured by Van Vechten. In the context of the essay in which it originally appears, the "No Manifesto" carries a different valence. Rainer herself revised the manifesto in 2008 to give greater flexibility to "the rules and boundaries of my own artistic game of the moment," as she had described the litany of refusals in 1965, pointing to an anxiety about the way an excerpt from her essay had been received, taught, and distorted as dogma. If anything, my confrontation with Van Vechten's images revealed a bridge between these hitherto antithetical practices, an unexpected juncture allowing for the implications of each philosophical proposition to come into greater relief. During the final edit of the book, *Transmissions*, I had the opportunity to participate in the reconstruction of Rainer's 1965 *Parts of Some Sextets*, in the context of Performa 19, a collaboration between Rainer and Emily Coates, in which I performed movements originally intended for Robert Morris. Subsequently, Rainer, Coates, and I produced a book that documents the "life and the after-life" of this complex dance and its reception(s): *Remembering a Dance: Parts of Some Sextets, 1965/2019* (New York: Performa; Hartford, CT: Wadsworth Atheneum Museum of Art, & Milan: Lenz Press, 2023). (The book comprises a facsimile of Rainer's *Tulane Drama Review* essay.)

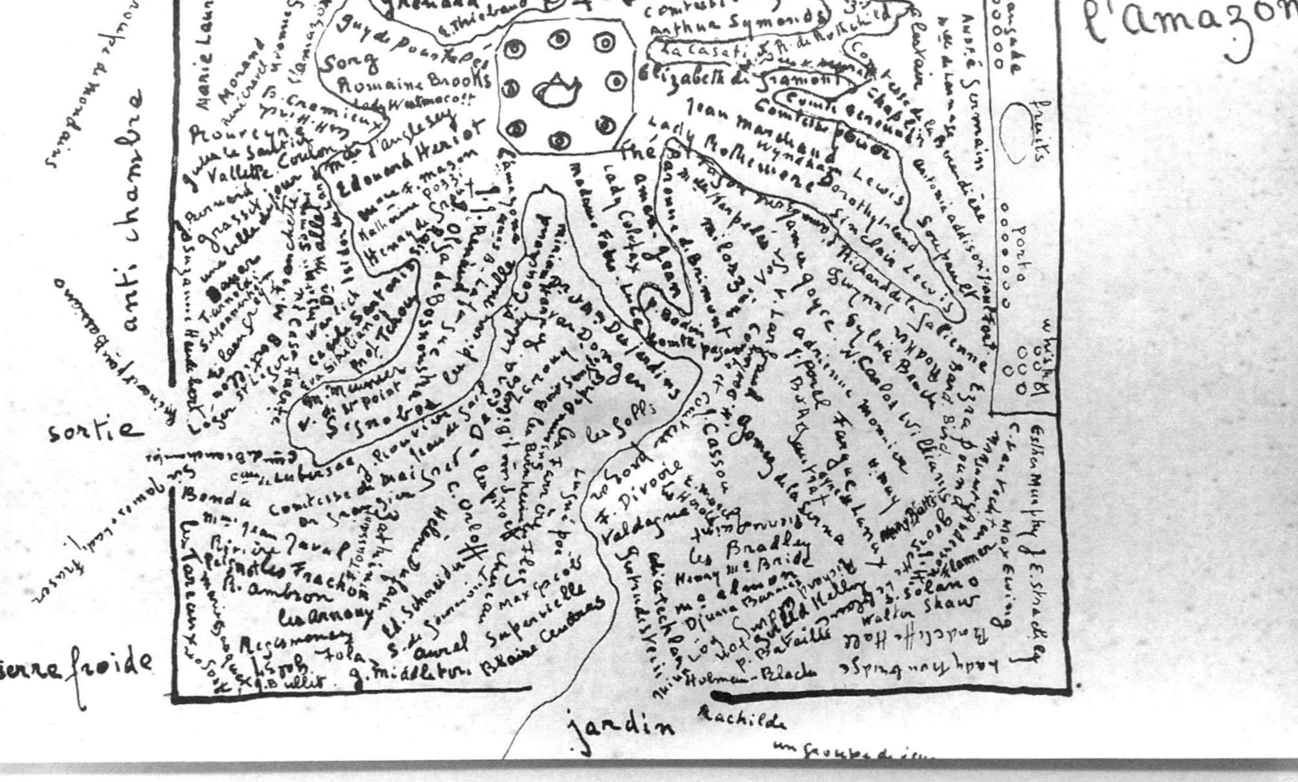

l'amazone
anti chambre
sortie
serre froide
jardin
Rachilde
fruits
porto
whisky
orangeade
Marie Laurencin
Morand
B. Cremieux
Song
Romaine Brooks
Lady Wstmacott
Guy de Pourtalès
Grenard
E. Thiébaut
Jean Giraudoux
Edouard Herriot
Mme de l'Anglesey
Valette Couton
Julie Sabiee
Fleureyns
Renard
grassy
Katherine Pozzi
Henry de Saut
Isidore
De Mallet
mol Tchou
V. Signo Goa
Lr. Poiret
M. Meunier
Sibilano
Lupin-millo
amazone Jean
La Casati
Anthna Symonds
A. de Rothschild
Elizabeth de Gramont
Jean marchand
Wyndham Lewis
Dorothy Ireland
Comtesse Power
André Germain
Lady Rothermere
Thé
Lady Colefax
Madame Fabre Luce
comtesse de Maison
Comtesse du Maigner
en Saxe
Katherine Mansfield
La Duchesse d'Uzès
Bonda
Rivière Javal
R. ambron
Les annony
H. Schneider
St Sauveur
St aurel
Superville
Blaise Cendrars
g. middleton
Messmoney
Fola
W. B. Wellit
R. Toussaint
Les Sofis
F. Divoire
Casso
E. Hacock
Valdagne
Suhudi
les Bradley
Henry Mc Bride
mo alonon
Djuna Barnes
P. Bataille
Holmen-Black
Walter Shaw
Esther Murphy J. E. Strachey
Max Ewing
Radcliffe Hall
Lady Troubridge
J. Joyce
V. Vost
Carlos Williams
admiral
Richard Aldington
Sylvia Beach
Gwyn
Bryher
Bricktop
Mary Butts
un groupe de...

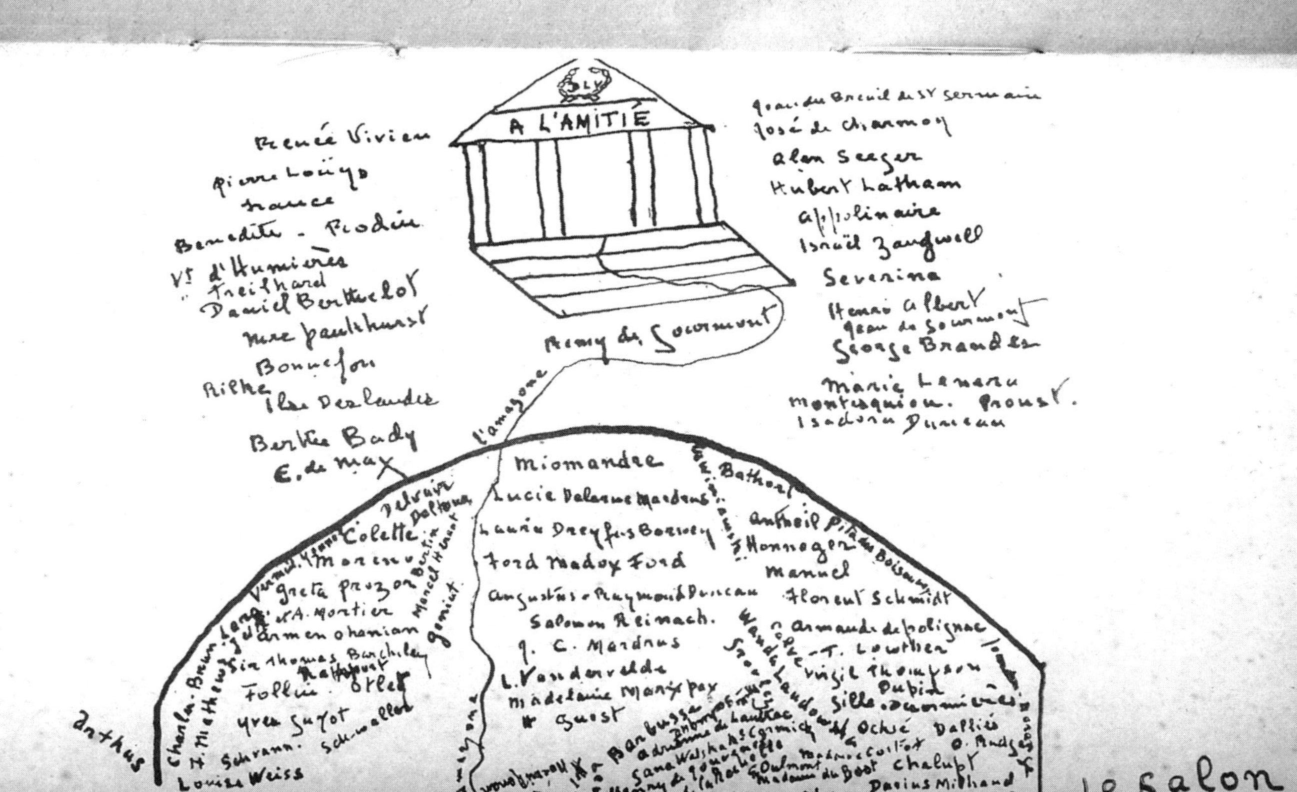
A L'AMITIE
Renée Vivien
Pierre Louÿs
France
Bénédite - Rodin
V. d'Humières
Treilhard
Daniel Berthelot
Mrs Pankhurst
Bonnefon
Rilke
Ilse Deslandes
Berthe Bady
E. de Max
Remy de Gourmont
l'amazone
Jean du Breuil de St Germain
José de Charmoy
Alan Seeger
Hubert Latham
Appolinaire
Israël Zangwill
Séverine
Henri Albert
Jean de Gourmont
George Brandes
Marie Lenéru
Montesquiou. Proust.
Isadora Duncan
Miomandre
Lucie Delarue Mardrus
Laurie Dreyfus Barney
Ford Madox Ford
Augustus & Raymond Duncan
Salomon Reinach.
J. C. Mardrus
L. Vandervelde
Madeleine Mony Pay
M Guest
Colette
Greta Prozon
A. Mortier
Armen Ohanian
Thomas Barchley
Follen Otlet
Yves Guyot
H. Schirann. Schwabe
Louise Weiss
Anthus
Bathori
Antheil Pitaud Boissier
Honneger
Manuel
Florent Schmidt
armande de Polignac
T. Lowther
Virgil Thompson
Dubin
Sille
Barbusse
Lautrec
Sana Walska McCormick
Henry de la Roche
Ochsé Dallies
Gourmont McCullot
Madame du Bost Chalupt
Darius Milhaud
le salon

When I came upon the dedication in Charles Henri Ford's volume of selected poems from 1972, *Flag of Ecstasy*, I found remarkable its address not to one but to many distinct individuals from the author's past and present who may or may not have known each other—and may or may not have even liked each other if they did. It is not a list of people one would necessarily think of as associated, and it gives its many unknowns the same weight as its luminaries. It begs questions: who are they, and how are they all related? In Ford's configuration, even those I was already familiar with had new significance. After some time spent reading the list over and over, I couldn't help but notice that nearly all these artists and writers seemed to be linked into this transatlantic network/milieu via Gertrude Stein: the mother of us all.[13]

I drew multiple webs of interrelationships, elective affinities, and echo waves of influence, focusing as much on the social, professional, sexual, and collaborative points of contact as on transhistorical resonances that were in some cases perhaps fantasy—eschewing standard mappings of modern art. To contravene the bizarre authority invested in Alfred H. Barr's diagrams of art of the modern period, I embraced anachrony and distortion over apparent objectivity. Ultimately, the most inspired social diagram arrived in the form of a drawing by Natalie Clifford Barney, inserted between the endpapers and frontispiece of her 1929 collection of essays, *Aventures de l'Esprit*. Barney's map details the many guests who came over the years to the salon she hosted in the Doric "temple of friendship"

---

13. Stein was a "mother" to a number of figures in *Transmissions*, including Charles Henri Ford, George Platt Lynes, Virgil Thomson, and Carl Van Vechten, to name only a few of the figures who she introduced to one another and whose work she supported.

beside her house in Paris starting in 1910. It's nearly impossible to read or figure out. As such, it not only represents the open form of this kind of gathering but also indexes with humor and charm and in a kind of chaotic complexity the passage of a few people through a particular place in time (notice the teapot around the tiny table at the center). The map admits its own insufficiency. I can decipher a few names: here too are Gertrude Stein, as well as Djuna Barnes, Colette, Eileen Gray, Rainer-Maria Rilke, and even some who moved from this social scene in Paris to the overlapping New York circles of my research: Isadora Duncan, Darius Milhaud, Virgil Thomson, and Carl Van Vechten. This *Temple de l'Amitié* gave me a conceptual model for the swarming that I hoped to picture in the form of an exhibition. I was beginning to understand that I wanted neither to conclusively portray early ballet in New York nor to glorify a lost sensibility but to transmit multiple simultaneous relations (among works of art and among people). Though punctured by voids and elisions, this construction would have to hold up against the irremediability of certain histories, figures, anecdotes, circumstances, artworks, dances, gestures, events, speech acts, and biographies.

It occurred to me that the history of dance in America, like the history of modern visual art that was ringing increasingly false, was marked by a rift: the most daring practitioners of dance in the United States in the first half of the twentieth century were women, many of whom made their careers abroad.[14]

14. Josephine Baker, Isadora Duncan, Katherine Dunham, and Loie Fuller are among the American dance makers who left an indelible mark on early twentieth-century visual culture in Europe.

These were makers of modern dance, even if some of what they made was termed ballet (in the US, the blanket term tended to be thrown on almost any artistic arrangement of bodies on a stage). Jill Johnston, the radical public intellectual who began her career as a dance critic and had worked in the dance division of the New York Public Library, narrates the fissure in the story of American dance as follows:

I had a powerful subconscious understanding of dance in America as a matriarchal tradition. Isadora Duncan was our founding matriarch. I saw her at the head of some family tree consisting of women. The story I had developed, and at length updated, went something like this: There had been something awful going on in Europe called the ballet, which was punitive toward women. But the ballet was the only form of respectable professional dance that existed for women. In the meantime, women in America were tasting greater freedom through the early feminist movement. The ballet had not taken hold here. A woman from California called Isadora, who knew all about ballet and had a free sort of California spirit, invented a dance that didn't bind the body or depend on men to look good. She was succeeded by other pioneering-type women, St. Denis, then Humphrey and Graham, who applied their intellects to dance making to invent whole techniques and formal approaches to choreography. . . . Then somewhere along in there the European ballet got a foothold in America. Modern dancers welcomed the opportunity to go to ballet classes and strengthen themselves or increase their range, but were powerless to stop an invasion that eventually obscured the through line of the American modern dance. . . . Ballet companies sprang up everywhere. The money went to ballet. Modern dance became a poor sister. And women were returned to the pedestal and made to appear silly in tutus and dependent on men to look good.[15]

Johnston's intentionally partisan account rhymed with my own initial aversion to ballet as a restrictive tradition, but by now I was convinced that the story of modernist ballet was much more lawless and unconventional than received ideas would have me believe. Dance historian Sally Banes dispels the assumption that ballet and modern dance developed in opposition to one another, suggesting a relationship of reciprocal parasitism: "More like a sibling rivalry than the unadulterated hostility of enemy camps, it has been threaded through with similarities as well as sharp distinctions, love as well as envy, collaborations and incessant jostling for dominance."[16] Thanks to a novice audience, American ballet was freed from the strictures of European protocols and could try out anything and take from anyone. The resulting magpie aesthetic often made it difficult to discern the frayed borders between ballet, modern, and social dance.

In the 1920s, decades before ballet's naturalization into the culture, the form was "colonizing the sister arts in various ways: borrowing techniques, styles, moves, structures, themes, ideas, and values, as well as composers and designers from modern dance and synthesizing it with classical ballet, as well as jazz

15. Jill Johnston, "How Dance Artists and Critics Define Dance as Political," in *Secret Lives in Art: Essays on Art, Literature, Performance* (Chicago: A Capella, 1994), 96.

16. Sally Banes, "Sibling Rivalry: The New York City Ballet and Modern Dance," in *Dance for a City: Fifty Years of New York City Ballet*, ed. Lynn Garafola with Eric Foner (New York: Columbia University Press, 1999), 74.

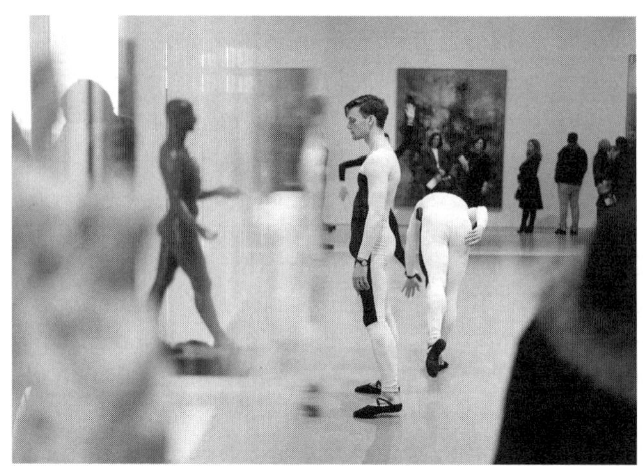

and social dancing."[17] I find Banes' use of the term "colonizing" in this context astute, in that it names the problematics.[18] Modernist ballet's ascendancy roughly coincided with the waning of the Jazz Age, and many of its productions were laced with quotations and appropriations from African American dance forms and their derivatives. Such "borrowings" may have been motivated by a certain American flair for the exotic as much as by an urgent desire on the part of choreographers to articulate, desegregate, and revise what constituted American concert dance or even American art in general. The questioning of all terms, including the term "American art," carries into *Transmissions* in emphasizing the crucial cultural contributions made by artists who were not considered wholly American—owing either to exile or emigration from their country of origin

17. *Ibid.*, 78.

18. It is the problems in history that are interesting to me, not the ways in which a cleaned-up past might affirm our fantasies about a desired present.

or to the fact that they live(d) as second-class citizens in "America." And though ballet has been yoked to an ideology of "whiteness," many images of modernist ballets in America attest to a reality in which deep-seated segregation came up against earnest (and often problematic) endeavors to create modern dances that reflected the totality of a riven yet miscegenated culture, both in its dancers and in the gestures they articulated. The fact that American ballet was often produced by European or Russian émigrés working with American ("American" here meaning performers of the African diaspora, as well as of Caribbean, European, Japanese, and Native American descent), European, and Russian dancers to broadcast a jumble of national themes through various caricatures makes it difficult, from our current vantage point, to adequately parse the tangled politics of these productions.

The question of black influence and of what Erin K. Maher terms "black self-representation in concert dance"[19] under Jim Crow laws is also hard to track, especially given the number of avant-garde dance productions featuring all-black casts during the interwar period (from Gertrude Stein and Virgil Thomson's opera *Four Saints in Three Acts* (1934), notable for its casting of performers in roles that were not race-typed, to Agnes de Mille's first ballet, an exoticist production called *Obeah* (1940), also known as *Black Ritual*, featuring sixteen African American female dancers who were not trained in ballet). These productions coincided with the emergence of "performances of theatricalized African diaspora social dance" by Katherine Dunham, one of several independent black choreographers with all-black

19. Erin K. Maher, "Ballet, Race, and Agnes de Mille's Black Ritual," *Musical Quarterly* 97, no. 3 (Fall 2014), 415.

companies.[20] Needless to say, critical scrutiny of a modern visual culture addicted to exoticism and primitivism must extend to modernist dance in order to assess the more brutal terms of representation and embodiment in these interconnected fields.

My decision to insist on ballet as the fulcrum in *Transmissions* was also a response to the ubiquity of postmodern dance derivations within the contemporary museum environment and the reductive version of modernity that these prequalified dance idioms signify and cement. Contemporaneity is reduced to a "look" of modernity. Modernist ballets make for engaging historical documents precisely because their own relationship to history is a kind of suspension of disbelief; they are intrinsically modernist, even if they don't "signal" modernity to contemporary eyes. But I had also noticed an undeniable difference in the images produced by ballet as compared to those produced by modern dance. While modern dance appeared enigmatic, cold, and intellectual, ballet was allowed to be highly sexualized and eclectic. Ballet images also tend to focus on and exalt the individual dancer/subject, whereas the modern dancer (unlike the auteur choreographer) was often made anonymous through universalization. The ballet dancer's headshot or full body shot—a new type of image convention borrowed from Hollywood—set in motion a peculiar ritual. Since this mechanically produced portrait was only "complete" with the depicted subject's autograph added, the image activated a circuit: seeing, admiring, dreaming about, seeing again, and finally being

20. Thomas F. DeFrantz, "Visualizing Dance of the Harlem Renaissance," in *Dance: American Art 1830–1960*, ed. Jane Dini (New Haven, CT & London: Yale University Press, 2016), 185.

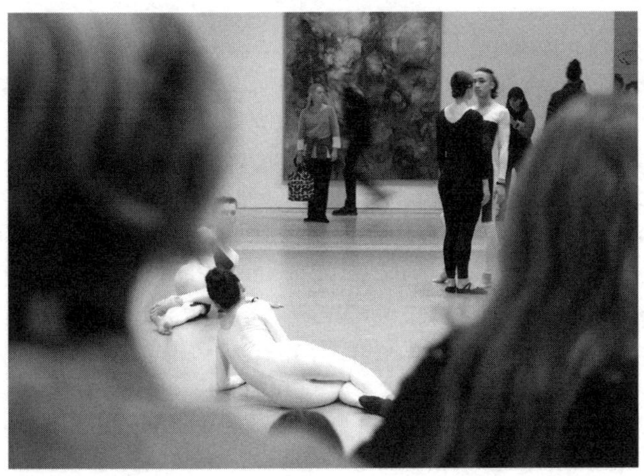

with the photographed subject, obliging the dancer to autograph their likeness as proof of the completed cycle.[21]

In ways I didn't anticipate, *Transmissions* became a historical recoding of a particular genre not only of art dance but also of art photography. Debates around photography's status as an art form (as in Man Ray's self-ironizing multipart text "Photography Is Not Art," published serially in View magazine)[22] dovetailed with the contestation of this other new art form, which happened to be a central subject of modern photography: the work of the dancing body. But the nascent status of photography as art meant that the schism between commercial and

21. Prephotographic ballet fetishes include the collecting of feathers, blossoms, and sequins that had fallen from costumes and, in one apocryphal instance, the boiling of the slippers of cult ballerina Marie Taglioni by her devotees to make a soup for their delectation. See Molly Engelhardt, "Marie Taglioni, Ballerina Extraordinaire: In the Company of Women," *Nineteenth-Century Gender Studies* 6, no. 3 (Winter 2010), www.ncgsjournal.com/issue63/engelhardt.html (last accessed March 8, 2024).

22. Man Ray, "Photography Is Not Art," *View* 3, no. 1 (April 1943), 23, and no. 3 (October 1943), 77–78.

high-art photography was not yet entrenched, so that photographers made use of all venues and surfaces, from catalogues and magazines to galleries and museums. That kind of porosity allowed for poses to filter back and forth between ballet, fashion, and high art in a style gradient that relied heavily on neoclassicism spiked with commercialized Surrealism and a penchant for the "unusual"—the invention of modern glamour paving the way for camp.[23]

By the end of World War II, thanks to the efforts of innumerable ballet academies and companies both imported and native, ballet had established itself as a vastly popular form of entertainment in America. An article in *Fortune magazine*, published just months after the end of World War II, "The Boom in Ballet," announces triumphantly:

There can be little doubt that the most striking artistic development of the past American decade has been the new popular success of ballet. . . . The total audience for these troupes may be estimated at over 1,500,000, and the gross take at $2 million. . . . Even Hollywood has been infected; some of the leading ballerinas have been seen along Wilshire Boulevard. . . .

Some people feel the magic at once. Others require considerable educating as to what they are supposed to see. But learning has been proceeding rapidly in the past decade. A whole new American audience has been discovering the fine art whose diaphanous graces have been rugged enough to

---

23. In this way, the dates of many photographs included in *Transmissions* might cause flashes of surprise. For example, images from the 1940s might, at first glance, be misrecognized as from the 1960s or even 1980s.

withstand every world upheaval since 1700. Aside from the audiences on the road, it is estimated that at least half the ballet's metropolitan public are people who had never seen a pirouette ten years ago.[24]

The delirious prose describing America's newfound balletomania abruptly swerves to warn of the underlying threat posed by the practice of this art form, by which dancers might easily be "infected":

In Virgil Thomson's classic observation: "Dancers are autoerotic and have no conversation." They are professionally obliged to have a preoccupation with their own bodies, and there can be little doubt that a narcissistic degree of it has often helped to promote the extraordinary graces the great soloists achieve. But if dancers spend much of their time in that erotic direction that Sigmund Freud declares is natural to all in infancy, it is a truism that many male dancers are also homosexual. This is perhaps very largely due to the middle-class prejudice against dancing as a male profession; few boys are encouraged in a dancing bent that might lead to a ballet career. In any case, the androgynous effect provided by many male ballet dancers is not admired by ballet specialists any more than it is by steam fitters who have wandered in out of curiosity. The ideal is the pliant vigorous masculine air.[25]

24. "The Boom in Ballet," *Fortune*, vol. 32, no. 6 (December 1945), 226.
25. *Id.*

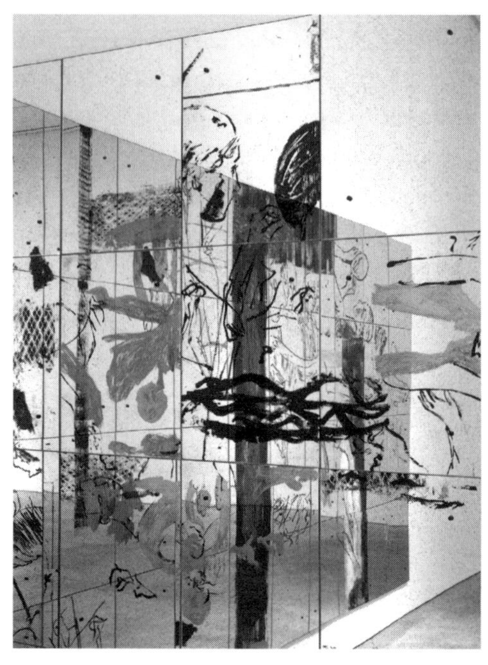

A surprisingly public reckoning with the specter of homosexuality, the fear of aberrant sexuality (and its class inscription) elaborated in this fantastical diatribe threatens to "out" dancers deemed too androgynous or even "feminine"—evidence of the tacit, though fragile, cover that ballet provided homosexual men on many fronts. To spectators, it offered a meeting place at a time when public congregation by homosexuals was forbidden; to performers, amateurs, or fans, it gave license to a complex negotiation of image, self, and desire behind the strict hetero-binary coding of ballet's narratives; to visual artists, it gave free rein to an erotic object, more naked than nude but appropriately cloaked in culture.

The world of the spectator, the receiver, was a primary lens through which I constructed *Transmissions*, and the flux of the exhibition's daily audience over the course of two months took on a central role within it. This book is similarly directed at the wholly different—private, rather than social—negotiations of the reader. A number of visitors commented that the eighth-floor gallery of the Whitney Museum felt more like a studio or some other space between public and private than like a museum. The visitors to *Transmissions*—their impressions, anecdotes, memories, questions, and consternation—completed what was from the outset an experiment in juxtaposing protocols of an historical exhibition with more porous artistic processes (including a collaboration with sixteen dancers).[26] And in my interactions with visitors, I understood the subject of *Transmissions* to be the memory of the body against the memory of the institution.

Transmissions became an exhibition (in its literal sense: a public display) of what the museum, as an extension of the culture, had repressed. This book is intended as a continuation of that project. I also would like to state emphatically that the histories addressed in *Transmissions* are not, as many people would like to continue to believe, minor histories. These artists and performers operated at the very center of American culture, with a high degree of visibility, popularity, influence, and support. What I laid bare in *Transmissions* is the process

26. See Allie Tepper, "Legacies of Exchange," in Nick Mauss, *Transmissions*, exh. cat. (New York: Whitney Museum of American Art & Dancing Foxes Press, 2020), 170–71; and "Nick Mauss in Conversation with Dancers Alexandra Albrecht, Kristina Bermudez, Maggie Cloud, Brandon Collwes, Jasmine Hearn, Elizabeth Hepp, Forrest Hersey, Alexandra Jacob, Burr Johnson, Maki Kitahara, Evelyn Kocak, Benedict Nguyen, Matilda Sakamoto, Quenton Stuckey, and Anna Thérèse Witenberg," in *ibid.*, 172–80.

of my own realization that American modernism is constituted by the very forms and protagonists that are claimed to fall
outside its scope. In treating ballets as connective tissue, I began to see a kind of looping correlation everywhere. The myth
of single authorship evaporated in countless collaborations, as
did the phantom of purity that seemed to enshroud ballet and
modern art. Every object I looked at opened up a new set of social, professional, sexual, and intellectual affinities and contradictions among protagonists who were often also spectators of
the multiauthored, time-based artworks they contributed to, so
that the cliché of an artist-as-set-designer proved too one-sid-
ed to account for the dedicated synergy and tension between
these imbricated worlds. I searched through collection data-
bases for works of art that emerged from this pluralized moment, works that are usually put in the service of a neutralized
history. But it was the artifacts of dance history that uncovered
what had been obscured by art history, pronouncing how false
it is to speak of one without the other. ♦

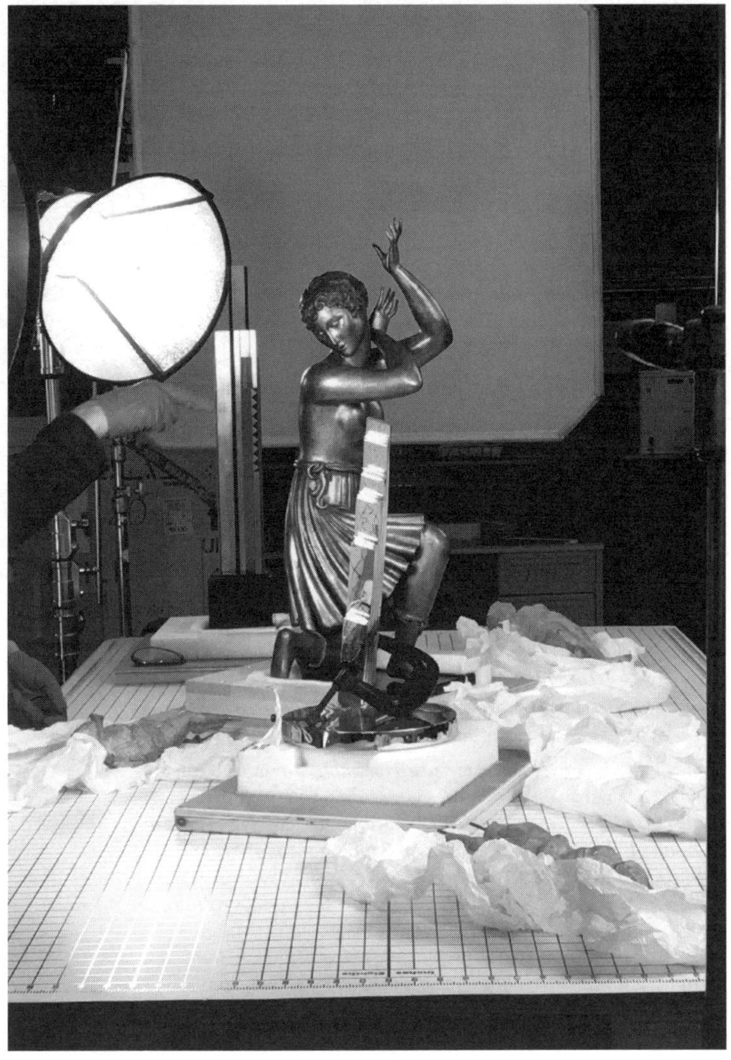

This conversation took place on May 13, 2018, in the context of Nick Mauss' exhibition Transmissions, *at the Whitney Museum of American Art.*

"I made the seemingly counterintuitive choice to invite Fran Lebowitz to reflect on ballet, AIDS, and the changing cultural landscape of New York City. But, as Megan Heuer, Director of Public Programs and Public Engagement at the Whitney, explained: 'Although the explicit focus of Transmissions *is on the decades around the Second World War, the show is equally a meditation on postmodernist questions about reception, repetition, and appropriation. Nick's interest in the historical materials he has brought together doesn't reside only in the past but also in the unrealized presents and futures that these artists and their work might have and might yet still produce. I think that's why when I asked Nick who we should invite to speak about ballet on the occasion of the exhibition, he said, in my memory, almost immediately, 'Fran Lebowitz.'"*

We Mostly Lived in Public:
A Conversation with
Fran Lebowitz at the
Whitney Museum
of American Art

FRAN LEBOWITZ: Hi.

NICK MAUSS: *Thank you, Fran, for being here on this grey Mother's Day. I've been hanging on to your every word since I moved to New York City, essentially. So it would be an understatement to say that I'm thrilled to be here with you.*

— Thank you.

— *Obviously, the historical framework of* Transmissions, *the exhibition I've made around modernist ballet as a cultural nexus in the 1930s to 1950s, predates you . . .*

— Just.

— *. . . but I began to feel as though the artistic achievements of this period cast long shadows forward. What drew me to this period is not so much the time itself but the way in which we are connected or disconnected from the ways of living that made this culture and why. You have this incredible memory and an uncanny ability to zoom very far out and also to recount the* *most minute and crucial details. So when I was thinking about who could speak as a witness to New York and to other kinds of participation and spectatorship, commentary, criticism, and discourse that stand apart from the situation we now find our-selves in, I thought immediately of you.*

To begin, I'd love to hear about what first brought you to the ballet. I know that you liked to go see silent movies at MoMA as a kid. Did you also go to the ballet then? Or did that happen later?

— No. I went to the ballet, I suppose, a few times when I was a kid. When I first came to New York, the New York City Ballet was the most important thing practically in New York. So some-times people would bring me. It was expensive. I did not go on my own. I went, I would say, not routinely but I went, because also Maria [Tallchieff][1] was dancing. There's nothing happen-ing now in New York that's so central. Although New York is bigger than it was before, because it now includes Brooklyn, the world of things like that that people were interested in was in a way smaller. In other words, there were certain people inter-ested in this stuff, not everybody. Museums, for instance, didn't really care how many people went to them. Something that if I was in charge, I'd bring back. No one really thought, how can we lure all these people with strollers into museums? How can we bring in all these people who really don't care about being in museums? Ah, restaurants!

1. Born on an Osage reservation in Oklahoma, Maria Tallchief (1925–2013) joined the Ballets Russes de Monte-Carlo in New York at seventeen. She met George Balanchine, who was then the company's resident choreographer; the two were married briefly. When in 1946 Balanchine co-founded the New York City Ballet, Tallchief joined the company and rose to prima ballerina. After retiring in 1966, she served as director of ballet for the Lyric Opera of Chicago and founded the Chicago City Ballet in 1974. [Editors' note]

The people who went to ballet all the time were not just fans of the ballet. They were literally fanatics. A lot of things are almost accidental. You had [George] Balanchine and Jerry [Jerome Robbins] at the same time.[2] You had for a period [Rudolf] Nureyev and [Mikhail] Baryshnikov at the same time.[3] None of those things would have happened without those people being at the same time. That's just happenstance. We apparently don't have a moment like that now.

Once I met Jerry, which I don't really remember when, but it must have been, I would say, sometime in the early '80s, then I went to ballet all the time. I went practically every night. I went with Jerry, which was very different from going with not Jerry, for instance. I didn't just go to the ballet with Jerry: I also went to rehearsals and things like that. Although I really liked the ballet before, my understanding of the ballet was incredibly enriched by my friendship with Jerry. I mean incredibly. One of the rich experiences in my life was knowing Jerry in this way.

Also, to me, a very odd thing happened when Jerry was making *Glass Pieces* which I don't remember when that was.

2. One of the most influential choreographers of the twentieth century, George Balanchine (1904–1983) joined the Ballets Russes in Paris, at the invitation of Sergei Diaghilev, in 1925. He moved to New York in 1933 and together with Lincoln Kirstein, he founded the School of American Ballet in 1934, and then the New York City Ballet in 1948. He conceived ballets with composers such as Igor Stravinksy and Paul Hindemith—but also worked in Broadway and Hollywood. A dancer, choreographer and director, Jerome Robbins (1918–1998) was as successful in his career in ballet as in Broadway. He worked with Balanchine and the American Ballet Theatre as early as 1940, and then at the New York City Ballet; in parallel, he conceived and choreographed musicals, notably *West Side Story* which he directed on stage in 1957, and then on film (in collaboration with Robert Wise) in 1961. From the 1970s, he mostly worked in classical dance as the ballet master of the New York City Ballet. [Editors' note]

3. Mikhail Baryshnikov (b. 1948) was principal dancer at the American Ballet Theatre from 1974 to 1978 and then at the New York City Ballet until 1979, a period when Rudolf Nureyev (1938–1993) frequently performed in New York. They appeared onstage together on a few occasions in the 1980s for gala benefits. [Editors' note]

But I'm sure someone could look it up on one of your modern devices. By the time I finish this, you're going to tell me when it was.

— *In 1983.*

— 1983. Thank you. You didn't even need it yourself. When he was making it, he said to me one night . . . One of the things that we had in common was constant endless complaining. Sometimes, I couldn't even hear him complain because I was complaining. What Jerry always said was, "I can't do this. I can't do this. This is going terribly. It's awful. It's horrible. I can't do it. I can't." He was saying this about *Glass Pieces*. They had a date for it to open.

Deadlines that choreographers have are different deadlines that writers have. The deadlines that writers have is if it's not there, it's not there. There's not going to be people sitting in an audience waiting to see it. So he was very concerned about this. He said, "It would really help me if you would come to the rehearsal." I said, "How would that help you?" He said, "I want you to come, because I can't do this. Could you just come?" I said, "I can't imagine how this would possibly help you because I don't really know how to choreograph. I know that I seem like a person who would. But in fact, I really don't know how to do it." And I said, "What do you mean come to the rehearsal? I thought you hadn't written it yet." He said, "What do you mean write it?" I said, "Don't you write a ballet?" He said, "How would you write a ballet?" I said, "I thought there was some system like, you know, of notation, hieroglyphics." He said, "No, you have to make it on the dancers." I was so shocked by this.

Instantly the idea that writing was the worst thing in the world disappeared for me, because I went to the rehearsal or whatever, and Jerry was not popular with the dancers or, in fact, with most people . . . We were in the studio; there were the dancers, all of them hated him, sitting there, glaring at him. That would be, to me, as if you were sitting at the desk, and all the words in the dictionary were sitting on the desk glaring at you. Because very often in my life, I'd looked at my dictionary, and thought, "All the words you need, Fran, are there. They're just in the wrong order." That is also true of the dancers, except they're people. Also then, dancers smoked. So this studio was like, you couldn't even see. Everyone was like [puffs] glaring at him. He would try it. If they didn't like it, you would see on their face that they don't like it. He would try one thing after the other. After the first rehearsal, we went across the street to eat or something. I said, "That's the worst thing I've ever seen in my life."

I said, "I don't know how I can possibly help you with this. I don't even know what you're doing." He said, "Here's how you can help me. You are the most judgmental person I've ever known in my entire life. All I have to do is look at your face." I said, "Except that my face, expressing whatever I think about this, really, is not that knowledgeable." He said, "It doesn't matter. It'll help me." So he did it. I don't know if you've ever seen *Glass Pieces*. We did a fantastic job. It's really good. I went to the opening of it. I felt really that I contributed quite a bit. I don't know if that's what you asked me but here's my answer.

— *What do you think it was that Jerry needed from you?*

— I guess the same thing that my mother used to call, "That look on your face." But I guess he profited from it. I have not.

— *What about the scene at the ballet? What was the audience like? What kind of a social space was it?*

— The audience in the New York City Ballet was an incredibly discerning, knowledgeable, critical audience. It was an audience so . . . I knew some of these people. Some of them were friends of mine. It seemed to me it was amazing that they got anything else done.

What I'm going to say now is a quote, so I do not want to be killed for this. But there was a man named Herbert Muschamp. He's dead. He was, for a long time, the architecture critic at the *New York Times*.[4] At intermission, you would hear the audience talking about, say, Suzanne Farrell,[5] who everyone was obsessed with. They would be saying, "Suzanne has a cold. Do you see that? I could tell that she went [sniffs] like that. She has a cold. That is why when she's supposed to go like *this*, she went like *this* instead." "No. She didn't go like *this*. She went like *this*." They were just completely obsessed with this. I once said to Herbert, "It's like listening to men talk about baseball statistics. In 1921, Babe Ruth is . . ." He said, "Yes. The ballet is baseball for fags." In a way, that is true, although I did not say that, of course. But he said that.

I was always thinking of money-making schemes. I was always saying no to people offering me actual money, then thinking of these money-making schemes. I said to Herbert, "Let's make baseball cards with all the dancers on them. Then, we would sell them to these four hundred people who cared about

4. Herbert Muschamp (1947–2007) was the architecture critic for the *New York Times* from 1992 to 2004. [Editors' note]

5. Susan Farrell (b. 1945) joined the New York City Ballet in 1961. She left the company in 1969 and went to Europe, joining Maurice Béjart's company, before returning to the New York City Ballet in 1975. She worked again with Balanchine then, who continued to create new ballets for her until his death in 1983. She retired in 1989 and worked as a dance teacher before she started the Suzanne Farrell Ballet in 2000. [Editors' note]

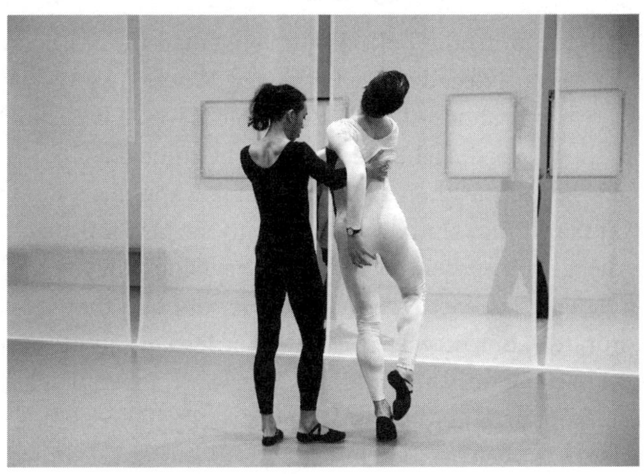

it." So people were very obsessed with it. My feeling was that the reason for it was they so idolized this talent that the dancers had that they did not have. They thought of it as the greatest talent you could have . . . They were probably the last generation of people that understands what talent is, which is that you just have it or you just don't. It doesn't matter how much your mother likes you or tells you how great you are or if you go to writing school. You either have it or you don't. So they were so reverent about this talent that if they felt someone was misusing it or getting a cold, they were very distraught by this.

I think that this is a good thing, this kind of audience, because I think that, although I did not know Susan Farrell, she certainly knew what this audience was like. It could not do anything but make you better. If you know that everybody in the audience really understands what you're doing and really understands how well it can be done, that if you're not doing it at the peak of your ability, they will know it.

I did not go to the ballet after Jerry died for really a long time, at least, a decade, maybe longer. When I went the first time, I was just shocked at how horrible it was. I was shocked. One of the things that shocked me was the audience. The second the first dancer put their foot on the stage, applause. I am telling you that if Baryshnikov had hung in the air for fifteen minutes, the former audience would have been like "Maybe . . .," and when he came to earth, it was like "He *could* do that for eighteen minutes, but he was only there for fifteen minutes." Now, they were constantly applauding. Afterward, I went backstage. I was talking to Sara Mearns[6] who is a young dancer. She's a little older than she was then but she is still young. Of course, she never knew that other New York City Ballet. But I said, "Doesn't it bother you, this constant clapping and applause?" She said, "Well, we can't hear the music." Well, really, if they can't hear the music, that's really a problem. The audience applauding, this is every audience now. If you go to see a play, everything is a standing ovation. Every single thing gets a standing ovation. Clearly, what is the audience applauding? Themselves. And where did they learn this? Oprah Winfrey. I have nothing against Oprah Winfrey, but really, the New York City Ballet audience should not be copying Oprah Winfrey. There's not going to be a car under your chair either at the New York City Ballet.[7]

— So, this loss of a discerning audience . . . Well, first, actually, I'd like to ask you, back then, were there people that you saw regularly at the ballet?

6. Sara Mearns (b. 1986) is a principal dancer at the New York City Ballet, that she had joined as an apprentice in 2003. [Editors' note]

7. "You get a car!" On September 13, 2004, TV talk-show host Oprah Winfrey surprised the 276 members of her studio audience by offering each of them a brand-new car. [Editors' note]

— Yes. They were the regulars. I'm certain it wasn't 100% the same people there every night, but there were a lot of the same people there every night. I was not that young in age. I was in my 30s. But I don't think I realized it was a moment. I don't think I realized that it was going to end.

The ballet, of course, is incredibly susceptible to the human lifespan, because the ballets disappear. The people disappear. They die. It disappears. Now, there certainly could be no one dancing who worked for Balanchine or who worked for Jerry. So you lose these. They get literally lost. That would happen even if the entire audience didn't die all at once from AIDS, which is really what happened. Almost the entire audience died within not very many years. If you would bomb Lincoln Center that would have had the same effect. That is not just the ballet audience. That's the audience for a lot of other things, too.

I really think that the loss of this audience has hurt everything. Of course, the loss of the artist is what everyone pays attention to, but these artists of that era and the eras before would not have existed at the same level without that audience. It's just like now. You didn't have the same thing with writers, for instance. Unfortunately, many of them are still alive. But truthfully, the way people talk about books now or talk about a book they read is idiotic. They literally don't know what they're talking about, mainly because they learned to talk about this in school. This is not something you can learn. In school, there are things you can learn. I didn't learn many of them but they're available to be learned. But there are things you cannot learn in school.

With films, for instance, obviously, all the people die. Sometimes, I'm watching a movie, and I realize every single person has been dead for fifty years. It doesn't matter because the movie is still there. But the ballet disappeared, and other things like that, too, the theater. To me, the fact of Charles Ludlam[8] dying wasn't a tremendous difference in the theater in New York. It would never have occurred to Charlie Ludlam or to anyone who ever saw his plays that there would be a time where you could have that kind of thing outside of that tiny group of people. No one could have imagined that if he had stayed alive, and all those people had stayed alive, then we would have *that* instead of the junk that pretends to be that.

— *I was talking to the artist Elaine Reichek the other day. She said, "In the '70s, we would go to the ballet. We would go see the Theatre of the Ridiculous.[9] We would go to see downtown dance, the movies, and go to the disco." All these things were sort of a part of . . .*

— Every single night, all the time, that's what we did. We did that all the time and had sex with five million people. How did we have all this time? No one was making money. No one thought about money. No one ever talked about money other than the way that I still think about money which is the way a child does. Like, do I have enough money? To me, there was such a thing as enough money. See, that's the problem. To me, enough money meant, could I pay my rent. The second I would

8. Born 1943, Charles Ludlam died of AIDS in 1987. He was an actor, director, playwright; an important figure of the experimental theatre scene in New York, he worked with Ronald Tavel and John Vaccaro before he founded his own Ridiculous Theatrical Company in 1967. His most successful play, *The Mystery of Irma Vep* (1984), is a camp pastiche of gothic tales. [Editors' note]

9. Actor and director Ronald Tavel (1939–2009) founded the Theatre (or Play-House) of the Ridiculous in 1966. He was the screenwriter for many Andy Warhol's films, and several members of The Factory played in Theatre of the Ridiculous productions. [Editors' note]

acquire enough money to pay my rent, I stopped working for that month. Because why would you keep working? Why would you keep working when you didn't need any more money? The amount of money that I thought I needed was literally $120. It wasn't like I had other things. I just thought, here's what you trade for money: *time.* I'm allowed to waste my time, nobody's allowed to waste my time just because they're giving me money. But now people have to make money all the time and talk about money all the time. It interferes with life. It's the opposite of life. For me, I know this sounds like a crazy thing, but I hate money. Unfortunately, I love things. This is a horrible combination. It's okay if you hate money, and you're a Buddhist monk. I am not. Okay?

We did, all the time, go to the ballet if we could. It was expensive to go to the ballet. Someone had to take you to the ballet. The upside, of course, of being young is that if you're cute, people take you to places. So there would be two kinds of people at the ballet: people who had money and then all the cute people who were being taken there.

I met Ellsworth Kelly at the ballet during intermission. This man came over to me. I didn't know what Kelly looked like. It wasn't like now where everyone knows what everyone looks like because they look you up on the internet or whatever. This man came over to me and said, "Oh, I just want to introduce myself to you because I see you here all the time." He was there all the time. I recognized him just from being there. He said, "I'm really a fan of yours. I'm Ellsworth Kelly." I said, "I'm a fan of yours." He said, "I thought you would be."

The same thing if you went to see the Theatre of the Ridiculous. They were the same people all the time. People went to see John Vaccaro[10] all the time. People went to see even much more ramshackle things than that, because I try to level them as much more organized than most of those people.

We went to the movies all the time. We went to the Elgin which is now the Joyce. I recently said to someone, "I'll meet you near the Elgin." They said, "The what?" It hasn't been the Elgin for like, thirty-five years. But in my mind, it's still the Elgin. It's the Joyce Theater now. This stuff was better when it was the Elgin.[11]

So Elgin was a movie theater. It was literally falling apart. It was dangerous to sit in those seats. There were pieces of steel sticking up. They had all the movies that we wanted to see. Terrible prints, the prints always broke in the middle of it. The Elgin, for a period, had movies all night. Max's [Kansas City][12] would close at four o'clock. We would go to the Elgin. We would stay there until like, ten in the morning. At ten in the morning, the Museum of Modern Art started showing movies. We go uptown to the Museum of Modern Art. We did this all the time because we could. Why wouldn't you do this?

St. Marks had these old movies as well. Most of the movies we saw were in terrible physical condition. A movie would

10. Actor and director John Vaccaro (1929–2016) worked with Tavel at the Theatre of the Ridiculous, then developed his own productions. His approach to theater, using cross-gender casting, camp provocation and humor, influenced 1970s music and counterculture. [Editors' note]

11. The Elgin Theater was located on the corner of 19th Street and 8th Avenue. From the 1960s it showed underground films as well as revivals of classics and auteur films; it also pioneered midnight movie programming. It closed in 1978 and reopened in 1982 as a dance theater, ran by the Joyce Theatre Foundation. [Editors' note]

12. Max's Kansas City was a nightclub and restaurant located at 213 Park Avenue South; opened in 1965 it quickly became a gathering place for musicians, writers, and artists. In the '70s Max's Kansas City became a base for the glam rock scene, and then the punk scene. It closed in 1981. [Editors' note]

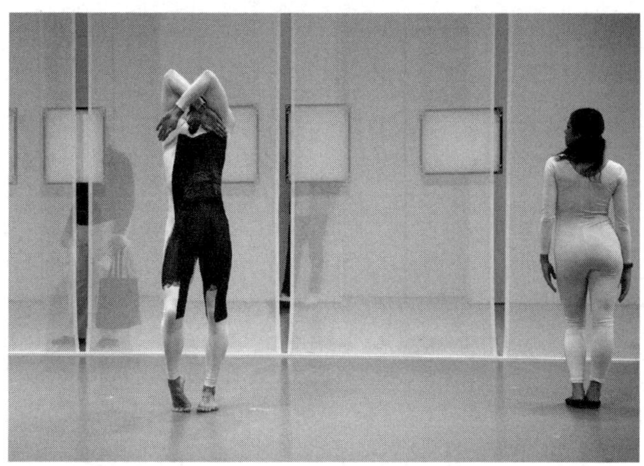

routinely break in the middle of the thing, and everyone would sit there waiting for it to . . . In the Museum of Modern Art's theater, movies didn't break. That was the other thing: "Let's go to the Museum of Modern Art because their movie is not going to break in the middle of it." Also, by the way, it was very cheap to get to the Museum of Modern Art. It didn't cost however much it costs now, $40, some crazy amount of money.

When I say "we," I mean all the people that I know and people like me. We did that all the time. That's one of the reasons we moved to New York, because in other places, they didn't have the stuff. That's why. The museums were empty, by which I mean the only people in the museums were people who liked museums. There aren't many people who like museums. When I was young, if I was uptown and I had forty-five minutes between two things I had to do uptown, I would just go to the Museum of Modern Art, because you could just go there for forty-five minutes and you could just look at, say, one painting because they have a lot of paintings and stuff there and not just a lot of restaurants. That is true. You could just walk in.

— *What you're talking about describes a really different way of being in the world ... I mean, as an audience, it was probably a smaller group of people who really had a wide range of passions and moved through many different worlds. Now, it does seem that people are much more compartmentalized and have a kind of narrow field that they like to move in.*

— Also, a different kind of person comes to New York now. Most of these people lived in New York because they weren't allowed to live anywhere else. You came to New York because you could live here. Now, people, especially gay people, they can live anywhere. I mean, there are gay people who were born in, say, St. Louis, and they stay there. They get married. They have children.

There was a . . . I don't know what the word is. Camaraderie is really too sweet a word to describe it. But that was your connection to these people even if you didn't like most of them, of course. There were different groups of people, of course. All of them hated each other. Human nature is always the same. Bad. But it is true that everyone I knew was interested in all this stuff. If someone would tell you about something, "Oh, you should go see this thing." It would be in someone's apartment. "What is that?" They would tell you, "Oh, this guy makes puppets." "Oh, yes. Let's go see that." Every single thing sounded good even if it wasn't good. Most of it was bad, because most things are bad. Most of these people were not Charlie Ludlam, who was immensely talented. They thought they were, but they were not. But they were very interested in the same thing.

Now, it's not like that anymore. Also, because it didn't cost us a million dollars to live here. When I was young, some of the people I knew had money. I didn't really realize that. I never really thought about it. But for people who did have money, meaning their parents or their family had money, it was not really a very stylish thing to have money. So they pretended they didn't. We mostly didn't go to each other's apartments unless you had sex with them. We mostly lived in public. So I didn't really know whether people had money or not. Some people had to work like me. Not everybody drove a taxi or was a waitress or whatever. We weren't really very interested in that part of people's lives. I had a girlfriend when I was young who lived in Beekman Place.[13] I never thought, how do you get to live in Beekman Place? Until I realized she was a hooker. Well, let me say a very expensive call girl. Someone said, "How could you not realize that? She's at Beekman Place," which was a place to me where Fred Astaire lived. Even now, if you go to Beekman Place, it looks like you're going to see Fred Astaire tapping down the street. We weren't really even curious about that.

Interestingly enough, the actual currency had no currency. It didn't have any currency. It carried no status among the people I know at all. So now, there are no competing values to money at all. None. Of course, things are different. Even if these people had not died, it would still be different. Although it's hard for me to imagine that they've not aged, I don't think having all these talented people alive would have kept capitalism from devouring democracy.

13. Beekman Place is an exclusive cul-de-sac in the East Side of Manhattan, associated with old money. [Editors' note]

— Right. But still, what you've said about the sudden eradication of all these talented people and their audience . . . I grew up in Germany, so I know what it's like to be in a culture that punched a hole in itself and doesn't understand why the hole won't fill up again.

— I could tell you.

— The way you framed was such a revelation to me in terms of: why is there no connection to some of the things that are in this exhibition. For example, our detachment from a certain style of camp or sophistication and wit that sparks sensibility.

— Because it was actually broken. A generation was lost, so it was broken just the way that could even happen in a family. Like it happened, say, in your native land. If a whole generation of people dies, then that connection is broken. The kind of thing you're talking about relied completely on kind of a voluntary passing down of something, because it wasn't a family. Okay? It's not a family. People are saying, "This is my family." It's not your family. Your family is your family. That's the bad news about families. These people that you say are your family, they're your friends. The difference is you chose them. That was broken.

When I went to the exhibition with you, you asked me, did I remember this or read that. But people would teach you. The older people have taught the younger people. But literally like, "Have you read this?" No. People sometimes say to me, "Did you ever read this?" I say, "No." "You never heard of this?" "No." "Why not?" "I lived in Morristown, New Jersey. That's why I never heard of it." But then I came here, I heard this person say it, and I heard of it. Then, I got the book. Then I went to see the thing. It was passed on to people. Just the same way, in your exhibition, that calling card, that Lincoln Kirstein . . .

— [Sergei] Diaghilev's calling card, which Kirstein kept on permanent display in his drawing room, and then passed on to one of his close friends.

— As I said to you, the present way of life of gay people, getting married and having children and stuff like that, would have been very bad for these people and it would have been very bad for the world: if, say, Lincoln Kirstein had children, when he died, his children would have inherited all this stuff and sold it. Okay? Museums and libraries are filled with the estates of gay people. The really important estates of gay people. You know, drawings, manuscripts, all these things were given to libraries, universities, and museums because there were no children to take them and sell them. Think about this before you make a bad decision.

— I mentioned that I had once noticed a David Wojnarowicz photo on the wall of a friend's apartment, who told me they'd found it in the garbage in the late '80s. It must have belonged to somebody who had died, and all their worldly belongings were thrown out on the sidewalk. There's a number of things that just vanished in addition to . . .

— These things were lost because . . . I mean, David's photograph probably did not have a high monetary value when it was thrown in the street. But what happened was when people in New York died of AIDS, it might be the first time that their family had seen them or maybe had not seen them. One thing is AIDS outed people. You couldn't pretend you weren't dying. Sometimes the families would come here after someone died. They would go into the apartment of the person who died, who perhaps they haven't spoken to for ten years, and they would throw their stuff out. Say, you were someone who had not spoken to your son or your brother or whatever for years because he was gay and he'd been thrown out the house, that kind of thing, like a David Wojnarowicz photograph, would have been thrown into the street. That happened a lot. I mean, with all kinds of things, with books, with photographs, all that kind of stuff that people had. Whoever owned it—it might have been a friend of David's or maybe it was given by David. That happened to a lot of that stuff. It got thrown away. I mean, that was right after the first wave of AIDS.

For instance, my first book had a first printing of 6,000. It was almost entirely bought by gay people because I was only known to people who read *Interview* then, which were only gay people.[14] Initially, after that became successful, those first edition copies were very expensive. I wanted some. I couldn't buy them. They were too expensive for me. And then at a certain point, they started turning up by their dozens and dozens and dozens because they were in these people's apartments, and their families came in and they threw them out. So they became much more inexpensive for a time. That's one of the reasons I knew about this. It happened also that the person would disappear. Another person died, and their friends had no access to their things even though they may have been shared things because the family just came in and took it. I mean the family was there because they were hoping there would be something valuable like a television set.

— Once you really let it sink in that loss of the audience is so significant, because it points to things that are not tangible, the

14. *Metropolitan Life* (New York: E.P. Dutton, 1978) is a collection of texts Fran Lebowitz had notably published in *Interview*, in which she held the column, "I Cover the Waterfront" during the 1970s. [Editors' note]

erasure of knowledges and certain kinds of sophistication or interest or the passion that you spoke about earlier. I mean, that really seems to be the greatest loss, and the reason why I think for people of my generation there has been no sense of a continuous history. The connection to anything that happened before Stonewall and AIDS is very difficult to locate.

— But also you can't make people who are young understand what it was like to be gay then. The loss of this culture is the downside of freedom. I mean, the personal freedom that you have that we did not have. That culture was a culture of marginalization. People say oppression. I think that's too strong a word. I think it's terrible to equate that, for instance, with slavery. I mean, it wasn't that bad. In fact, it was pretty fun, which you never hear slavery being called fun.

When I was young, there were two upsides to being gay. You didn't have to go in the army, and you didn't have to get married. The first two things that gay rights activists fought for were gays in the military and gay marriage. The two most confining institutions in the world. This is what they most wanted. Really, you want to go in the army? I mean, this just struck me as bizarre. So now, people get married. I guess they go in the army. At first this whole thing of gays in the military was so shocking to me because I was in the generation of had I been a boy, I would have gone to Vietnam. That was a way to get out of going to Vietnam, by the way. Someone I know, a very rich man, gave a lot of money to the campaign for gays in the military. I said, "How did you stay out of Vietnam?" And he said, "I told them I was gay." Most people didn't do that, by the way, because you then could never get a job if you were officially gay, which you would be if that was your reason for not going to

Vietnam. So you have that. You have gay marriage and you have children. What could be more distracting? What could be more or less likely to result in, say, the Theater of the Ridiculous or *West Side Story*? These things are what you had instead of children. To me, this doesn't seem like much of a contest. It's not like there aren't enough people in the world. Everyone acts like the biggest problem we have is there are too few people, so we have to keep thinking of more and more ways to have children. "Oh, you're a woman? You're 60? No, we can fix that." No, no. I don't know what you asked but there's my answer. Yes, it's gone. It's lost. It's not coming back.

It's probably very hard for someone young to understand the feeling that you had, that feeling of recognition from looking at certain things from the past . . . This is one of the ways that certain things get into the popular culture, is that people don't know where they came from. For instance, Madonna did all that voguing stuff. The people who liked Madonna, and there were many of them, although I personally knew none, didn't know where that came from. They thought she invented it.

On a higher level, the same thing happened with Susan Sontag. Susan wrote all these things and all the people in France thought she was just promoting their ideas. And everyone in the United States said, "They were her ideas." She knew that. So that's what happens when people don't realize where something comes from.

I went to see the caves at Lascaux. And my first thought was, when did Picasso see these? So even something like Picasso comes from somewhere. It doesn't just come out of the blue. Now people can see everything, not me because I don't have these machines, but everyone else has them. And you can see every single thing in the world, but you see it all at once. If you see it all at once, it has no linear quality. So that for me the things that I know, which is not everything, close, I at least know them in order. I think it's so important to know things in order. It doesn't seem to be at all an interest anymore to people to know what came before this or what came before that. To me, it's centrally imperative that you know what order things came in.

I think one of the great things about your exhibit is that in a way, it shows you where it came from. It's very electrifying to me to see where things came from. It's really important that people know this. And it's certainly not just important for artists, of course, but I mean, when people don't know this . . . I don't know what they're seeing when they look at this stuff. If you don't know what you're seeing, what is the point of seeing it? They don't have to keep these museums so crowded. Stay home.

— *What you're talking about is also a question of context.*

— It's totally about context. There's no context for this, if you don't have a context for it. For instance, Marty [Martin Scorsese][15] knows every single frame of every single movie ever made. That sounds impossible, but let me assure you that's true. He knows these things. He knows them in order. So it's an incredibly enriching experience to go to the movies with Marty. And if you say to Marty, "I don't like this movie," that he thinks is a great movie, he says, "You're wrong, I'm going to run it for you again." And then he runs it for you again, and then you realize

---

15. Martin Scorsese and Fran Lebowitz worked together on two documentary projects: the much-acclaimed 2021 series *Pretend It's a City*, in which Lebowitz talks about living in New York City; and the 2010 documentary film *Public Speaking*. [Editors' note]

you're wrong. And believe me, "I'm wrong" is not something I like to say very often.

Jerry was like that with ballet, although you can't know the ballet in that way, the same way. And also because Jerry was unable to see things that happened before. There's so little film in the ballet. I would recommend that you see this movie about Tanny Balanchine [Tanaquil Le Clercq][16] just because there's some film of her dancing. Hardly anyone ever saw her dance. She danced for like five minutes. So I mean, that movie is very valuable, I think, because there's some film of her dancing, even though there's very little film of dance. It's a horrible way to see dance, by the way. It's like looking at pictures of architecture. It has nothing really to do with what you're seeing, but it was at least some chance to see it, especially since every single person had always described her to me as the greatest dancer ever. I asked Jerry once, "Who was the greatest female dancer you ever saw?" And he said to me, "Tanny Balanchine," and she only danced for five minutes. Jerry saw a lot of dancers. He said it like that without hesitating even one second.

— *Did he say why?*

— If he did, I don't recall. He was very devoted to her. I knew her because of him. He was extremely devoted to her. But she really danced very briefly. Everyone who saw her said the same thing, but not everyone is Jerry. And also, Jerry was not filled with praise for people. He said it like that, which is also part of the reason why it was such an exceptional tragedy that she got

16. The last wife (1952–1969) of George Balanchine, Tanaquil Le Clercq (1929–2000) joined the New York City Ballet at its beginning, when she was 17, and became principal dancer at 19. Her career ended brutally when she contracted polio in 1956. She is the subject of the 2013 documentary film, *Afternoon of a Faun: Tanaquil Le Clercq* by Nancy Buirski. [Editors' note]

polio. I asked him too, "Who was the greatest male dancer?" And he said, like that, "Baryshnikov." When Baryshnikov was dancing, there were camps, no pun intended, as to who was the better dancer. I mean, Baryshnikov was clearly the better dancer. He was not, however, the beauty that Nureyev was. He was so beautiful. He was just like an astounding physical presence and a great dancer. But there were really warring factions. I mean, if those people were still alive, they'd still be fighting over it, believe me. I've witnessed many, many brutal verbal confrontations, but confrontations about Baryshnikov and Nureyev were among the bloodiest I ever saw.

— *When you were watching* Glass Pieces *being made, was there any way you felt that you could get inside of Jerry's head?*

— No, I never understood what he was doing. I mean, I really tried. It's like it's a language that either you have or you don't. I had more ability to discern, in some way, having seen it when it was finished. I understood more what he was doing in retrospect. But no, I have no . . . I am monolingual. I speak no other languages. I would say I have a little more access to the language of a choreographer but not much more. But while he was doing it, no. But the dancers do. That's the interesting thing to me. I noticed that while they were making this, the dancers do, even though they're not choreographers. I mean, some dancers become choreographers, but they understand it in a way because they speak that language. They also know what he's asking of them. Something has to be pretty extraordinary to me in ballet for me to see how extraordinary it is. But every little thing they do is very painful, physically, it's hard to do. And they know how hard it is. Like, if he would tell them to do this and I would see them go like this, I would first think they thought it was a bad idea. It wasn't that they thought it was a bad idea, although they may have, it was that they knew it was hard, that it was going to be hard to do. To me, I can't do any of it. So of course, it'd be hard to do but they knew the difference.

— *I found this really interesting quote. This is a bit of a jump aside, but I wanted to hear your reaction to this statement, which is from a conference in 1949, called "The Western Round Table on . . .*

— I'm not that old.

— *I know. Frank Lloyd Wright is wondering out loud, "You would say that this movement we call modern art and painting has been greatly in debt to homosexualism?" Duchamp responds, "I believe that the homosexual public has shown more interest or curiosity for modern art than the heterosexual."[17] In one of our earlier conversations you talked about how you moved to New York, the people you knew, you knew them because they were gay. You had to be kind of covert about it. But those were the people you knew that you gravitated towards, and they were also the people that you shared interests with.*

— You knew people just because they were gay, was the point I was trying to make to you. In other words, I mean, the same way that I know people now just because they smoke. Actually, homosexuality and cigarette smoking have changed places completely. They just traded places. I mean, if you told me when I was like, 13 years old, that the thing that would give me the most trouble in my adult life was cigarette smoking, I would have said you're crazy. When I was young, you could smoke

17. "The Western Round Table on Modern Art," ed. Douglas MacAgy, in *Modern Artists in America*, ed. Robert Motherwell and Ad Reinhardt (New York: Wittenborn Schulz, 1951), 30.

everywhere, but you couldn't be gay anywhere. Now, you can be gay anywhere, St. Louis, Atlanta, but you can't smoke anywhere. I know people now just from standing outside restaurants smoking. That is how we know them. The same way I knew people when I was young just because we were gay. That is why I knew them. So that most of the people that I know because we were gay were like me, by which I mean they were writers or artists or whatever.

I knew this man, who was a very eminent scientist, and he was a friend of Jerry's. He was more the age of Jerry than my age. He was elected to—I forget what exactly it's called—the American Academy of Science or something like that, which is kind of like the French Academy. There's only like, forty people, someone died so he was elected to this, and they gave him like this medal and a ribbon. And I said to him, "David, why don't you wear this?" And he said he would never wear that. He's a very kind of conservative guy. So I said, "Well, give it to me, I'll wear it." One of the things is a little ribbon that you put in your lapel, which I wear all the time when I wear a dinner jacket.

I once wore it to some benefit for some disease, some illness or something. I was in the elevator with a lot of doctors and scientists and one of these men looked at me, and he looked at my lapel, and he said, "Aren't you Fran Lebowitz, the *writer*?" I mean, I can't tell you, like, the contempt. "The writer?" So I said, "Yes." He said, "Where'd you get that?" Because he recognized the ribbon. So I said, "Oh, a friend of mine got this, and he gave it to me because he didn't want to wear it." "A friend?" So I tell him the guy's name. And he goes, "How would you know him?" I couldn't tell him, because he's gay. That's how I know him. You're right. I would never know this guy otherwise, not in a million years. That's how I knew him. And I now know people just because they smoke. So, the same way that I know the people who are gay like this famous scientist, I know the people who smoke.

— *Was there any crossover between disco dancing, which you told me you liked to do, and ballet?*

— Yes. I mean, the crossover just was that we went dancing all the time. It was a craze. I loved to dance so much when I was young, and I was a very good dancer, not a good ballet dancer. Most of these places were illegal, where we danced, because you needed licenses and all those kinds of stuff, which they didn't have.

It was the same people. I mean, I never saw, like Ellsworth Kelly dancing at 12 West.[18] It doesn't mean he was ever there. I don't know. But I mean, it was mostly people who were young, who were dancing. I know people who are young dance now. I still am an excellent dancer, but I would never dance in public now because I just remember what it was like, if I would see someone like older dancing, I would think, what? Why would you be dancing? You're thirty-five.

The hatred by the way that straight people had for disco music . . . I mean, straight artists, especially. Straight artists were so contemptuous of disco music. I remember I had a girl-friend who had just been the girlfriend of a straight male artist and was still parroting what he said instead of what I said. That came later. She said something like how horrible disco was, which is what they used to say. And I said, first of all, "You're wrong." I said, "Because disco music is black music. Black

18. 12 West was a disco club in Greenwich Village, active between 1975 and 1980. [Editors' note]

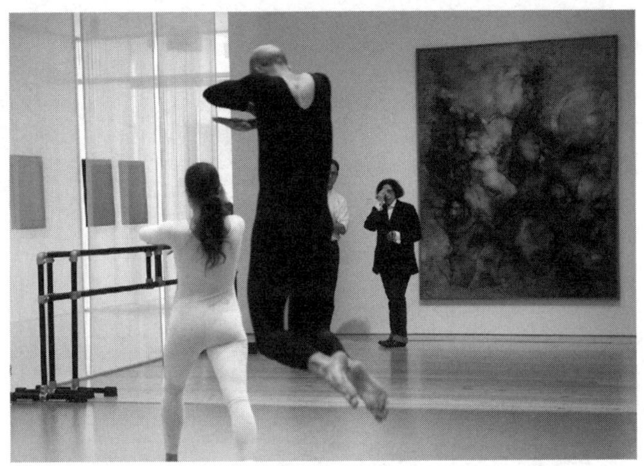

music is never not good. Okay? Period." And so this guy, who's now of course a quite well-known artist, is wrong. And here are the people who are least likely to know what good, popular music is. Straight white guys. Who cares what they think? I mean, really about anything.

— *I think that's a great place to end. Thank you, Fran.* ◆

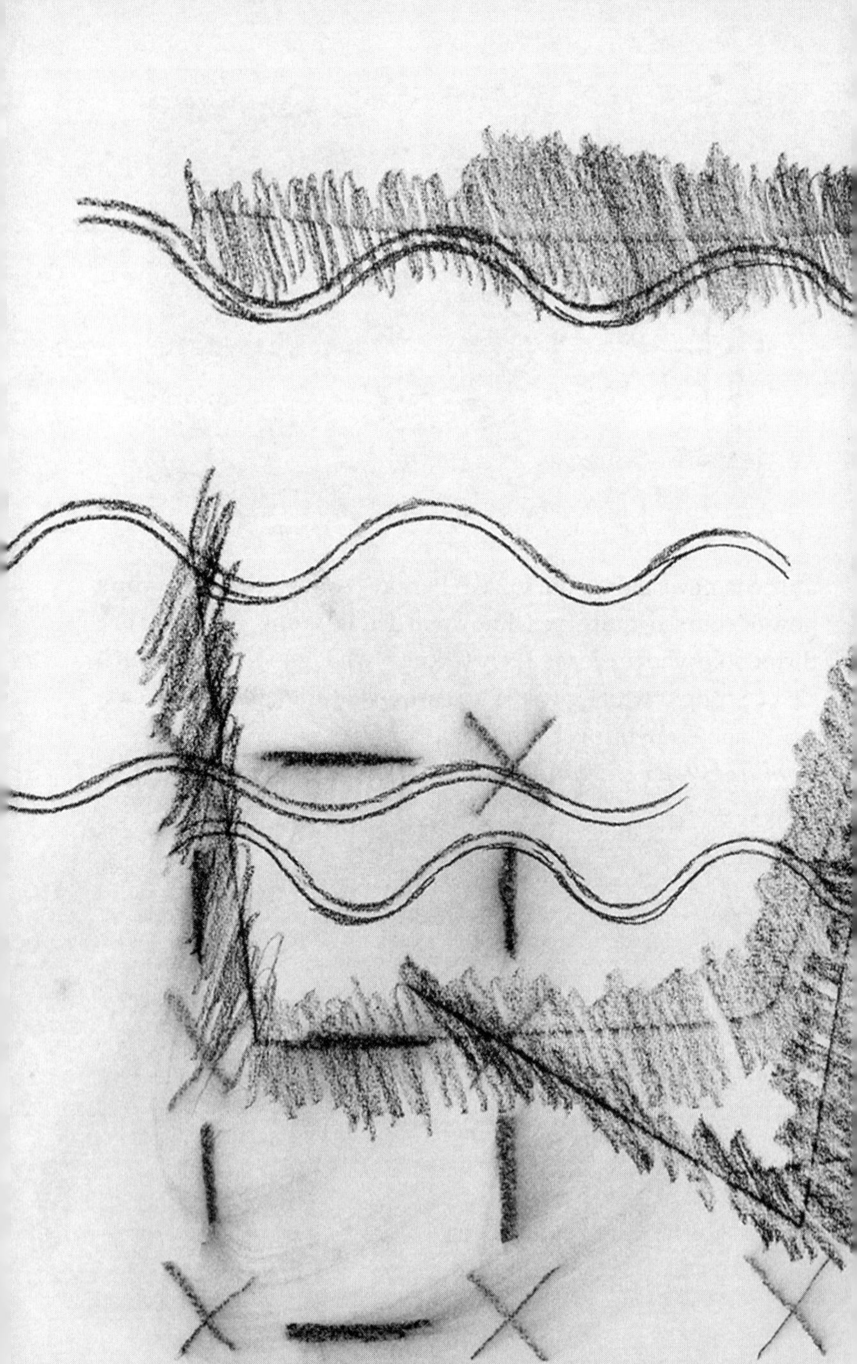

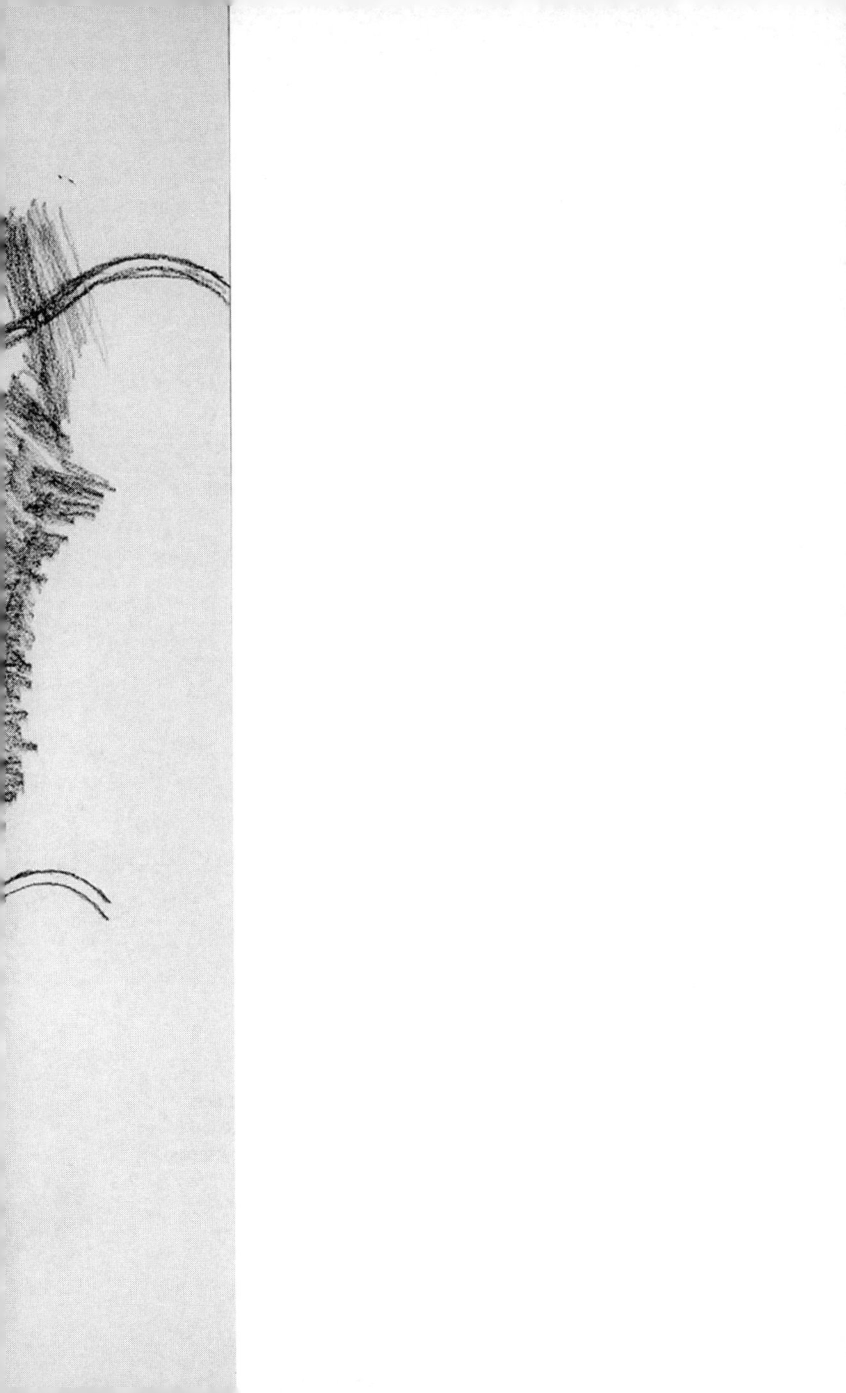

This essay is an adapted version of a talk, given upon the invitation of Visual AIDS and Bidoun as part of the symposium International Mutant: Nicolas Moufarrege in Time and Space, *on February 15, 2020, in the context of the survey show,* Nicolas Moufarrege: Recognize My Sign *at the Queens Museum (October 6, 2019–February 23, 2020), curated by Dean Daderko. The text has been subsequently published in* octopus notes, no. 10 (June 2021).

I Always See Relationships.
On Nicolas Moufarrege

In 1998 I had just moved to New York City to study at Cooper Union and my friend April Lee, who was an intern at PS1, pressed a copy of the catalogue of the 1987 Nicolas Moufarrege memorial exhibition at the Clocktower gallery into my hands—not just because the cover was emblazoned with my name, but because she sensed that I would be interested in this work, which nobody I knew at the time could tell me anything about.[1] Just over a decade had passed since Moufarrege died of AIDS-related complications at the age of 36, but only the faintest traces remained of the East Village whose art scene he had celebrated, co-created, and found a home in. I tried to make sense of this present overlaid on an invisible past, and flailingly pieced together a picture of what had happened—how this blunt erasure had been carried out. I noticed, for example, that an older friend of mine had a David Wojnarowicz photo in their apartment, which they said they'd found on an Avenue B sidewalk, mixed in with the trash. They went on to describe a time when coming upon the abandoned remains of a lifetime's worth of belongings tossed to the curb—presumably by an indifferent landlord or by family members cleaning out

---

1. *Nicolas A. Moufarrege*, exh. cat. (New York: Institute for Art and Urban Resources, Inc., The Clocktower), 1987; with texts by Brooks Adams, Michele Cone and Bella Meyer, Carlo McCormick, Rene Ricard, and Pierre Restany.

the apartment of a relative who had succumbed to AIDS—was a regular occurrence. Part of the landscape. I had a job working at the Strand and found a copy of *Needlepoint News*, which featured, among other things, a needlework pattern for a kitten, a rondel of Arabic calligraphy, and on the last spread: a remembrance of Nicolas Moufarrege, composed of biographical details interspersed with his own writing and reproductions of his work. Over the years there were just a few opportunities to see individual examples of his art in person, for example at La MaMa Galleria, just down the street from where I lived, in an exhibition organized by Sur Rodney (Sur).[2] I met Chuck Nanney, and then Elaine Reichek, also artists I admired, only to realize later that they all knew of one another, and had been intimate with Moufarrege. I'm grateful to Chuck, Elaine, and Sur for all the ways in which they have brought his work closer to me and to others, and to Moufarrege's brother Nabil, who was kind enough (when I wrote to him out of the blue to send me pictures of any works of Nicolas' he still had) to share snapshots with me of Nicolas' works proudly hung around Nabil's family home, where they have been looked after and preserved so that they can be seen by new audiences today.[3]

The modest Clocktower catalogue was a kind of talisman for me. I came to know its reproductions by heart. In their bravado, sophistication, and generosity, these embroidered

2. The exhibition *NOT OVER: 25 Years of Visual AIDS*, organized by the nonprofit organization Visual AIDS and curated by Kris Nuzzi and Sur Rodney (Sur), presented at La MaMa Galleria Galleria (June 1–30, 2013).

3. The exhibition *Nicolas Moufarrege: Recognize My Sign*, curated by Dean Daderko at the Contemporary Arts Museum Houston (Nov. 10, 2018–Feb. 17, 2019), travelled to the Queens Museum (Oct. 5, 2019–Feb. 16, 2020), was the first institutional solo exhibition of Moufarrege's work since his posthumous retrospective at The Clocktower Gallery, New York, in 1987.

illuminations spoke to me directly, as if I was in on the joke—a joke that was about to get serious. I was both lured and slightly repelled by the deliberate weaponization of kitsch and sentimentality: to confuse the polarities between art and craft, to trample a notion of the avant-garde in celebration of decoration as a serious gesture; flouting (as if each stitch were accompanied by constant laughter) the gender binaries that are encoded in false aesthetic hierarchies. I also had another job at the time working for a publisher whose bookshelves—which I was meant to alphabetize—were inconveniently modeled after the irregular grids of Mondrian paintings, making my straight-forward-seeming task close to impossible. But on these meandering shelves I discovered for the first time Owen Jones' *Grammar of Ornament*, as well as Hogarth's *The Analysis of Beauty*, featuring the fantastic emblem of the "Line of Beauty," otherwise known as an arabesque, suspended in a pyramid whose base is inscribed with the word: "Variety." All this to say that I was primed to receive Moufarrege's message (or messages), to enter into the gesture of embroidery as a way of dwelling on, elaborating, or even overturning existing images, ideas, and codes. I was also still buzzing from the shock of having recently seen my first Sturtevant painting of Warhol's *Flowers*, and unsure what to do about it. But I knew I believed her statement: "Commentaries, commodities, copies, appropriation, authorship, death-talk, originality. . . these are for 'heroes,' hot dog boys, and bubble gum chewers."[4] In Moufarrege's work I found detours around the rigid certainties that the bros in my art school liked to lean on, those hot dog boys and bubble

4. Elaine Sturtevant, *Sturtevant* (New York: Stux Gallery, 1987).

gum chewers—instead emphasizing confusions, uncertainties, and conflicted readings. At the moment when I was casting about for gay antecedents who had not been prepackaged, Moufarrege suggested a wildly inscrutable web of lineages. It was exhilarating to encounter an artist who was willing to show his cards, to revel in his influences, to say: all of this is equally inconsequential, valuable, permanent, fleeting, and interdependent; history is a chaos that you must make your own.

In an untitled work from 1985, the name "NICK" is rendered in all caps stencils—the same plain symbols used by Jasper Johns to signal the evacuation of the painter's personal touch, corrupted by Moufarrege to announce the intentions of his excessively personalized art in glittering, hand-embroidered thread. The superimposed name disobeys the guidelines of its support, a readymade design "after" Fragonard that has been pre-printed on embroidery canvas for use by hobby artists. This given image, however, is not only "after" Fragonard, but "after" so many subsequent derivations of Fragonard's image of the young woman beginning to carve her name (or her lover's) on the bark of a tree. The support signals many degrees of both the artist's and viewer's belatedness, not least in the "after" implied by the derivative pattern of Ancient Egyptian hieroglyphics which serve as an incongruous backing (and frame) to the embroidery canvas, and alludes casually to the artist's Egyptian childhood. In effect, "NICK's" signature becomes the subject as well as the effacement of a deeply layered image, and this vandalism exceeds the tentative gesture captured in the Fragonard motif rendered kitsch (of a young woman leaving her tag, the line of beauty): Moufarrege writes his name boldly on a support of his choice. His act of overwriting is an additive negation—rather than applied art, Moufarrege is making mis-applied art. And his deliberate use of this now-kitsch motif renders it something else, bouncing back the questions: what do you know about kitsch, about value? Who determines, who draws the line?

Moufarrege's embroidered paintings showed me a way out of the stultifying—and still abiding—specifically post-war American glorification of painting as defined by an opposition between abstraction and figuration, as if these terms really still needed to be defended, or as if a picture could not be something else entirely. In Moufarrege's work, figure, ornament and text inhabit the same plane in a kind of meticulous clamor, staking out a trans-historical, and trans-cultural territory, complicated by what Monique Wittig, in her critique of the straight mind called, "a multiplicity of languages which constantly act upon the social reality":

> *Thus, the entire world is only a great register where the most diverse languages come to have themselves recorded, such as the language of the Unconscious, the language of fashion, the language of the exchange of women where human beings are literally the signs which are used to communicate. These languages, or rather these discourses, fit into one another, interpenetrate one another, support one another, reinforce one another, auto-engender, and engender one another.*[5]

In Moufarrege's own words (riffing on the work of graffiti artist Frederick Braithwaite, aka Fab 5 Freddy): "Where writing and

5. Monique Wittig, "The Straight Mind," in *The Straight Mind and Other Essays* (Boston: Beacon Press, 1992), 21 and 22.

painting mingle and mix, the image develops into ideogram, hieroglyph, and calligraphy."[6] Or, as he wrote in his two-part essay "Intoxication": "The language of the image, the experience spelled out: figurative writing and the writing of the figure; form and word, figure, letter, numeral; story, dot, dot, dash, dot, message; speech and figures of speech."[7]

Who, or what, then, are the figures in Moufarrege's work? I've heard people discuss the canvases of the early 1980s as figured by homoerotic desire, but that insists on a false symmetry between an artist's sexuality and their work, forestalling the possibility of other readings. While Moufarrege's figures often appear to be male, they are only as gay as Michelangelo (there are also countless female protagonists borrowed from Lichtenstein, and all of the figures engaged in acts of reading or writing are female muses dragged out from other chapters of art history). Idealized, more than eroticized, they are figures of art, like anatomical models dropped into pictures to which they don't belong. To me these characters always appeared like atlantids, the counterparts to caryatids, usually framing doorways and windows—but atlantids off the job: relaxing or in revolt. Even if some of these torsos read as "beefcake" they are exaggerated to baroque absurdity, as in an untitled work in which the corporeal fragment invades the visual language of Lichtenstein's citation of Mickey and Donald's cartoon world to propose a new set of terms. Moufarrege himself wrote, in an essay responding to a show about gay "sensibility" that, "fantasy is androgynous." In that same essay, "Lavender: On Homosexuality and the Arts,"

6. Nicolas Moufarrege, "Another Wave, Still More Savagely Than the First: Lower East Side, 1982," *Arts Magazine* 57, no. 1 (September 1982), 70.

7. Moufarrege, "Intoxication," *Arts magazine* 57, no. 8 1983), 71.

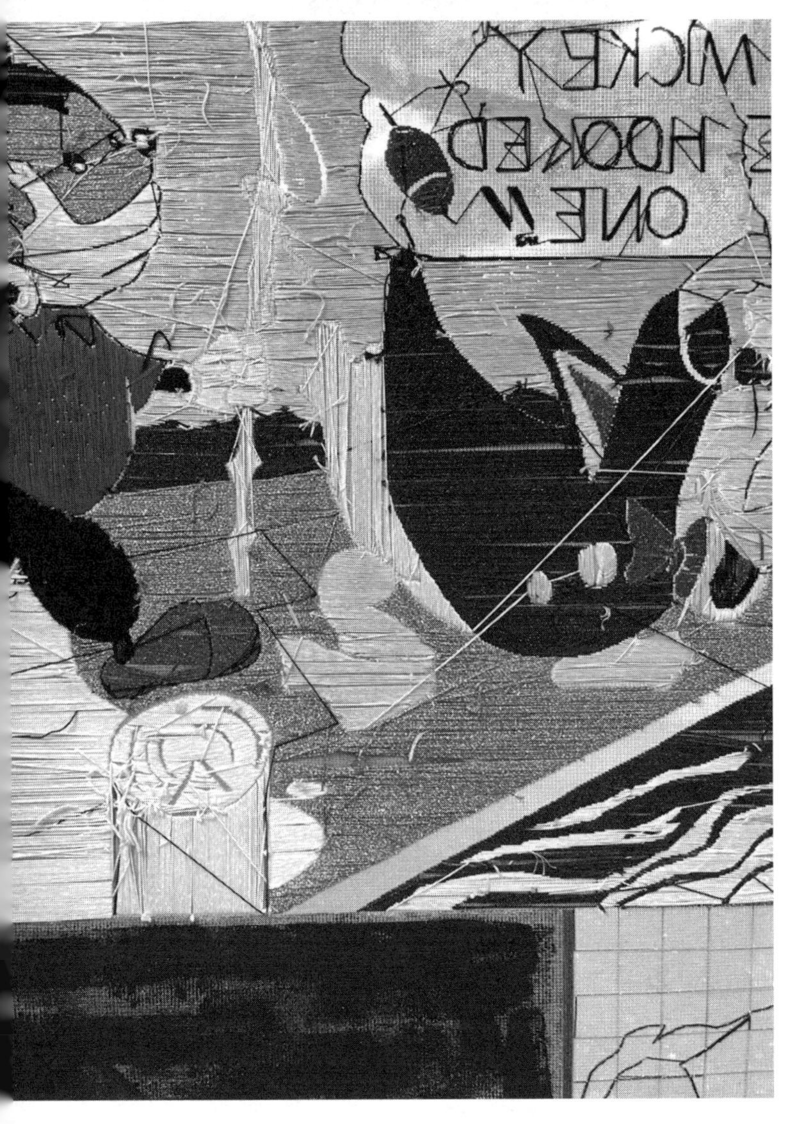

View of the reverse of Nicolas Moufarrege, *Untitled*, n.d.

published in *Arts magazine,* he goes on to reject the mapping of essentialized identities onto works of art:

> *... my perception of an extended sensibility does not restrict itself to gay or lesbian artists—it is a liberatory seal, a state of mind, maybe occasional, more often constant. It is important to draw on one's total self to become the person one is and to divest oneself of any sense of shame in reaching that goal. Extended sensibilities comprehend links to one's roots, to childhood and things past, the rejection of all forms of oppression, an inebriated compulsiveness and an equally inebriated search for beauty, the abrogation of masculine and feminine stereotype models, a certain sense of style that may incorporate a quirky aesthetic, a surrogate self, but ultimately and always a strong sense of personal affirmation ... This article is colored by the writer's sensibilities. I sleep on white sheets, prefer chocolate to vanilla, and happen to be a homosexual. The paintings I do used to conform to traditional rectangular formats ...*[8]

Moufarrege's pointed use of embroidery—the "subversive stitch," as Rozsika Parker called it[9]—should not overshadow the work's emphatic reengagement with a history of painting (and with history painting as a genre) through its connection to tapestry (the tapestries produced after cartoons by Nicolas Poussin and Peter Paul Rubens, for example). Moufarrege also insists

8. Nicolas Moufarrege, "Lavender: On Homosexuality and Art," *Arts Magazine* 57, no. 2 (October 1982),

9. Rozsika Parker, *The Subversive Stitch: Embroidery and the Making of the Feminine* (London: Women's Press, 1984; London, New York & Dublin: Bloomsbury Visual Arts, 2019).

on painting's initial bond with architecture, citing the painted architecture of tombs and ancient interiors, with their mixture of symbolism and trompe-l'œil. The gryphons in *The Importance of Being Evergreen* (1980), for example, also appear in the Villa Agrippa Postumus in Boscotrecase, in a Roman Third Style mural that has absorbed Egyptian iconography. In *Nikki* (1976), an arrangement of broken columns reveals a human profile dovetailing with a column's base, not unlike Jacques-François Blondel's eighteenth century analyses of architecture as measured against the human body, which elaborate on Vignola's sixteenth century renderings of Tuscan entablatures. Moufarrege's visual fitting together of human and architectural profile poignantly compresses memory with a landscape of loss whose tragic structures are animated by the echo of speech. In lending his own familial nickname as a title to this painting, Moufarrege calls back to the locales of a childhood that can never be revisited: Alexandria and Beirut. The profile in *Nikki* first appears (many of Moufarrege's works reappear in different guises across different works) in a work titled *The Blood of the Phoenix*, made in 1975, the year of Moufarrege's emigration to Paris, and of the outbreak of the Lebanese Civil War. It is one among just a few of his works that registers the violence of deracination, iconoclasm, and war, in a composition of tatters, floating eyes, visual blurs, and a fist punching through the bleeding ground.

In later works from Moufarrege's New York period (1980–85), windows of untouched embroidery canvas are left blank, allowing light to pass through the open mesh, shadows to cast on the wall, giving a sense of air behind the image, and exposing the stretchers. These zones of difference, some worked to opacity with needle and thread, others just touched by a pencil, heighten the sensual dimension of encountering the work as a conceptual object—the emphasis on the limits of the frame, the play between illusion and anti-illusion, the creation of a new frame of reference extending in multiple dimensions. Throughout his work Moufarrege also leaves visible the draughtman's grid—a method for faithfully copying or enlarging an existing image—as a persiflage on the grid as a transcendent emblem of modernity. In an untitled work from 1984–85, half of the picture plane is left "naked," except for its delicate graphite gridding and an idealized, possibly Renaissance, figure delineated in thread. Seen from the back, this figure mirrors our own disposition as viewers in relation to the picture plane—we merge as subjects. The other figure faces in the opposite direction, "looking" directly out of the picture: composed of an empty t-shirt over which a mirror hovers, it stares back at us blankly, offering no reflection.

In many instances, Moufarrege's canvases recall the strain and wonderment of Enlightenment visualizations of new concepts and technologies, such as the construction of pictorial illusion, which carries in itself a narrative of borrowing, miscegenation, and appropriation: pictorial perspective, "invented" in Renaissance Florence, derived its name as well as its theoretical underpinnings from a twelfth century Arabic treatise by the mathematician Al Hazen, which was translated into Latin in Spain. Many of Moufarrege's figures are positioned at the precipice of the perspectival field like demonstrative bodies in instruction manuals, serving as both witness to and agents of the picture's coalescing and dissolution. The gridded, veil-like nature of the open passages recall the optical device known as Alberti's veil, or Dürer's draughstman's net—devices that allow for the connection between the hand and the eye—or Abraham Bosse's seventeenth century treatise whose title translates to *The Universal Way to Practice Perspective*—in which multiple 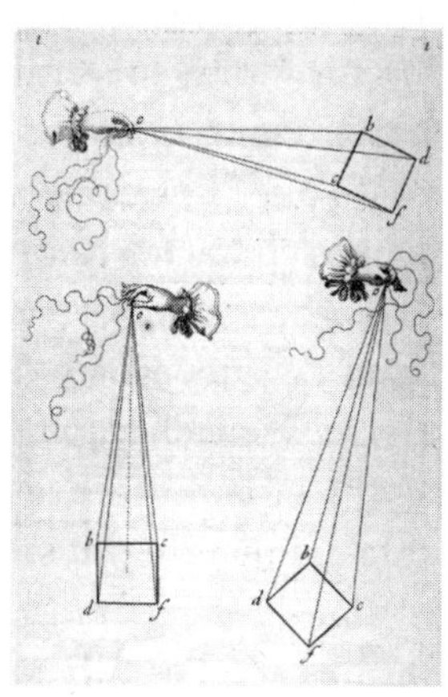 figures are depicted as situated in the same space, the rays of their distinct gazes producing different, isolated frames of vision.

In Moufarrege's seven-part free-form essay on a growing, trans-historical circle of artists he named the "Mutant International"—a rejection of all labels, groupings, and -isms currently in fashion in 80's New York—the artist, curator, and critic wrote:

I am Penelope, Spiderman, and Santa Claus. I am the mad painter with 53 names. My initials, in Arabic, my mother tongue, spell the word meaning "yes"; my mother's family name is hayek, meaning weaver. I am not timid. I've been knocked around. I have wandered; I have gone from place to place.[10]

If Moufarrege is Penelope and Spiderman, he is also Arachne, who challenged Athena and was changed into a spider, just as much as he is also the young Watteau girl reading. Moufarrege's

10. Nicolas Moufarrege "The Mutant International," *Arts Magazine* 58, no. 1 (September 1983), 20.

prose continues: "For many years my art raged in isolation. One piece of 1978, *Sunday, Bloody Sunday*, is in a Paris cave; hopefully there are spiders weaving solitary carpet-webs around it."[11]

What I have not yet really touched on is the aspect of embroidery as translation, which in Moufarrege's work can often take the form of a mis-translation, or false legibility, such as *The Truth About St. John the Baptist* (1983), in which a portentous swath of Arabic calligraphy looms in the sky next to the Marvel comics character Rom (along with the numbers 3 7 1 2, a code that recurs across several other works). In translation, the calligraphic superscript deflates deliciously to: "My father taught me Arabic calligraphy." Again and again, Moufarrege pierces myths of an authentic, original, or self-identical subject. The stitched picture transports a sense of purpose, care, and deliberation in its adaptation of an existing image to the limits of various stitches threaded through a standard mesh. Such pictures, while withholding the sense of the sole authorial gesture that inheres in paintings, also communicate the presence of a generally unknown maker who nevertheless communicates: I was here, I fixated on this, I transposed it, I passed my time in this way. The encoding of time and individual effort in needlework is certainly one of the reasons it is so affecting as a document, though some of Moufarrege's pictures were realized by multiple hands. Alanna Heiss, in her letter to the deceased Moufarrege that serves as the introduction to the Clocktower catalogue writes:

11. *Id.*

Remember when you organized a group of women from the Long Island City area into a sewing group to work on some of your embroidered and appliqued paintings? I was appalled when you first suggested the idea, but it worked wonderfully. The image of 7 or 8 older women and you dressed in a black leather motorcycle jacket sitting around your studio chatting about life has never left my mind.[12]

In *The Autobiography of Alice B. Toklas*, Gertrude Stein writes through Alice's voice to make her own self-portrait. One passage always jumped out at me, and seems fitting here:

Picasso had just written to Gertrude Stein announcing his marriage to a jeune fille, a real young lady, and he had sent Gertrude Stein a wedding present of a lovely little painting and a photograph of a painting of his wife. That lovely little painting he copied for me many years later on tapestry canvas and I embroidered it and that was the beginning of my tapestrying. I did not think it possible to ask him to draw me something to work but when I told Gertrude Stein she said, alright, I'll manage. And so one day when he was at the house she said, Pablo, Alice wants to make a tapestry of that little picture and I said I would trace it for her. He looked at her with kindly contempt—if it is done by anybody, he said, it will be done by me. Well, said Gertrude Stein, producing a piece of tapestry canvas, go to it, and he did. And I have been making tapestry of his drawings ever since and

12. Alanna Heiss in *Nicolas A. Moufarrege*, *op. cit.*, 5. Heiss founded The Institute for Art and Urban Resources, Inc. in 1971 (which became PS1 Contemporary Art Center in 1976) and The Clocktower Gallery in 1972. [Editors' note]

they are very successful and go marvelously with old chairs. I have done two small Louis fifteenth chairs in this way. He is kind enough now to make me drawings on my working canvas and to color them for me.[13]

I am not sure how likely it is that Moufarrege knew of Russell Lynes' article "The Mesh Canvas" published in *Art in America* in 1968.[14] Lynes' article and accompanying image spread suggest that embroidery provided a trajectory of art from the realm of the specialized to the popular, and also from the public to the private, so often coded as the domain of the feminine. Aiming to reframe needlepoint as a practice with serious high-brow artistic merit, Lynes showcased Lichtenstein's 1963 *Ball of Twine*, translated into an embroidered cushion cover by Mrs. Leo Castelli. Lichtenstein's ball of twine does make a cameo appearance (together with a Lichtenstein golf ball, *Betsy Ross' Flag*, and Jasper Johns' *Green Target*) in an untitled, undated Moufarrege work —so if he hadn't seen the article, I'm sure he would have thrilled to the idea of "Mrs. Castelli" taking up needlepoint to turn works by artists in her husband's stable (not only Lichtenstein's but also Frank Stella's work has been converted to needlepoint) into pillow covers. Coincidentally, embroidery was also an important pastime for the author's brother, artist George Platt Lynes, who took up the pastime with and under the influence of artist friends such as Bernard Perlin and Jared French in the 1940s. An undated photograph

13. Gertrude Stein, *The Autobiography of Alice B. Toklas* (New York: Harcourt, Brace, 1933), 228–29.

14. Russell Lynes, "The Mesh Canvas," *Art in America* 56, no. 3 (May-June 1968), 28–49.

(likely from the early 1950s) showcases a number of embroidered pillows—though they are not exactly the punctum of the photograph. Lynes also worked out a pillow design on which the contorted bodies of naked men spell out his monogram, and he translated paintings by Jared French into needlepoint pillows. As a gift to his lover, Monroe Wheeler, Lynes adapted a motif by Paul Klee on a little piece of embroidery canvas. Several of these embroideries also included strands of pubic hair, invisibly encoding the material evidence of affections that had to be publicly repressed. None of these examples of needlework have direct ties to Moufarrege, other than following his lead to "always see relationships: a fatal destiny, an unpremeditated appropriation, an intoxicated appropriateness,"[15] and to place Moufarrege within an unwritten history of avant-garde embroidery, overlapping with a practice of appropriation "before" appropriation.[16]

The long horizontal formats Moufarrege turned to in the early 80's are his most complex and coded. Featuring frieze- or panorama-like parades of characters, these paintings are also festooned with jeweled brooches as if to accentuate the magpie-like tendencies of its maker—Chuck Nanney told me that Moufarrege took great care in selecting and placing the brooches on the canvases. There is a lot to read and to string together in these panels—cultural and personal signs—direct, opaque, inverted, and purposely misleading. Nanney also

15. Nicolas Moufarrege, "Intoxication," *art. cit.*, 76.

16. And yet, in "Intoxication," Moufarrege credits George Platt Lynes' "human alphabet" as inspiring the following ekphrasis: "Naked in Time I tumble, body and letter, stage without mask, a pile of words, specters, barges, easels, and wheels (George Platt Lynes, *The Human Alphabet* series, c. 1945)." *Ibid.*, 75-76.

recalled an incident when Jean-Michel Basquiat visited Moufarrege's studio and became incensed by his use of Arabic calligraphy, accusing him of cultural appropriation, and Nanney had to explain that Moufarrege's play with signs corresponded to a world-view shaped by his acculturation in plural societies: born in Egypt to Lebanese parents, raised in Beirut by Christians, and living peripatetically in Cambridge (Moufarrege earned a Master's degree in chemistry at Harvard), back in Beirut, and Paris, before arriving in New York. The anatomical figures of the earlier works appear in these horizontal works as Marvel superheroes alongside many other characters—most of whom are doubles for Moufarrege (certainly Spiderman and Santa Claus, the Americanization of St. Nicholas)—in conjoined pictorial spaces defined by the directionality of text. Moufarrege best describes the function of these works, and their sources, in "Intoxication":

> *These words, dovetailed with Egyptian dancers and sumo wrestlers, flax and Flaxman; the lightning breaks haywire, berserk; a serpent coiled on a mound, the lion, the eagle; Christmas trees off of Second Avenue and Persian horses from* A King's Book of Kings. *Mishima's fan waves to Baudelaire and Poe; deciphering García Márquez and Nietzsche, poets and scientists; the wind wipes out the city of mirrors, stars die, dawn.*[17]

These works circle back to Fragonard's unwitting graffiti artist whose future is foretold in the adjoining panel by Lichtenstein's

17. *Ibid.*, 76.

spraycan, recoded from the disinfectant spray of the housewife to the brush preferred by the "painters" whose work Moufarrege admired so much. In his text "Another Wave," covering the burgeoning arts scene in the East Village, Moufarrege draws the explicit link between graffiti and painting, and the operation of the signature that is so often skewed in his work: "Five years ago I timidly scribbled my tag on the wall of the Vavin subway station in Paris; I then went home and recorded the date in my notebook. I'd spent years peering into the corners of paintings attempting to decipher the artists' names; then the names disappeared—they were on the backs of the canvas."[18] These late horizon panels—among Moufarrege's final works— are affiliated with, and perhaps even an homage to the paintings on trains—artworks that have since vanished—by artists like Lady Pink, Lee Quinones, or Fred Braithwaite. In an interview with several New York graffiti artists, Moufarrege mounted a defense of graffiti, proclaiming the written word as:

. . . The subject which has fascinated artists since time immemorial—from Islamic art to Japanese calligraphers to the French automatic writers. The list of people even currently involved with the written word is so extensive and various; look at Twombly, Ruscha—the list is endless. The written word is no way a trap. Look back, it was through it that Magritte liberated the image. Why can't it be art? I see it as a source of inspiration, and it is at least as mobile and dynamic as the human figure.[19]

18. Moufarrege, "Another Wave," *art. cit.*, 70.
19. Nicolas Moufarrege, "Lightning Strikes (Not Once But Twice): An Interview with Graffiti Artists," *Arts Magazine* 57, no. 3 (November 1982), 89.

So many of Moufarrege's works are landscapes—even the earlier conjoined canvases in which he proposes cousinages across centuries and styles turn portraits into landscapes. As Moufarrege moves into the stretched format of the decorative frieze, the written sentence, they turn into a kind of urban pastoral, sentences and terrains that can be read backwards and forwards, full of signs meant to be seen, but not necessarily disclosing their entire capacity for meaning to everyone.

Images snow down on skyscrapers. Manhattan, capital of the century and landscape of living monoliths, where the Act accomplishes itself as it rejoins the atoms of our ancestors. This city draws the Mutant International in as a giant magnet or lodestar. What is the dream, what kind of folly: Is this the isle of You-kali? Via Trieste, Bucharest and Paris, Leo Castelli landlights in Manhattan. Europe is blue. I read Yves Klein better now. Hello there, buddy on the nightshift, the Schickelgruber rages in Germany. Leo Castelli arrives in New York. In his own words, the first Jasper Johns painting came out of the blue. It was Green Painting; *it was at the Jewish Museum; it was 1955. Quantum leaps and the treasure of Tutankhamen flashed in Leo Castelli's mind. Something very mysterious. How can you explain? It's altered states, or Memory, that drew him to Garouste's work, years later. Merry Christmas, Mr. Castelli. How many languages do you speak? Welcome to the Mutant International . . .*[20] ◆

20. Moufarrege, "Mutant International," *art. cit.*, 128.

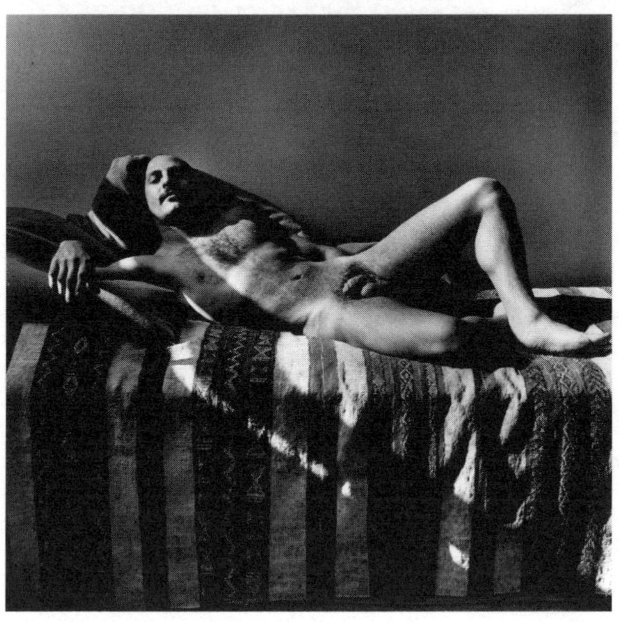

Peter Hujar, *Nicolas Abdallah Moufarrege, Paris*, 1980.

Why Is a Dress.
On Susan Cianciolo

The impossibility of Control
tofu kequishe
CORN muffins
SeaSOR Salad
Reflections of ouRself
IMAntations of ouR Iife
Dream of Different tomorow
—FROM A DRAWING BY SUSAN CIANCIOLO FOR RUN RESTAURANT'S MENU

I went to the RUN Store in the fall of 2001. I didn't know what to expect. The shop had been set up for one day in a storefront on 8th Avenue near 14th Street, and its opening was preceded by rumors and fantasies, the sense of private anticipation that remains the ineffable emblem of Susan Cianciolo's brand of agitprop. This was way before pop-up shops were everywhere, and though it seems strange to bring up that historical detail, it's important to remember that, at the time, it actually felt like an experimental thing to do, this temporary store. I remember it now like a film played at the wrong speed, one in which people enacted various attitudes of service in uniforms that were delicate travesties of utility and futility, ready-made T-shirts that had been cinched and clipped to resemble shrunken waitress aprons with scalloped hems. It was unclear what, if anything, was for sale in this store run by what appeared to be a nonhierarchical all-ages commune or the cast of Robert Altman's film *3 Women.* Models and nonmodels acted like absentminded shopkeepers, as if under a spell or beholden to an oblique subtext. And for a moment, everyone was participating in this projection of an alternate site of exchange and attention, and I caught glimpses of details: ethereally weird makeup, talismans, words emblazoned on clothes held together by spiderwebs and altered with hedge clippers. "It's like couture made by people who really really can't sew and grandmother master tailors simultaneously," a friend offered, as an explanation of how something could seem at once so sophisticated and so wilfully naive. Each garment bore the traces and decisions of many authors, and ways of making, of learning and unlearning.

Fashion houses have always been collaborative, but Susan Cianciolo's RUN emerged in a climate in which they were being streamlined to the point of airlessness. Under the pressure of corporatization, designers were becoming carefully marketed caricatures of "the artist"—neoliberal avatars of bohemian creativity—while the clothes themselves were being drained of interest in order to facilitate mass consumption based on predictable trend patterns. RUN, a label that produced eleven collections between 1995 and 2001, went directly against the grain of these developments, proposing a model for generating clothes with many voices and with a disregard for efficiency. Cianciolo's clothes were handmade for particular individuals, designed, assembled, and adorned in a process that pooled various types of knowledge, techniques, skills, and nonskills, in a punk-constructivist reimagining of the production line; couture as collective improvisation. "I have always collaborated with many people," she once told an interviewer. "I have made things with other artists. But everything was like this. Historically, and in everyday life. A bakery bakes bread with everyone.

You can't live alone. . . . I feel that I am always collaborating with somebody in everyday life. . . . It is opening yourself up and accepting other people's ideas using you as a filter."[1] For many RUN collections, a group of collaborators would come together to develop and produce the garments—from DIY "kits" to one-of-a-kind ensembles carefully pieced together from an archive of found and altered textiles. These sewing circles were composed of friends, students, even relatives. Cianciolo acknowledged her indebtedness to the matrilineal transference of knowledge and skill by folding her mother's and grandmother's work into her own. Perhaps the most disarmingly uncool thing Cianciolo ever did was directly implicate her own family in her work, making those relationships explicitly visible yet ambivalently coded. Recently, her most intimate and daring collaboration has been with her now-seven-year-old daughter, Lilac Sky, whose hand and touches of glitter were visible all over Cianciolo's 2015 exhibition at New York's Bridget Donahue gallery, *if God COMes to visit You, HOW will you know? (the great tetrahedral kite)*. As Cianciolo gathered her daughter's notes and sketches to include in a work, she asked Lilac Sky for permission to use them and was surprised by the answer: "You can do whatever you want, as long as we split fifty-fifty." Her daughter also appears in the 2015 video *Queens and Kings and Working Class Heroes* (shown along with five of Cianciolo's other moving-image works in the 2016 edition of MoMA PS1's Greater New York).

The handmade collective deconstruction of what a body can be does not work with factory production. The only way to

---

1. See "Susan Cianciolo", *Bijutsu Techo Magazine*, vol. 54, no. 822 (July 2002), 9–28.

produce truly new fashion is to inhibit the industrial production of clothes. When Cianciolo says that she makes "costumes" rather than engaging in the "designing of clothes,"[2] one thinks of what it could mean to wear a costume every day, to activate a form of interpersonal ritual within a stream of global trends. On the one hand, *fashion* connotes an originally Western tradition that is only about five hundred years old, while *costume* is used by curators and academics to refer to the practices of making and wearing clothing in every place and period. Cianciolo's chosen term therefore suggests that the wearer of her clothes is somehow outside fashion but still very much embedded in histories. On the other hand, costume is also meaningful in a specific historical context: the 1990s was the era of the Gap uniform at the low end of the market and of understated "minimalism" at the high end, styles that posited attire as a kind of transparent frame that lets the wearer's authentic self shine through. The idea of a costume—of clothing as performance—violates this logic. Cianciolo's work seems to aspire to a state of permanent dishabille. Her costumes require a new kind of reciprocal engagement from her clients, who must learn how to wear a piece, how to incorporate it into their lives, and how to acclimate to its constraints over time. In 1996, discussing RUN 3—each collection was simply called RUN and numbered consecutively—Cianciolo stated: "There's personality in each person's movement, it's like any other type of expression. And the industrial fabric [I used in this collection] collaborates with that expression. It doesn't just become part of the body, it's like the two are almost fighting together. For that fabric to meet

2. Interview by Alex Fleming, "Susan Cianciolo," *Flash Art*, vol. 48, no. 303 (July–September 2015).

the body is so difficult. It's a sharp object—you know some of [the clothes] have metal and Kevlar in them—meeting a soft one. Technology, the computer versus the human."[3]

I first heard of RUN through word of mouth. I was working for Mended Veil, a tiny apartment operation that made fantastical dime-store-meets-*Salammbô* jewelry. Some of those pieces were shown in Cianciolo's early collections. Nearby, at Colin de Land's gallery American Fine Arts, artist Patterson Beckwith's mother, Jane, was organizing crafting bees called Bee-Ins; American Fine Arts was a few blocks from Cianciolo's studio. Danny McDonald, the genius behind Mended Veil, ran the gallery; I remember Lizzi Bougatsos playing receptionist, waiting for band practice to start, while, in the basement, I drilled holes into quarters from 1984 for necklaces. There was a lot of antic collaboration across disciplines and vested interests, and, more important, injections of eccentric motives into seemingly stable frameworks. It's relevant that some of the most interesting collaborative projects happening at that time, like Art Club 2000 (the artists' group that seven Cooper Union students, including Beckwith and McDonald, had founded with de Land in the early '90s) and the artists' collective Bernadette Corporation, used fashion as an avenue for cultural critique. AC2000 parodied the sartorial monoculture of the Gap in a deadpan performance of selling out, while clothes with the Bernadette Corporation label could be found for sale in Ludlow Street boutiques. But if Bernadette Corporation was performing its own now-famous mystique as part of a critical investigation of the

3. See Ameena Meer, "Dressing Lazarus," *Big Magazine*, no. 15 (1994).

cultural and economic co-optation of "downtown," for Cianciolo the earnest openness of *un*coolness was an operative method.

As time went on, RUN became an umbrella for a wide range of propositions that have operated sometimes in tandem with collections and sometimes independently of them, and that continue to this day. One of the earliest was RUN Restaurant, an establishment that existed for a month at New York's Alleged Galleries in 2001 and that, in documentation, looks like a piece of experimental theater, the enactment of a social ideal and an exercise in suspension of disbelief, much like RUN Store. People sit on the floor around a low, cobbled-together table-cunt-stage, near a freestanding fence, close to a small hut. Someone is "cooking"—actually, it looks more like they're decorating hors d'oeuvres. The food doesn't have to be real. A man wears an apron with an outsize handpainted gingham motif. Cianciolo's other ventures have included the alternative currency RUN Money, with which people could pretend to purchase RUN kits at the RUN 11 collection presentations; the housewares line RUN Home; a perfume, Chevalier; and, most recently, YaIoRUN, a project space in Water Valley, Mississippi, founded by Cianciolo with artist Coulter Fussell and designer Kiva Mornyk, which also functions as a store for textile-craft supplies.

In retrospect, it becomes apparent how defiantly Cianciolo has played with commerce in order to rethink value, insisting on the way ideas, feelings, and intimacy inhere in both production and day-to-day life with garments and objects, on touching and looking rather than being looked at. Functionality is given dreamlike new valences or thwarted completely; often, to use one of Cianciolo's products, you have to love it irrationally,

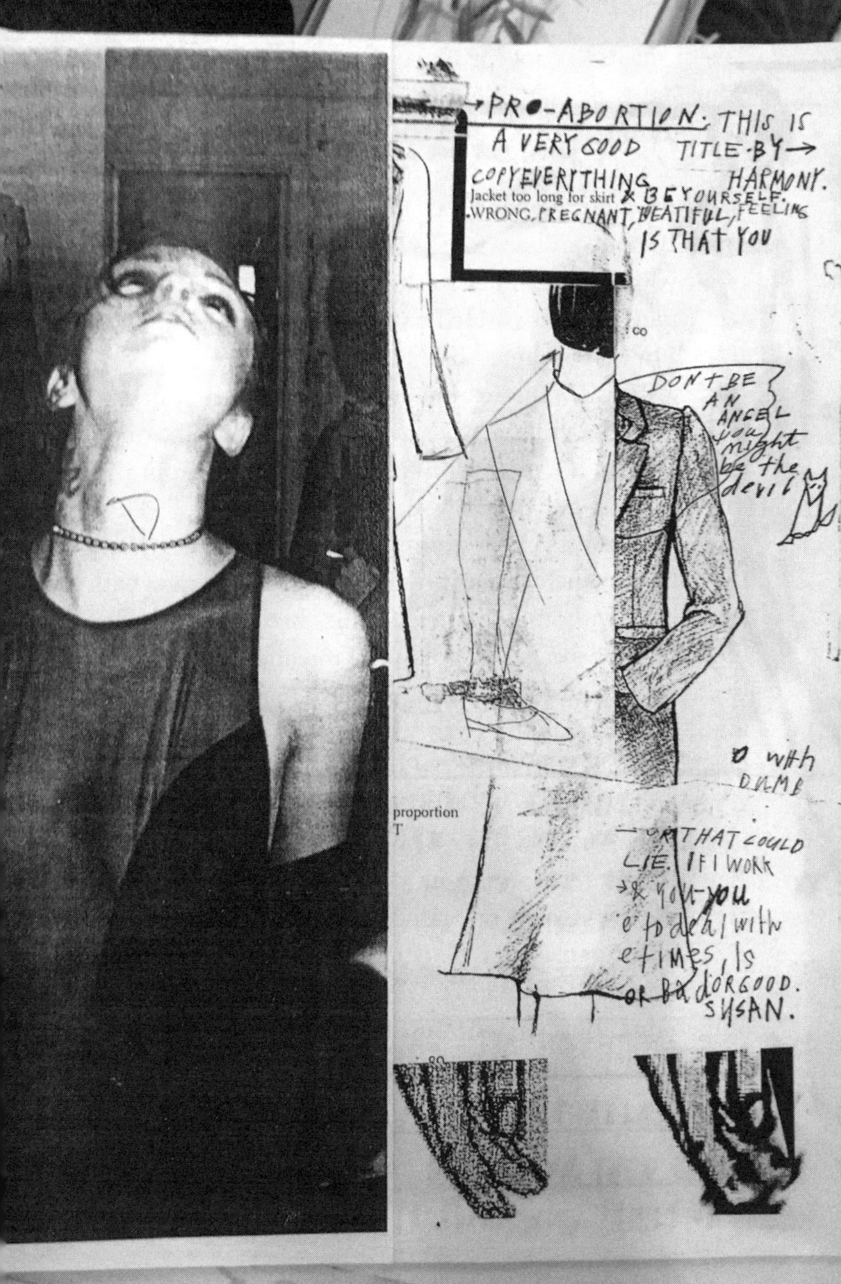

→ PRO-ABORTION: THIS IS
A VERY GOOD   TITLE·BY →
COPYEVERYTHING   HARMONY.
Jacket too long for skirt X BE YOURSELF.
.WRONG, PREGNANT, BEATIFUL, FEELING
IS THAT YOU
DON'T BE
AN
ANGEL
you
might
be the
devil
proportion
T
O with
DUMB
OR THAT COULD
LIE. IF I WORK
→ & YOU YOU
e to deal with
e times, Is
or Bad ORGOOD.
SUSAN.

love it for itself (not for its usefulness or for the way it ratifies your status or your identity), even love it enough to sacrifice comfort or security or sense. Shoes are covered in white feathers that will fall off if you wear them as often as you'd like. Sacks made of veiling provide only the thinnest, most porous boundary between your bare foot and the floor—they are just volumes of air with a long zipper to close them up. A swimsuit kit is in fact a canvas book with slits into which your hand disappears to pull out a crocheted bikini. In a 1999 essay, fashion editor Nakako Hayashi quotes Cianciolo: "Most of my work is about happy and sad memories." Hayashi continues, "She once made a skirt where a long, narrow cloth hung down from the waist 'to wipe your eyes when you cry uncontrollably.'"[4] This affective "script" hints at the complexity of Cianciolo's vision of peformativity, which in her work is deeply inter-twined with lived experience without necessarily being "live"—for her videos and films have always gently pressured the line between performative presence and the moving image. One of her earliest fashion shows, for example, was not a show at all, but a screening of her film *Pro-Abortion/Anti-Pink* (1996), while her hauntingly elliptical *Queens and Kings and Working Class Heroes*, shot in the Cloisters in New York City and in more bucolic settings in New York State, Maine, and Mississippi, evokes—and features performers who have appeared in—her live shows.

The story goes that Cianciolo "left" the fashion system at the moment it claimed her, when her brand marketability was burgeoning. But it's clear now that she has used fashion as an exploratory vehicle for an ongoing multidetermined perfor-

4. See Nakako Hayashi, *Paris Collection Individuals 2: 1999–2000* (Tokyo: Little More, 2000).

mance work that allows for numerous collaborators, experimental venues, and layers of conflicting messages. Still, for a long time, except among true devotees, it really did seem like Cianciolo had disappeared in 2001. And so excitement greeted the announcement of Cianciolo's "return" exhibition at Donahue's gallery in the summer of 2015—an appearance that would be followed in quick succession by outings in group shows at Rodeo Gallery's Istanbul and London locations in September and in Greater New York in October, with solo shows planned for 2016 at 356 Mission Road in Los Angeles and Yale Union in Portland, Oregon.

The Bridget Donahue show, curated by Donahue and artist Alex Fleming, featured thirty-two found or newly made boxes, or kits, laid out on the floor in a loose grid. In the late '90s, Cianciolo began studying Fluxus and developed a relationship with movement historian Barbara Moore. Cianciolo's first group of kits, which she has referred to as "Fluxus boxes," grew out of this engagement; since then, the kits have become a central feature of her work. Each unique kit contains a highly personal constellation of objects. Offering her reconfigured archive in the form of distinct devotional cosmologies, Cianciolo created a complex dramaturgy of intimate tactile conversation, improvised ritual, and hypothetical transaction. She also reimagined the role of the gallerist for this scenario: Donahue became docent, interpreter, archivist, and oral historian. On entering the gallery, at your request, she would begin describing and interpreting, while carefully laying each artifact on one of the small quilts or rug-like textiles on which the boxes were decisively positioned—a tactic that delimited a zone of focused activity in which the boxes became reliquaries, conceptual models, sliced sediments of a life given up for perusal, theater stages, libraries, lamps, even utopian cities. (In a sequence *in Queens and Kings and Working Class Heroes*, Lilac Sky performs a similar role, unpacking one kit's contents on a cloth that has been carefully laid on a bench.) The nonlinear "purpose" of each kit—*Hologram Box* (2015); *Documentary of Conversations Box* (2013–15); *DIY Blouse Kit* (2001)—is expressed by artifacts from different points in time, atomizing chronology to illuminate other kinds of relationships among the various items gathered within and across boxes. In this context, Cianciolo's "costumes" became historical events annotated with snapshots and notes. Everything became an asterisk referring the viewer/handler to some other item among a battery of social memories of a particular set of events, casting webs of cross-references throughout the space. Where one box might contain an elaborate necklace-like collar that can also be hung on the wall for decoration, you could discover in another box a photograph of that piece as worn in what looks like a procession through a forest. A pandemonium of artists, filmmakers, photographers, musicians, designers, and stylists from the New York scene were conjured in a zone that connected to other historical legacies: of avant-garde costume design, Futurist books made of sandpaper and wood pulp, and the collaborative modus of Sonia Delaunay, who also reinvented books, blankets, and boxes in her own explicit language of citation, collage, decoupage, and patchwork. As an event, and as a history, the exhibition made sense the same way Cianciolo's clothes always have—obliquely, with an intense vulnerability.

As in other Cianciolo projects, this investigation of the retrospective format not only functioned as a reevaluation of old conventions but also generated its own momentum as a pretext for the production of new images and satellite occasions: a series of posters, a screening of Cianciolo's films at Anthology Film Archives, and a presentation by Moore of never-before-shown slides of the Fashion Show Poetry Event, organized in 1969 by Hannah Weiner, Eduardo Costa, and John Perreault at the Americas Society (then the Center for Inter-American Relations) on Park Avenue and 68th Street. The last of these side events was particularly interesting, as it folded other important microhistories of the art-fashion dialogue into this one. Described by the poets who organized it as "a fictionalized version of a real life event that would appeal to an audience accustomed to sophisticated perception of visual phenomena,"[5] the Fashion Show Poetry Event included among its participants Andy Warhol, Claes Oldenburg, and Deborah Hay, all of whom made clothes following sets of instructions provided by the organizers. The poets in turn retranslated these ensembles into "typical fashionese" and read their texts during the catwalk presentation. The audience was asked to contemplate a "slightly insolent creation . . . for the young man about town" as Rene Ricard modeled Marisol's paint-smeared underwear on the runway, while Weiner's design, "Wear Your Own Luggage," was modeled by Bernadette Mayer.[6] "There is a difference between fashion copy and our 'poems' which are imitations of fashion copy," wrote Mayer, Costa, and Perreault. "There is a difference between a real fashion show and our imitation of a fashion

5. Hannah Weiner, "The Fashion Show Poetry Event Essay" (1969), in *Hannah Weiner's Open House*, ed. Patrick Durgin (San Francisco: Kenning Editions, 2006), 57.

6. Quotes from Barbara Moore's presentation on the "Fashion Show Poetry Event," June 14, 2015, in Cianciolo's exhibition at Bridget Donahue.

show. We are interested in these differences in spite of the fact that we have tried to eliminate them. . . . The Fashion Show Poetry Event is not only fashion, poetry, and art, it is where these arbitrary categories overlap and as categories dissolve and become irrelevant."[7]

The RUN presentations followed in this transgressive tradition—Cianciolo showed clothes in art galleries and public bathrooms, live and on film. For the 1997 collection RUN 5, she introduced life-size dolls, or "sleepers," alongside living models, followed by abstract bodies—neoconstructivist wooden armatures to support clothing, conceived by artist Aaron Lown—for RUN 9 (1999). But of course, Mayer, Costa, and Perreault's statement has a broader resonance for Cianciolo's practice, not just her fashion shows—she, too, has explored and activated the dissolution of cultural categories while, paradoxically, sustaining poetic difference. The invocation of the Fashion Show Poetry Event within the frame of Cianciolo's exhibition not only situated her in a particular lineage, intensifying the dialogue between "art" and "fashion" in historical terms, but underscored the singularity of her work, bringing into sharper focus her techniques of deconstructive intervention, her coquetry with expectations, and the multiple reimaginings and conflations of spectator-ship, consumption, and collaboration within her constantly shifting scenographies. ◆

7. *Ibid.*, 58.

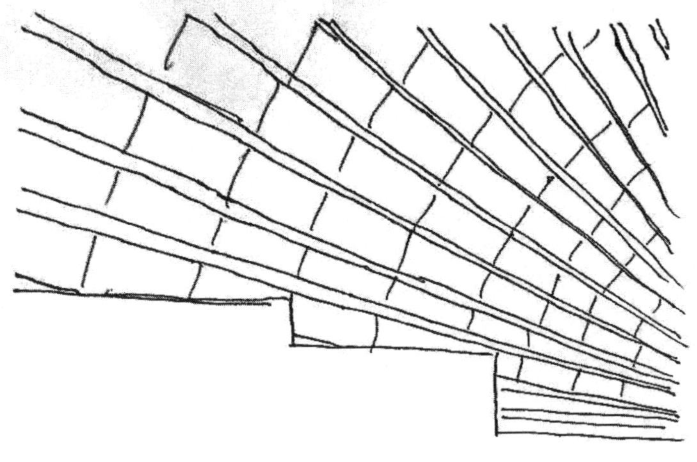

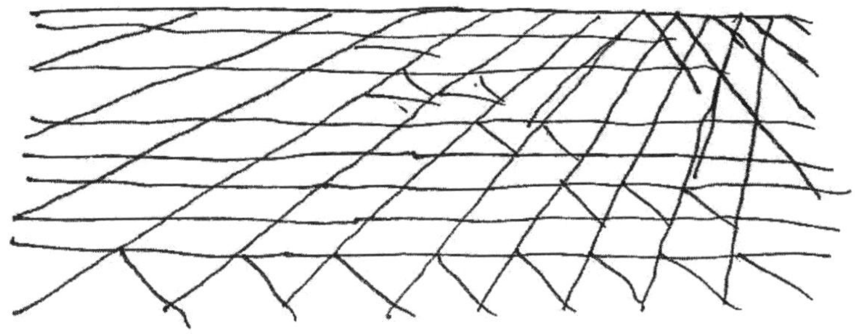

This essay was written for Christian Bérard. Excentrique Bébé, *ed. Célia Bernasconi, exh. cat. (Monaco: Nouveau Musée National de Monaco and Paris: Flammarion, 2022). Mauss also worked alongside curator Célia Bernasconi on the eponymous exhibition, presented at Villa Paloma, Nouveau Musée National de Monaco (July 9–October 16, 2022).*

The Painter of Inner Life.
On Christian Bérard

E. instructed me to recreate the model of a room I had built in her dream. As she described it: just like that Claes Oldenburg installation with the plush and the zebra, except the bed is covered in a grid of baguettes standing en pointe beneath a poster of the cover of *Tristes Tropiques*. "You still haven't made it?" she keeps asking me, incredulous.

The attempt to draw a relation between the present and the presence of something out-of-present (to show that presence persists) is generally misconstrued as too contingent, undefined. But in that dilating space of absence varying presences and intensities can be orchestrated. I find myself revisiting encounters in the flourish of their disorder and tangents. The structure is generally this: one experience interrupted by the passage into another experience.

Boredom is a warm gray fabric lined on the inside with the most lustrous and colorful of silks. In this fabric we wrap ourselves when we dream. We are at home then in the arabesques of its lining . . . who would be able at one stroke to turn the lining of time to the outside? Yet to narrate dreams signifies nothing else.[1]

1. Walter Benjamin, *The Arcades Project*, trans. Howard Eiland and Kevin McLaughlin (Cambridge, MA & London: Belknap Press of Harvard University Press, 2002),

This room is not a room, but a passage between spaces and functions. Now you can press on the velvet doors and get a facial, a massage, or, if you wait at the open fourth wall, beauticians in white lab coats may distribute cosmetics around the surface of your face. It was as an intervention into his stark interior for the Institut Guerlain on the Champs-Elysées that Jean-Michel Frank commissioned this antechamber from his frequent collaborator Christian Bérard in 1935, years before Frank took his own life in Manhattan and before this singular architectural scheme was mutilated by layers of renovations that spared only Bérard's anomalous velvet space. Based on a gouache projet, his persiflage of classicism was translated from paper to appliqué by Margarita Classen-Smith, the couture embroiderer who acted as a frequent intermediary in the dialogue between Bérard and Frank, converting what Colette called Bérard's "nonchalant hand"[2] into more refined materials, such as fabric or leather.

Awkward, un-peopled, Degas-colored, Bérard's countless renderings of "imaginary rooms" are free inventions described in just enough detail to give a semblance of decorated space, dashed off like autographs or thank-you notes. But they are not inventions so much as they are compressions of memory, literature, and historic period styles internalized affectionately. What appears to be a generic stand-in for "painting" in one of Bérard's gouaches of a wood-paneled room is his abbreviation of Caravaggio's *The Cardsharps* (visualizing a theme of deceit to which de La Tour also paid homage, and which Bérard would have studied at the Louvre as a pupil of Édouard Vuillard and

2. Colette, "Christian Bérard," in *En Pays Connu* (Paris: Ferenczi, 1950), 132.

Maurice Denis). Conversely, Bérard re-worked art history in paintings composed with specific rooms in mind, such as the one he fantasized in a letter to Jean Cocteau: "For the salon I'm envisioning a large Delacroix harem scene with young fishermen and thugs in *houri* poses."[3] Bérard's paintings of spaces tend to be constructed around absence, deriving their charge from those figures who have exited, or have yet to be painted in. Rooms suspended entr'acte. At times it is unclear whether these gouaches represent commissions for interiors (rooms to live in), or for the theater (rooms in which to perform living), though the distinction seems of no consequence to Bérard, whose painted carpets could end up in Nelson A. Rockefeller's apartment in New York, just as well as on the cover of *Vogue*.

Cruel	Brilliant
Humain	Enfantin
Rapide	Refoulé
Instructif	Aimant
Snob	Reclus
Théâtral	Dérasé [4]
Imaginatif	
Angoissé	
Noyé	

3. Christian Bérard to Jean Cocteau, illustrated letter (c. 1940). Our translation.

4. Christian Bérard's acrostic self-portrait, excerpted from Cecil Beaton, *The Glass of Fashion* (New York: Doubleday, 1954), 264. Beaton's transcript is actually erroneous: the first I stands for "Instinctif", the second for "Imaginatif" and/or "Intoxiqué," and the last letter, D, for "Dépassé." Which translates to: Cruel / Human / Fast / Instinctive / Snob / Theatrical / Imaginative [and/or] Intoxicated / Anxious / Drowned; Brilliant / Childish / Repressed / Loving / Recluse / Outdated. According to Beaton, the acrostic, "from an after-dinner game," was written on "a scrap of paper" kept by George David, fiction editor of *Harper's Bazaar*. [Editors' note]

"In the official annals of modern art, Bérard's name is missing. Or nearly so: sometimes he is mentioned in passing."[5]

I must have first seen his name cross-fading in the title sequence of the film *Orpheus* (1950), dedicated in Cocteau's hand to Bérard. Poulenc's *Stabat Mater* was composed to memorialize him the same year. And as late as 1972, Bérard features in the list of dedicatees of Charles Henri Ford's volume of poems, *Flag of Ecstasy*.[6] In other words, Bérard's name is not missing, but deliberately inscribed in filmic, musical, and poetic monuments that pay tribute to his irrepressible storm of costume designs, fashion illustrations, frontispieces, paintings, set designs, rugs, scarves, improvised stylings, and "looks" for legendary parties. The involuntary, signature-like quality of his promiscuous undulations and their clumsy "you-know-what-I-mean" shorthand constitute a form of painting as direct address, a disarming mode of speech that carries over into Bérard's preference for painting his notes to friends with a brush.

Once so ubiquitous, Bérard left an evaporating legacy dispersed among countless fleeting art forms (ballets, plays, festive occasions), magazines and books, gifts or throw-away gestures. And though his life opens like a door to a social history—people, sentiments, and convictions—it does not harmonize with the "official annals" of modern art, from which his name was slowly excised. Writing in 1980, the *New York Times* art critic John Russell grappled with Bérard's painting *On the Beach (Double Self-Portrait)*: "Where on earth could we fit such

5. Jean Clair, ". . . The Most Elegant Woman in the World . . .," in *Christian Bérard*, ed. Boris Kochno (London: Thames and Hudson, 1988), 81.

6. Charles Henri Ford, *Flag of Ecstasy: Selected Poems*, ed. Edward B. Germain (Los Angeles: Black Sparrow Press, 1972).

a painting in the didactic sequences of the Museum of Modern Art? And yet it speaks for a specific moment in the history of twentieth-century art, even if it is not one that at present has many admirers."[7] Only half a century earlier that same painting had graced the cover of James Thrall Soby's study *After Picasso*, in which the curator wrote of Bérard: "The very property of his magic makes him more difficult to understand than most contemporary painters. Nearly everyone is at first repulsed by the surface casualness of his painting and by its apparent atmosphere of chic . . . Bérard is by nature not an illustrator at all. Whatever he records is necessarily something that has touched him deeply. Except for his occasional fashion sketches, the surface appearances of society pass by him entirely; what he seizes is recorded in the fragility of its essence."[8]

Bérard's sudden death in 1949 while working on stage at the Théâtre Martigny prompted an outpouring of recollections of the artist who "bridged every world."[9] Elsa Schiaparelli's assistant, Bettina Bergery, evoked the image of "Bébé" gleefully spraying his beard with Schiaparelli's Schocking until the liquid ran down his neck and onto his soiled shirt. Dalì recalled that "his filthiness fascinated me quite as much as his mind."[10] The teenage Yves Saint Laurent attended a production of Molière's *The School for Wives* in Oran, Algeria, in 1950, and was so deeply moved by the sight of "Bérard's prestigious set . . . the most

7. John Russell, "Introduction," in "Christian Bérard," *op. cit.*, 7.
8. James Thrall Soby, *After Picasso* (New York: Dodd, Mead & Company, 1935), 39.
9. Diana Vreeland, *D.V.*, ed. George Plimpton (New York: Vintage Books, 1985), 179.
10. Salvador Dalì, *The Unspeakable Confessions of Salvador Dalì*, ed. André Parinaud, trans. Harold J. Salemson (London: Quartet Books, 1977), 172.

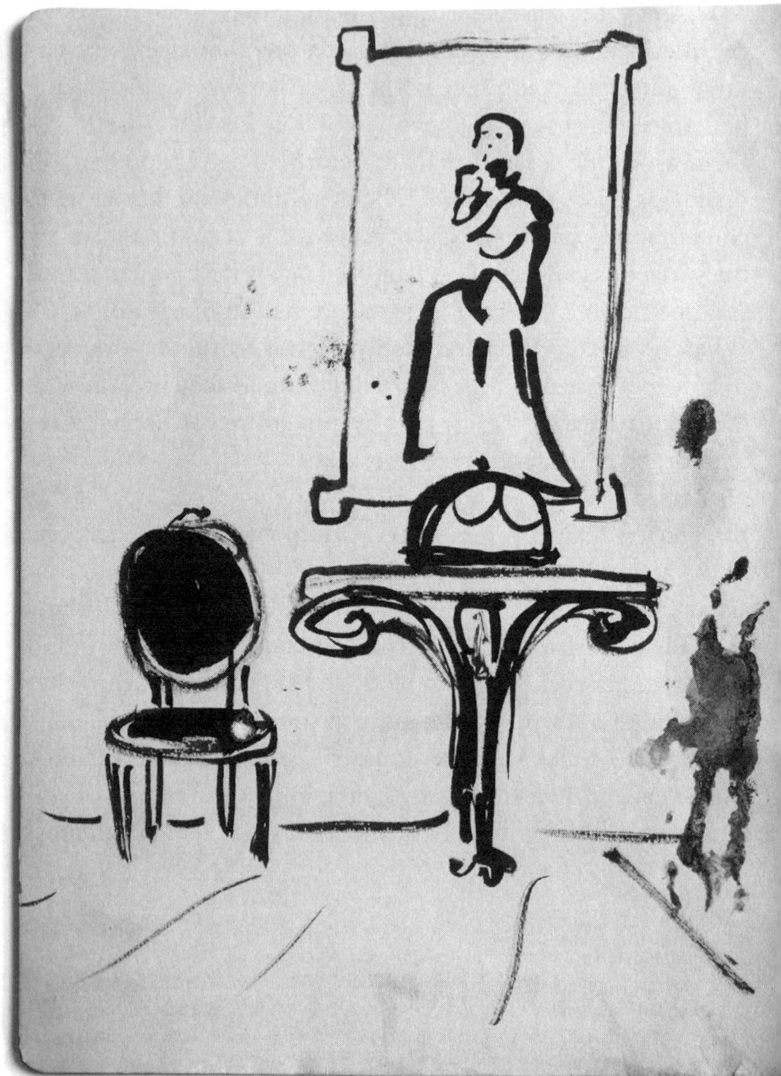

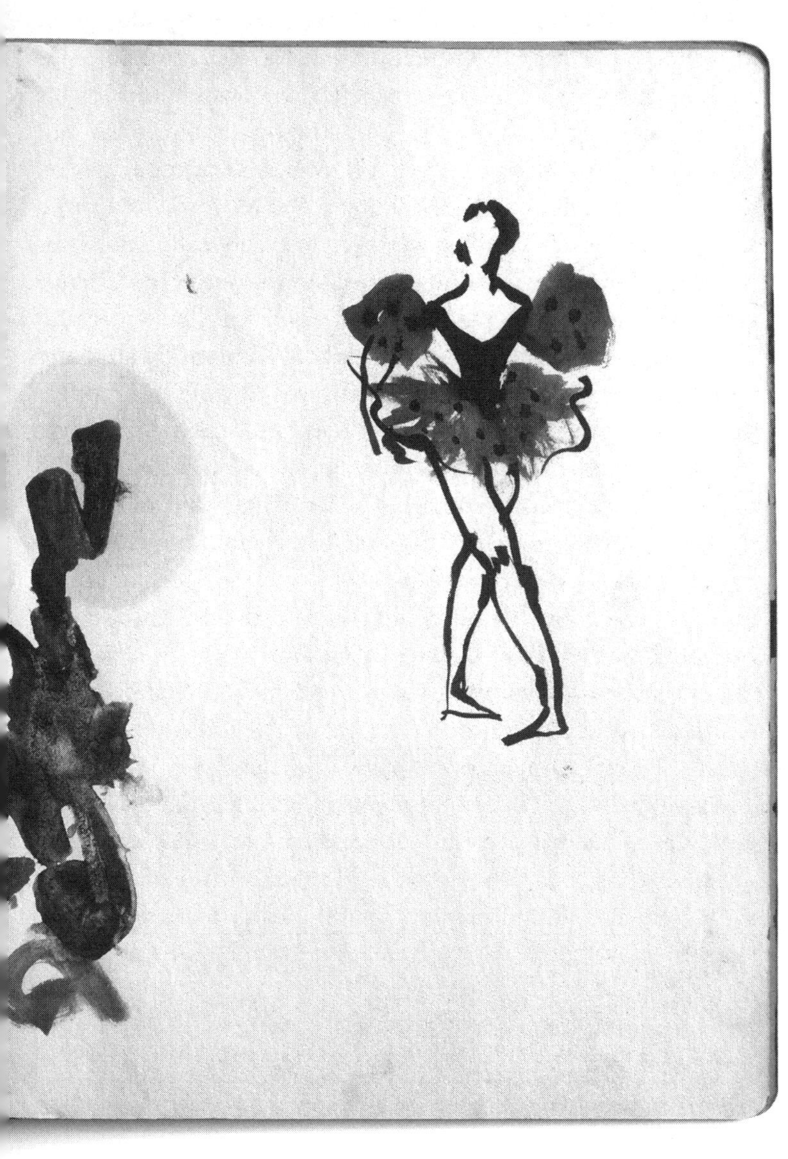

extraordinary feeling I think I have ever had in my life,"[11] that he went on to construct a miniature theater with moveable sets and paper dolls on which to stage his own productions for his family. A 1951 gouache shows just how totally Saint Laurent had fallen under Bérard's spell, ardently replicating his vision of the archangel in Jean Giraudoux' *Sodom and Gomorrah*, whose wings cross tantalizingly over his crotch. But notwithstanding Bérard's wide range of influence, numerous friends lamented the loss of a painter who "would have been" great, if not for his forays into the "minor" arts of fashion, theater, and décor. Julien Green, for example, delivered the following judgement: "It was the applause that led Bérard to success, with eyes closed, and prevented him from seeing the canvases he wanted to paint. Each of his decorations was a delight, but how many paintings have they deprived us of."[12] Cocteau seemed to echo him, but gave Bérard the benefit of the doubt: "If he had not let himself be seduced by the fashions he created for his designer friends, he would have been a great painter. But can Watteau be reproached for painting *Gersaint's Signboard*, and for the costumes of the *Embarkation to Cythera*?"[13] Today we can recognize Bérard's supposed trespasses against easel painting as an expanded vision of artistic commitment that flouts false hierarchies of painting versus set dressing, or of the avant-garde versus the decorative. Indeed, Cocteau's invocation of the sign Watteau painted in 1720 for the dealer Gersaint is apt, since this functional painting of the rococo no doubt served as

11. Yves Saint Laurent in *Yves Saint Laurent, tout terriblement*, dir. Jérôme de Missolz (documentary, France, 47 min, 1994).

12. Julien Green, *Dans la gueule du temps* (Paris: Plon, 1978), 42. Our translation.

13. Jean Cocteau, *Mes Monstres Sacrés*, ed. Bertrand Meyer-Stabley and Édouard Dermit (Paris: Encre éditions, 1979), 92. Our translation.

inspiration for the triptych "sign" Bérard painted for Jean-Michel Frank's store on the Faubourg Saint-Honoré. Prominently displayed amongst Frank's designs and those commissioned from his core group of artist-collaborators (the Giacometti brothers, Bérard, Emilio Terry, and Dalì) Bérard's painting of three enigmatic figures also represents a Giacometti plaster vase and one of Frank's trademark table lamps. Bérard's most striking paintings flourish in the dissonance between art and the social spaces it occupies. In decoration, he speaks fluently through ornament, abstraction, and corporeal gesture, vivifying architectures in which we are incited to act differently, spontaneously.

American audiences were more inclined to embrace Bérard's hybrid vocations. An exhibition of his work in New York simultaneously included oil paintings, designs for the ballet, book illustrations, and perfume branding. An article in *Art News* reported: "As if in defiance of the Puritan mistrust of the Jack-of-all-trades, Bérard can juggle his talents . . . Even if at some point he designs a tooth-paste tube, it will be immediately recognizable as a Bérard."[14] By the late 1940's he was well-known in New York as the designer of the sets for the popular production of Giraudoux' *Madwoman of Chaillot*, as well as for his affiliation with the *Théâtre de la Mode*, an elaborate work of cultural diplomacy that brought to Americans what they "sorely missed during the war—French art and fashions."[15]

14. Thomas B. Hess, "Spotlight on Christian Bérard," *Art News* 45, no. 11 (January 1947), 21.

15. Virginia Pope, "Fashion Pageant from Paris Opens," *New York Times* (May 2, 1946), 18.

Billed in the *New York Times* as a "FASHION PAGEANT FROM PARIS," intended to prove that "the years of occupation did not cause France to lose her creative spirit,"[16] the *Théâtre* featured a miniature opera designed by Bérard around "a central group that reproduces the opening night of the ballet," in addition to dioramas of "poetic Parisian life" conceived by the leading French scenic set designers. Like a modernist update of a baroque Neapolitan crèche, the *Théâtre*'s twelve scenes were populated by two hundred miniature wire mannequins designed by the young artist Eliane Bonabel, topped with minimalist, white plaster heads by the sculptor Rebull, dressed in the newest creations by fashion houses including Lanvin, Balmain, Balenciaga, Schiaparelli, Nina Ricci, Lelong, Worth, Paquin, Rochas, and Madame Grès. President of the Chambre Syndicale de la Couture Parisienne, Lucien Lelong stated: "At all times of difficulty in its history, when the mere idea of style might have seemed paradoxical, Parisian Couture has time and again had recourse to such little figures, which not only create by their size alone a fairy universe, but give an exact and subtle idea of technical perfection with the use of a minimum quantity of material."[17] The miniature ambassadors of the *Théâtre* went on to travel the United States, raising money for French war relief and promoting the cultural and economic importance and relevance of French fashion. Presumed lost after their tour of duty, the mannequins and dioramas had been forgotten in the storage of a San Francisco department store fittingly called City of Paris. Thanks to the concatenation of blunders we call his-

16. *Id.*

17. Lucien Lelong, "Introduction," in *Théâtre de la Mode*, ed. Boris Kochno (Paris: Aljanvic Publicité), 1945.

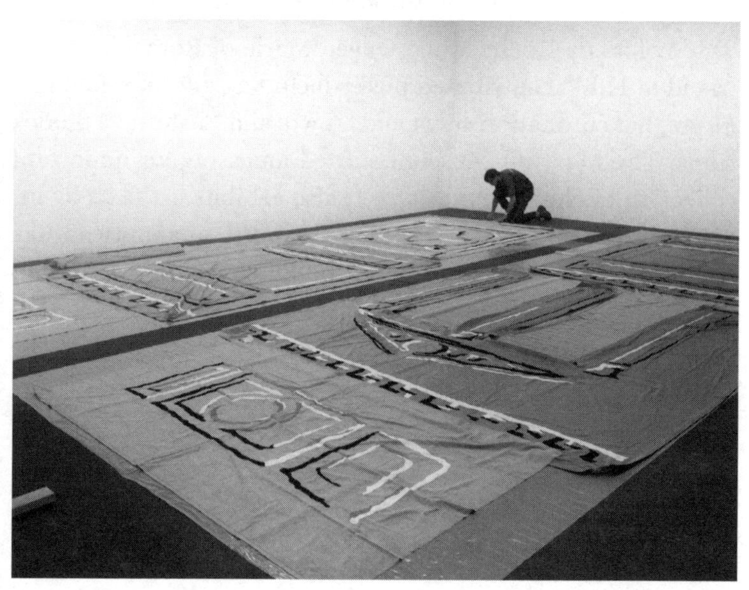

tory, and the efforts of a philanthropist named Alma de Bretteville Spreckels, in 1952 what remained of the *Théâtre* entered the collection of the Maryhill Museum of Art, in Washington State.

The museum is housed in the former mansion of Samuel Hill, a Quaker businessman and idiosyncratic philanthropist. Perched on a cliff overlooking the Columbia River gorge, the Beaux Arts-style building is surrounded by miles of austere terrain. Hill had intended for the area to become a Quaker community, but Loïe Fuller, the radically innovative performance pioneer, convinced him to turn the mansion into a museum after practical considerations halted construction of the community in 1917. Fuller helped form the collection in its initial stages, gifting artworks such as palm-size sculptures and erotic watercolors by Rodin, while Queen Marie of Romania, also a friend of Hill's, contributed pieces including gilt faux-folk furniture, her coronation gown and crown, and Eastern Orthodox icons. The Maryhill Museum started amassing an important collection of chess sets in 1957. It also exhibits artifacts by indigenous peoples of North America, and the panopticon-like twenty-four-car garage of Hill's building, transformed into galleries, displays items like baskets and waterproof sealskin shirts from Pacific Northwest tribes. This place couldn't be further from Paris, and yet the mannequins of the *Théâtre* are here, utterly out of place and time, arranged in gossiping clusters on low stages, dramatically lit, frozen in poses, still modeling the couture collections of 1946. A diorama called *La Grotte Enchantée*, designed by André Beaurepaire, looks like a vision of Piranesi crossed with Bob Fosse, a tempestuous setting for mannequins in sequined, embroidered, and feathered gowns. Another environment is more quotidian, depicting the arcades of the Palais Royal, its figures dressed in light day-attire, promenading, pausing, and throwing shade. My favorite is *Le Jardin Incomparable*, a nonsensical dream architecture of drooping cords, festoons, trompe-l'oeil painting, artificial trees, streetlights, niches, and a swing, in which numerous figures, dressed in gowns for a variety of occasions, interact while maintaining their icy distance, like characters in a Bergman film. The most vehemently political diorama is Cocteau's tribute to René Clair, in which a mannequin-bride in white rides a broomstick out of the bombed-out roof of her bridal chamber. The aerial views of Paris conjure its occupation, confronting war with fashion in a dramatization of "those nights which no one has yet forgotten . . . So that this scene of a devastated room, damaged, but in which figures of great elegance and style continue to move, might well be the very symbol of this whole exhibition."[18] In his role as artistic director of the *Théâtre*, Bérard assembled peers from every discipline, inadvertently encapsulating his own time in a memorial of exquisite care. ◆

18. *Id.*

This text was commissioned and published online by the Department of Media and Performance Art at the Museum of Modern Art (MoMA) in New York on the occasion of the presentation of Anne Teresa De Keersmaeker's Work/ Travail/Arbeid *at The Donald B. and Catherine C. Marron Atrium, MoMA, New York (March 29–April 2, 2017), organized by Ana Janevski with Martha Joseph.*

What Remains When You Take it All Apart? On Anne Teresa De Keersmaeker's *Work/Travail/Arbeid*

"Between a museum and a marketplace," is how Anne Teresa De Keersmaeker described the Museum of Modern Art's Marron Atrium, where her *Work/Travail/Arbeid* was performed for five entire days in spring 2017. The choreographer's take on the centerpiece of the Museum's 2004 expansion was intended, without irony, to embrace the idealistic potential of a space in which the classical functions of the museum and the marketplace as storehouses of public memory, culture, and exchange could overlap and be tested. On the evening of the premiere of *Work/Travail/Arbeid*, De Keersmaeker dedicated the upcoming five days of work to the memory of Trisha Brown, and acknowledged with barbed humor that it's not easy to work in a *fabrik* (factory) such as The Museum of Modern Art, reminding the audience that "dancers are not objects." Firm and self-evident, De Keersmaeker's statements laid out some of the tensions at play in this work: the disparate economies of art and dance, the oscillations of private and social memory, and the challenges of presenting dance in what Paul Valéry called a "house of incoherence."[1]

1. See Paul Valéry, "The Problem of Museums" (1923), in *The Collected Works of Paul Valéry, Vol. 12: Degas, Monet, Morisot*, ed. Jackson Mathews, trans. David Paul (New York: Pantheon Books, 1960), 202–207.

Work/Travail/Arbeid is De Keersmaeker's response to a two-way question: can choreography be performed as an exhibition? Both the question and its complex answer apply brilliant pressure, cracking open along the lines that define what constitutes choreography and exhibition practices at a moment when these forms—and the institutions that frame and validate them—have come into consistent, exploitative contact. De Keersmaeker refers to this period as the "second wave" of dance in the museum, after the "first wave" of the 1960s and 1970s. While notions of dance and the museum have certainly changed over the course of these decades, one of the most striking differences of this most recent re-introduction of dance to art hinges on how museums define and address their audiences at this moment—a relation that quantifies through "programming" and is distorted by a deep anxiety about fulfilling audiences' imagined expectations. De Keersmaeker observes the alienation that is often inimical to the way museums instrumentalize dance, and she implicates this strained relationship in a danced exhibition that demands a constant renegotiation of the terms of its viewing.

I saw the first iteration of this piece in Brussels, at Wiels Contemporary Art Centre, in 2015, for a few hours in the morning and a few more hours in the afternoon. In two bare, adjoining galleries flooded with daylight from high windows, I observed two dancers separate out from the meander of museum visitors to traverse overlapping circles traced with chalk on the floor. Within an instant, the room recalibrated, bodies organized themselves in relation to the dancers' conduct, and we observed each other and the two dancers walking, circling, uncoiling. I tried to read the laconic movements for traces of other dances—any accents, echoes, inflections, lifted phrases—but found none. The dancers and musicians had the stripped-down mien of Robert Bresson's "models" (the term he used for actors in his films). For lack of a better word (or feeling), the coherence was classical.

Abandoning origins, I began to sense a patterned vocabulary, and a precisely determined system of permeable rules that produced no experiential repetitions. I could sense it on the level of a floating pulse when the dancers performed noiselessly the memory of the voice of the instrument that had been played in the immediate past, the movements becoming the music's future memory of the dance. In this sense, the musicians' movements—before, after, and during their "work"—came into relief with a kind of pathos, as choreography of another kind. I saw a dancer "being" the voice of the piano, or another dancer "being," in silence, the just-past voice of the clarinet already eroding in my memory. This protracted space of pleasure in the not-yet-knowing, or of memory making contact again, resonates with what Gérard Grisey (the composer of *Vortex Temporum*, the musical work that catalyzes, structures, and permeates *Work/Travail/Arbeid*) calls, in musical terms, "pre-audibility." As a witness, one had the sense of being suspended between the dance and its music, observing their function as separate objects in the life-world, imposed on one another in the self as a private act of memory.

"We are going to the fields," the choreographer says when she describes working in the studio with her dance company, Rosas, as if the work they do is cyclical, innate, necessary. "The work is the rehearsal and the rehearsal is the work." In this way, *Work/Travail/Arbeid* can be read as De Keersmaeker's reflection on the lives of performers, a monument to their work, a meditation on the lengths of days, weeks, years, and seconds they spend together developing new work or rehearsing the old, as if the process had no goal other than the work of doing it. Each section lasts an hour. The entire cycle takes up nine hours. Its first performance took place on every consecutive workday for nine weeks. "How do you divide your time?" De Keersmaeker asks.

My instinct to ultimately capture the dance as I observed it was repeatedly frustrated by the radical austerity of the dramaturgy, and by the fact that I knew the dance would go on beyond my time as a spectator. Who dances all day? I noticed a clock on the wall, a piece of chalk hanging from a string, each dancer, each musician, each visitor, every piece of clothing, haircut, bracelet, decision trembling. Not even the sunlight was incidental. The slice down the wall and onto the floor seemed to hum in correspondence with dancer Igor Shyshko's carving of the space with his arm, the slowly jagged movements closely following liquid passages of running, suddenly at full speed, around the room along the chalk circles on the floor.

Remembering a passage from Wiels: the traveling sun burned into my mind forever through milk glass windows Balázs Busa's solo, which may have actually been a duet, but memory isolates around this sole figure. I had tracked this dancer all day, back and forth through the two rooms, until he performed what I understood to be the most devastating dance I will ever have witnessed, and I can't say why. Turning around his own axis with immaculate control of an almost plant-like slowness, unfurling, cleaving the space around his body repeatedly, caressing the millimeters above the floor where glinting

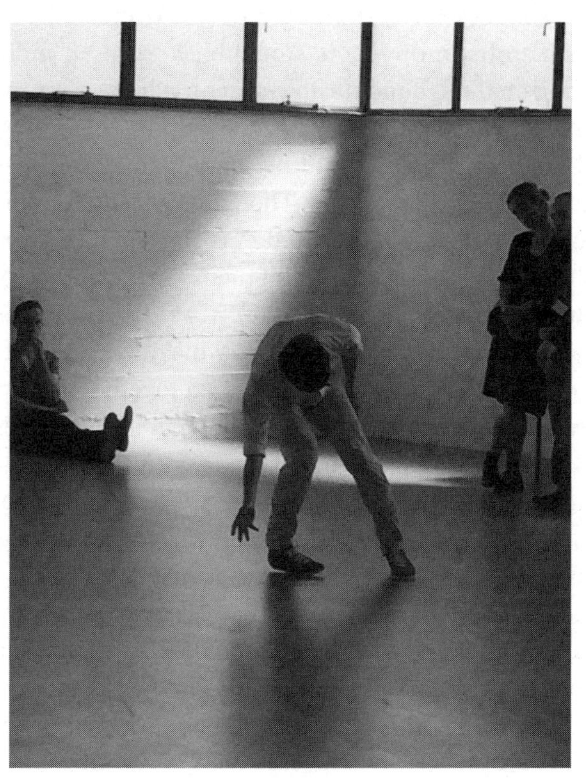

sweat gathered in a puddle running from his wrist after a long passage of high-velocity running in circles, truncated by violent stops and shifts in direction, stopping short of an indifferent child lying on the ground staring up at an iPhone. This moment of distance was simply sustained, hanging there. Invisible, agreed-upon thresholds could become distinct and razorlike, or suddenly wobbly, liquiform. Though it is by now common to find oneself "among" dancers and musicians in a performance, rather than at a remove in front of them— both in theaters and museums—the simple porosity of *Work/Travail/Arbeid* felt like an enduring risk. Something very moving appeared in the vision of performers and spectators seen together as an image, as different ways of being. On the one hand, the dancers and musicians were making their work in real time, and on the other, something else was being made between each distinct body in the room—a kind of modeling of new forms of courtesy and awareness.

As an "experience of dance," rather than an "evening of dances," *Work/Travail/Arbeid* has a family resemblance to Merce Cunningham's *Events* (1964–2011), a collection of works that were also born of the demand for performance in non-proscenium spaces and could be performed anywhere, from a museum in Vienna to Piazza San Marco in Venice. *Work/Travail/Arbeid* is, by design, a scalable work—the vortex of overlapping circles can be scaled up (or down) to fill (or even exceed) spaces. Its elegance and authority derive from an ability to be fastidiously transposed from one space onto another, allowing the work to expand to the gigantic conditions that have become the norm of contemporary art museums, while also suggesting that the work could be happening on a microscopic scale. Deformations of scale are also enacted through Grisey's score for *Vortex Temporum*, the three movements of which manifest distinct perceptions of time-scales: the human time of respiration, the glacial time of the whales, and the infinitesimally trembling time of insects and birds. The materials of the piece—chalk, dancers, clock, musicians, and instruments—suggest that the work could pack up and leave at any moment. There can be no props, no exoticism, no glamour in this surgical disarticulation of dance, presence, and audience: only the "workers" and whatever else is "found" or given. Each iteration is a reconsideration of the work through the architectural volumes, visitor traffic and behavior, and light conditions of a museum venue, taking on the notion of "composing around space," likened by Grisey to the work of sculptors, "whose hollows are not holes bored into the material, but forms in negative around which the volumes are articulated."[2] At MoMA, the monumental verticality of the Marron Atrium allowed for multiple layers of proximity and optics—from incredibly intimate contact with dancers flying by, or coming to rest between visitors up against a wall after the diminution of a jubilant moment of "tutti," to the bird's-eye views afforded by the gangplanks connecting the museum's upper floors, or the windows cut out of some of the higher galleries. The work felt like an unlocking of the Yoshio Taniguchi–designed building, or a full realization of its architectural transparency, maximizing the potential of this pierced, multivalent space as a volume of air and light through which the circulation of the museum moves in spirals. From a higher vantage point, one could observe the dancers and musicians

2. Gérard Grisey, "*Tempus Ex Machina*: A Composer's Reflections on Musical Time" (1980/1985), trans. S. Welbourn, *Contemporary Music Review*, vol. 2, no. 1 (1987), 258.

nested in the shifting frame of an attentive or quizzical audience, surrounded, in turn, by the faster traffic of visitors with an urgent itinerary, the crowded line at the coat check, solitary figures browsing in the museum bookstore, or museum goers standing at the windows in the painting galleries facing back down into the atrium. At times, sounds of Grisey's *Vortex Temporum* bled into even the furthest galleries, connecting every part of the building with the intense demonstration at its core, and piercing our unquestioned consent to silence in the museum.

De Keersmaeker often speaks about the "writing of the dance," by which she means the composition of dance and the writing that the action of dance itself creates. The writing of the dance is always impermanent and only experiential. In 2011, De Keersmaeker performed *Violin Phase* on a layer of sand in the Marron Atrium, revealing the writing of the dance—the accumulation of traces produced by her movement—as she was dancing. In *Work/Travail/Arbeid*, the writing of the dance is always written and rewritten and continually re-remembered, misremembered, and on the verge of dissipating, inciting a cycle of needing to be there, again and again, with the live work, to keep the channels of memory active. This ability to return, over and over, is singular to *Work/Travail/Arbeid*—no other dance work creates a viewer that can give in so readily to this extended space of work at attention. Grisey's treatise, "*Tempus Ex Machina*: A Composer's Reflections on Musical Time," the scaffolding on which De Keersmaeker's work is constructed, analyzes the perception of temporality in order to show that "it is in fact the listener who selects, who creates the changing angle of perception which will endlessly remodel, perfect, sometimes

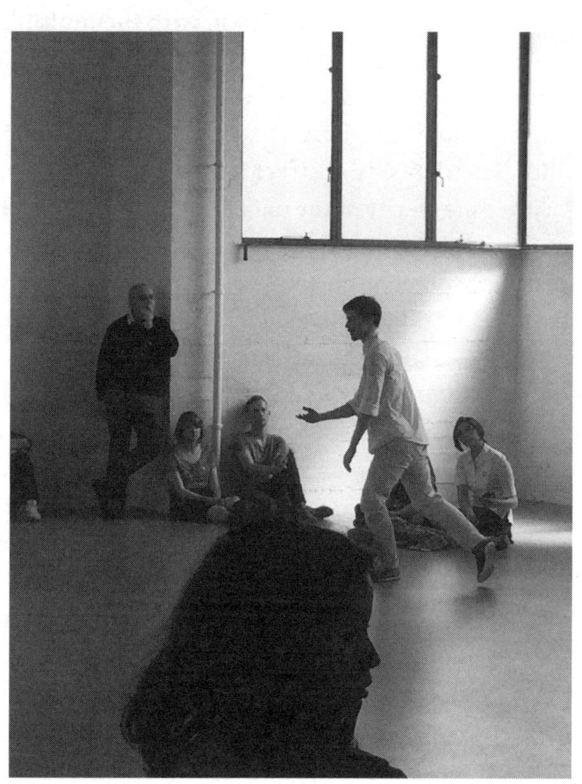

destroy musical form as the composer dreamed it. In turn, the listener's sense of time is in correlation with the multiple times of his native language, social group, culture, and civilization."[3] De Keersmaeker stresses the need to make the work abordable (approachable), and her dancers speak about the importance of legibility. The dance is abstract and the music is "spectral," but the crystalline clarity of the dancer's training and technique holds you for hours in an experience of multiple swelling, subsiding, distinctly perceptible temporalities. When the choreographer asks, "How do you divide your time?" she is also asking how you divide—or bring together— your attention.

The conceptual and spatial plasticity of *Work/Travail/Arbeid* seems to derive from a trust in instinct, or certain atavisms. At a discussion about *Work/Travail/Arbeid* at the Graduate Center, De Keersmaeker mentioned being inspired by the flocking of birds to use peripheral vision to maintain formations flexibly. Explaining the use of the circle in *Work/Travail/Arbeid*, De Keersmaeker suggested that it's "as if somebody starts to make a fire in an open space and people gather around in a democratic way." The circular structure of *Work/Travail/Arbeid* is an orchestral structure. It is a shape that distributes energy and power evenly. It is the form that is assumed when rehearsing parts of a dance in the studio. It is utterly matter-of-fact, yet enigmatic, like the deliriously willful whorl of hair at the top of a child's head. It returns to the word "choreography" through its Greek roots in *khoros* (a round dance; dancing place; band of dancers; choir) and *graphein* (to write). The circle lends itself to the spiral, which brings vertical movement

3. *Ibid.*, 273.

and velocity. "But when the movement is counter-clockwise," De Keersmaeker reflected, "you get this opposite feeling." At MoMA, I could understand how much the dance itself shaped the dynamics and positions of the audience in the atrium, the circular movements constantly reorienting and unsettling the assumption of a fixed position, shaping large swaths of bodies into new forms that contrasted with the socially inflicted obedience to forms like queues or clustering around furniture.

Work/Travail/Arbeid is a beautifully observed piece, not only on the level of the dance language, but on the level of internalized behavior: how people move, hesitate, risk, confront, and create a public. There is a deep understanding of gestures of invitation and blockade, of opening and closing, and a play with permission and refusal, vulnerability and violence—all of the boundaries left rigorously porous. Observing from one of the gallery windows as the piano swept across the floor below and gently coerced the seated audience out of its path like a giant broom, I thought of Temple Grandin's observations about fear and habit in herding animals:

Novelty is paradoxical. New things are both attractive and frightening. They are attractive when the animal is allowed to voluntarily approach and frightening when suddenly forced upon the animal. . . . Notice that the sheep are circling around the handlers while maintaining a safe distance and keeping the people in sight. Note that the sheep tend to move in the opposite direction of handler movement. Walking in the opposite direction of the direction of desired movement can be used to move groups of animals. Walking in the opposite direction tends to speed up movement and walking in the same direction tends to slow down movements. These principles work with all herding animals.[4]

Work/Travail/Arbeid should not be confused with tendencies toward immersion or interactivity. The spaces shaped by and with the audience are not necessarily inclusive. In reference to an earlier iteration of the piece, De Keersmaeker described chalk circles drawn on the ground "that invited people not to enter into that space." The uncountable minutiae of silent negotiations produced by *Work/Travail/Arbeid* pose the concept of democracy as a question, and De Keersmaeker seems to welcome the possibility that freedom might flicker into tyranny.

Ritual is often circular. Encoded structures become indistinguishable from the performer. In order to function, ritual communicates a set of terms and relies on the absorption of those terms. Watching the work accumulate in the time-space of the exhibition, and trying impossibly to construct its totality of voices and layers in the mind, produces a kind of intensified erotics, in which the ethics of *Work/Travail/Arbeid* are also located. If dance is a modeling of society, of how we live (together), how do we apprehend the bearing of the dancer Gabriel Schenker in his "Bernie" shirt, profoundly self-possessed, moving among us and subdividing the luxuries of air above him into angles and curves, slicing through planes with radial intentions: marking, specifying, articulating the dizzying variability of a deliberate sequence? In *24/7: Late Capitalism and*

---

4. Temple Grandin, "Behavioral Principles of Livestock Handling" (1989–2018), available online at www.grandin.com/references/new.corral.html and "Understanding Flight Zone and Point of Balance for Low Stress Handling of Cattle, Sheep, and Pigs" (1989–2022), available online at www.grandin.com/behaviour/principles/flight.zone.html (last accessed March 8, 2024).

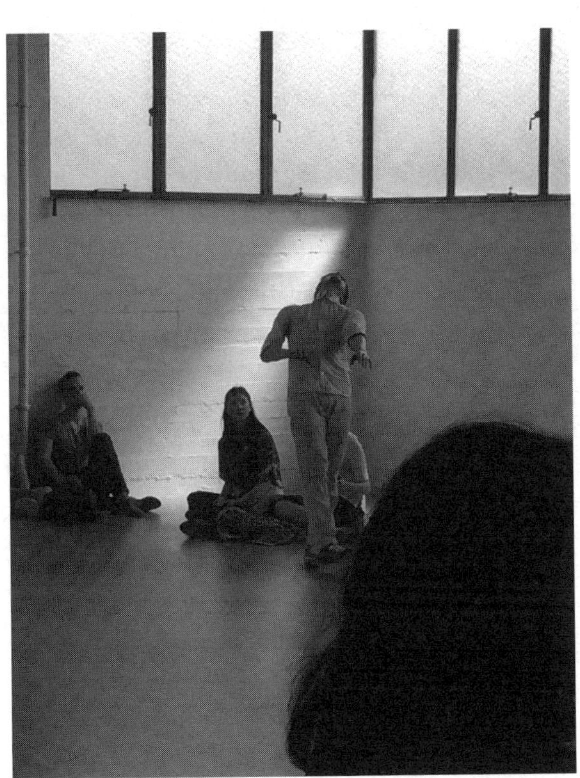

the Ends of Sleep, his essay on the "impossible temporalities" of the neoliberal timeframe, Jonathan Crary writes:

> *The frameworks through which the world can be understood continue to be depleted of complexity, drained of whatever is unplanned or unforeseen. So many longstanding and multivalent forms of social exchange have been remade into habitual sequences of solicitation and response. At the same time, the range of what constitutes response becomes formulaic and, in most instances, is reduced to a small inventory of possible gestures or choices.[5]*

Work/Travail/Arbeid generates a ritual that counteracts this immobilizing embodiment. We participate—in varying degrees of closeness and remove—in how work is made, how it is perceived, how it is remembered, felt, and enacted. ♦

---

5. Jonathan Crary, *24/7: Late Capitalism and the Ends of Sleep* (London & New York: Verso, 2013), 59.

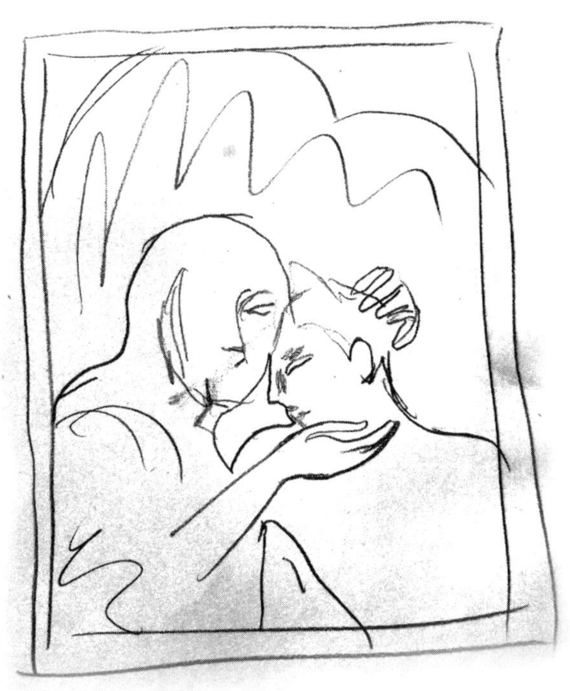

The Dissolving Line of Influence.
On Douglas Crimp

The books I most often revisit are Simone Forti's *Handbook in Motion* and Douglas Crimp's *On the Museum's Ruins*, which is a handbook in its own right.[1] Unlike those texts or works of art that assume an unassailable position and harden over time, *On the Museum's Ruins* has a vivid afterlife. It continues to surprise, structured by an intricate marquetry of nested frames of reference connected by corridors, trapdoors, and passages of openwork, where broadly traced questions, propositions, and proximities interlace. As a kind of armature, *Ruins* allows me to think with it, then through it—augmenting, undermining, and even doubting the structure. Like a Situationist slogan, its title reads as the writing on the wall. We suppose that ruins precede the museum, which was invented to showcase fragments pilfered from their sites. Crimp thinks this order of events beyond its conclusion to the inevitable future when even the museum has fallen into disuse, and is pilfered in turn, to

---

1. Simone Forti, *Handbook in Motion* (Halifax: The Press of the Nova Scotia College of Art and Design & New York: New York University Press, 1974; Middletown, CT: Wesleyan University Press, 2021); Douglas Crimp, *On the Museum's Ruins* (Cambridge, MA: MIT Press, 1993).

be absorbed into another kind of institution. Today, the question prompted by Crimp's title has still not been answered: can we imagine what comes *after* "the museum as an institution of confinement" and "art history as a discipline of confinement"?[2]

What surprised me when I first read the collection of essays was not just the particular synthesis relayed by them but that such an excess of pleasure could be smuggled into the decorous format of an academic book, distending its conventions and inventing an audience. (I would later learn that, as editor of the journal *October*, Crimp had gone even further to test the limits of form and audience by instigating the issue on "AIDS: Cultural Analysis / Cultural Activism" in 1987.) I came away with a new way of reading as a form of searching: behind, and around, the self-evident. Not only was this collection of essays my introduction to Crimp, it was also my first encounter with the work of Louise Lawler, and the repartee between Lawler's "pictures" and Crimp's essays remains one of the most startling collaborations across disciplines that I know of, recalibrating their roles as artist and critic. In this erosion of traditional notions of authorship, I fantasized about the social life of the work of art and began to think of the viewer as performer. I realized, as I read Crimp's invocation of Walter Benjamin, that I also had "to brush history against the grain."[3]

Though I came to Crimp as a belated reader—even the living artists he discussed were, to me, "historical"—his work occasionally folded into my life. I attended a film screening in

2. See Crimp, "On the Museum's Ruins" (1980), in *On the Museum's Ruins, op. cit.,* 48.

3. Quoted from "Theses on the Philosophy of History" (1940), in "The Art of Exhibition" (1984), *ibid.,* 238.

a Soho loft and was stunned when a friend introduced me to Joan Jonas, who happened to be sitting in front of us. In the momentary lull before the film, Jonas recalled having been in that space (or one like it) decades earlier and watching, through a hole in the floor, a Jack Smith performance transpiring in the loft below. The hole must have been cut by Gordon Matta-Clark, she said and turned around as the film began. It was then that I began to think about the value of anecdote—in its ancient sense of a thing unpublished, as information not yet written down. In the image conjured by Jonas' recollection my compartmentalized sense of history collapsed under enchantment, and artists I had envisioned as separate, even divergent, were now entwined as spectators, co-conspirators, collaborators, and participants, inhabiting coincident temporalities and even piercing my own present.

By the time I met Douglas, he was already in treatment for multiple myeloma, and we had to rush through the tentative beginnings of friendship. We saw a few films and went to the ballet and discussed important performances and screenings we had both attended before knowing one another. Being in an audience with others—disconnected in experience, and then reconnected in reflection—was crucial for Douglas, as an active mode of inhabiting and shaping the world. Douglas understood that concurrences were not the exceptions to history but its ligatures. His study of Alvin Baltrop's virtually unknown photographs of the illicit cultural activities that flourished in and around the West Side piers before the onset of the AIDS crisis did as much to position the significance of Baltrop's work as to cancel the romantic afterimage of Matta-Clark's aperture cut into a "vacant" ruin of deindustrialization, giving an entirely different valence to *Day's End*.[4] Similarly, Douglas knew how to zero in on the unlikely cohabitation in a film frame of turn-of-the-century "art dancer" Paul Swan, underground performer Tally Brown, Factory superstar Jane Holzer, and Jack Smith (in Warhol's 1965 film *Camp*) to draw out a genealogical arc marked by disparity.[5]

I never had the chance to explain to Douglas what his books meant to me, or that I had read *Our Kind of Movie*[6] on a night boat from Naples to Stromboli and then again on the way back. "Companions in pathos, who barely murmur, go with your lamp spent and return the jewels. A new mystery sings in your bones. Cultivate your legitimate strangeness," that book seemed to say, alloyed in my mind with René Char's 1967 poem "Partage formel."[7] In Douglas' work I found the license to foreground my own formation, to immerse myself in the techniques of antecedents, to take on supposedly extra-artistic functions to the point where my identity seemed to vaporize. I located my subject and my desire in trying to trace the dissolving line of influence. Douglas' greatest generosity and joy, I think, was seeing others make use of his thoughts. ◆

4. See Crimp, "Action around the Edges," in *Mixed Use, Manhattan. Photography and Related Practices, 1970s to the Present*, ed. Lynne Cooke and Douglas Crimp (Cambridge, MA: MIT Press, 2010); reprinted in Crimp, *Before Pictures* (Chicago: University of Chicago Press & New York: Dancing Foxes Press, 2016).

5. See the chapter, "Most Beautiful," in Crimp, *"Our Kind of Movie." The Films of Andy Warhol* (Cambridge, MA: MIT Press, 2012).

6. Crimp, *"Our Kind of Movie." The Films of Andy Warhol, op. cit.*

7. See René Char, "Partage formel," in *Fureur et mystère* (Paris: Gallimard, 1948; 1967).

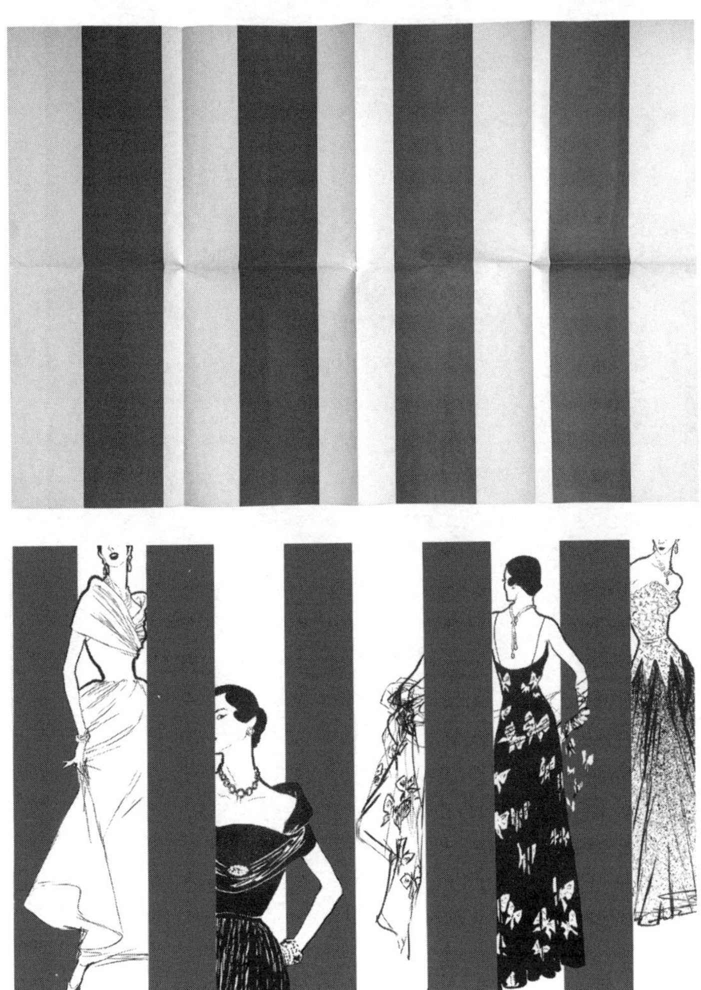

TOP: Daniel Buren, *Untitled (Wide White Space Gallery Announcement)*, 1969–74.
BOTTOM: René Gruau, illustration for *Flair Magazine*, 1951.

These three texts were originally published in Ways of Seeing: Writings on Drawings from the Jack Shear Collection, *ed. Hilton Als and Claire Gilman, exh. cat. (New York: The Drawing Center, 2021).*

Three Drawings

1

Souvenir Portrait

(Jean Cocteau)

The unknown subject of Jean Cocteau's 1933 "souvenir portrait" is pictured in pensive near-profile, like most of the poet's drawings. But whether this is a portrait in the conventional sense of a living likeness remains uncertain; Cocteau drew "from life" as much as from fantasy, memory, and myth. What is the nature of this souvenir? Is it Cocteau who is remembering (by drawing) the pictured subject, or is it the recipient of this drawing who is to remember Cocteau?

A striking intimacy and remove characterizes Cocteau's mode of drawing, similar to a cartographer's self-assurance in transcribing an internalized terrain onto paper. The pen, it appears, hardly leaves the page as it describes what it has committed to memory: a haphazard shirt collar, long-lashed eyes that can only be hazel, but then, an unexpected invention: the sensual transfiguration of an ear into cursive. The ear never ends, and the name "Jean" never begins—the autograph and the drawing are made of the same material, like an ingeniously bent wire. Cocteau himself would describe this singular fluency between drawing and writing in the dedication of his first published book of drawings (addressed to Picasso): "Poets don't draw, they unravel their handwriting and then tie it up again, but otherwise."[1] In his appreciation of that book in a 1925 issue of *Harper's Bazaar*, e.e. cummings admitted that Cocteau "the poet, the satirist, the Parisian, the literary idol," had now also proven himself to be a "draughtsman of first-rate sensitiveness."[2]

Along with Klee, Kandinsky, Picasso, Grosz, and Calder, Cocteau ranks among the early twentieth century's most inventive analysts of the line, which he deemed an expression of "the soul's style." He is rivaled only by Matisse in bringing the arabesque of handwriting into confusion with the non-linguistic register of drawing. "Writing is drawing in different apparel, and drawing is another way of writing," Cocteau wrote, "and when I draw, I write. Perhaps when I write, I draw."[3] His insistence on the inextricability of drawing from writing is a programmatic revolt against rationalization, that "constriction of thought" identified by paleoanthropologist André Leroi-Gourhan as the disappearance of "the dualism between graphic and verbal"[4] in the phase of human development that separated their functional coexistence.

Nobody can say how many thousands of drawings Cocteau produced "on blotters, tablecloths, and backs of envelopes"[5] during the course of his life, (not to mention the walls

1. Jean Cocteau, *Dessins* (Paris: Librairie Stock, 1924). Our translation.

2. e. e. cummings, "Jean Cocteau as a Graphic Artist" (1925), in *A Miscellany Revised*, ed. George J. Firmage (New York: Liveright, 2018).

3. Cocteau quoted in *60 Dessins*, exh. cat. (Paris: Galerie Bert, 2013).

4. André Leroi-Gourhan, *Gesture and Speech*, trans. Anna Bostock Berger (Cambridge: MIT Press, 1993), 210.

5. Cocteau, *Dessins, op. cit.* Our translation.

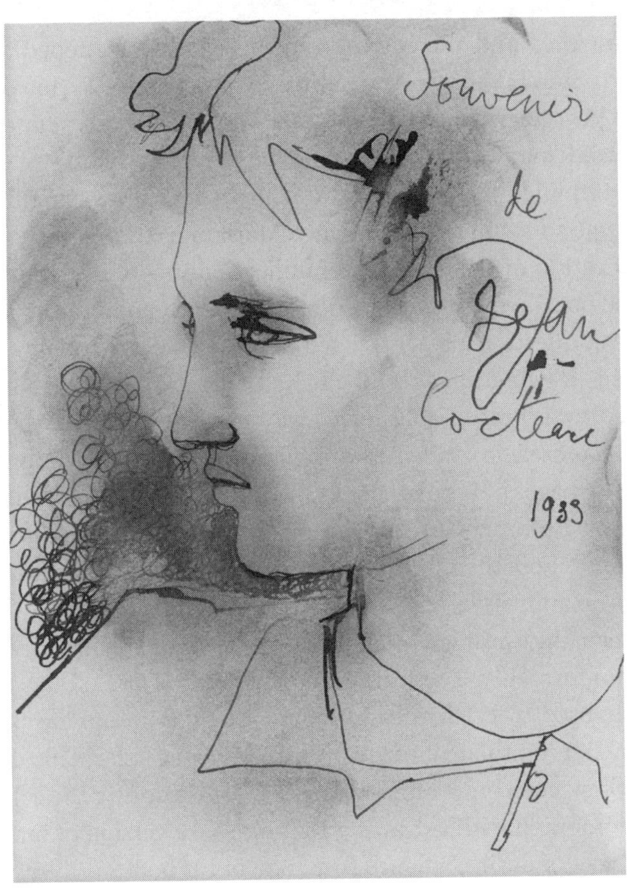

Jean Cocteau, *The Souvenir*, 1933.

of churches and the Mediterranean Villa he "tattooed" with drawn murals) but the souvenir portrait emerges as one of the most prominent, recursive formats, very consciously refined into a trademark, or even a type of currency that both reflected and amplified his celebrity status. Cocteau's drawn profiles of the 1930's morph over time, into Marianne (the symbolic personification of the French Republic, donning a Phrygian cap) or the poet-hero Orpheus, a double for Cocteau himself.

The question presents itself whether we are looking at a signed drawing, or an embellished autograph. This souvenir portrait was presumably given away as a gift, much like the many elaborately inscribed drawings Cocteau made to illuminate the title pages of his own books, dedicating them to friends and patrons. But Cocteau's inscriptions in books were usually more personal, and therefore signed, simply: "Jean." This drawing bears no addressee, and is followed by the full autograph: "Jean Cocteau," indicating a level of remove from the recipient, and a certain formality. The formulation *"Souvenir de . . ."* was commonly used by celebrities in France, such as Josephine Baker, when signing their photographs to admiring fans. This drawing, then, is an innovation by Cocteau, substituting the celebrity photograph with a drawing that may be a version of himself, an object of desire, a figure from one of his books or films, one of their sources in "real life," or a short-hand synthesis of them all.

2
Drawing Money
(Andy Warhol)

Much has been made of Warhol's indebtedness to Cocteau's line and homoerotic subject matter, given the clear affinity between Cocteau's drawings from the 1930's and Warhol's from the 1950's. But every artist knows that the most powerful influence is indirect and enmeshed with others. As Nathan Gluck, one of Warhol's early studio assistants explained in an interview:

> *... rather than saying that Andy had looked at Cocteau and had been influenced because I'm not sure that at the time that Andy mentioned this about the Cocteau book, he had been, you know, drawing like this for quite a while. It's just like when people tie it into Ben Shahn and think that Shahn was an influence. And I don't' think it was. I think that it's just that if you're going to look for an influence, you might go back to Picasso's* Blue Period *and Picasso's* Classic Period *when he was drawing in a fine line which, then, you could say was an influence on Shahn and an influence on Andy. And, of course, Picasso wasn't the first person to invent drawing in line. You can go back to Ingres."[6]*

Compared to his early "fourth generation Picasso by way of Cocteau"[7] drawings, Warhol's deadpan 1964 drawing of the back of a dollar bill appears un-stylized and asexual, verging

6. Nathan Gluck quoted in Patrick S. Smith, *Warhol's Art and Films* (Ann Arbor, MI: UMI Research Press, 1986), 328.

7. Henry Geldzahler quoted in *ibid.*, 307.

on the indifference of a sign (though its imputation of hand-made money feels taboo). But like even his earliest drawings it is marked by contractions and elisions, graphic decisions that seem to bring the drawing to its essence. Warhol's abbreviations allow us to see, as if for the first time, the strange graphic lay-out of this "paper promise," riddled with radiating symbols and derivative ornaments. A painting of money approaches trompe l'oeil and the counterfeit, a drawing of money tries to under-stand it. What makes this drawing hurt is the way it evades the inherent romanticism of drawing as the artist's direct registra-tion of an intense moment of encounter. It seems to counter the question it poses—what is drawing?—with the self-evident fact that money is drawing.

"When you see a big store and see so many of each kind of anything that is in it, and on the counters, it is hard to believe that one more or less makes any difference to anyone," Gertrude Stein wrote in her meditations on money in the *Saturday Evening Post*. "When you see a cashier in a bank with drawers filled with money, it is hard to realize that one more or less makes any any difference. But it does, if you buy it, or if you take it away, or if you sell it, or if you make a mistake in giving it out . . ."[8] As a subject in Warhol's work, money is linked to the advent of his use of silkscreen in paintings in 1962. Since his silkscreener ini-tially refused to make screens of money, Warhol had to draw the money that he wanted to reproduce on canvas. As a concept and material, money had already appeared a decade earlier in the Cocteau-like drawings, where extravagantly crumpled up dollar bills surround an elegant naked calf and foot. Flagrantly

8. Gertrude Stein, "Money," *Saturday Evening Post* (June 13, 1936).

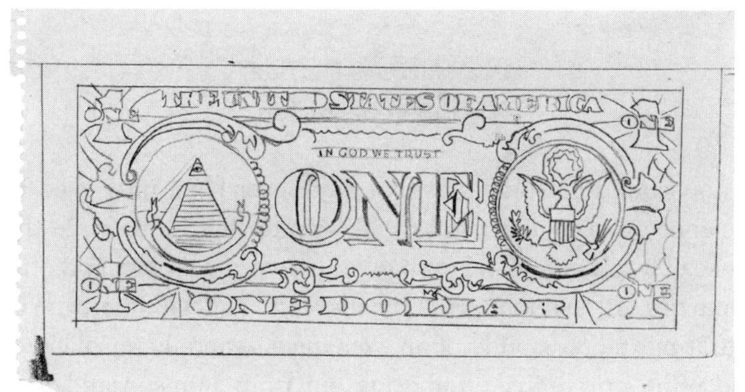

Andy Warhol, *Dollar Bill*, 1964.

coupling desire with stupid excess, Warhol renders money absurd, the way an alien visitor might not be able to naturalize its use value or symbolic function. In his *Philosophy* Warhol declared: "The best way I like to carry money, actually, is messily. Crumpled wads. A paper bag is good."[9]

9. Andy Warhol, *The Philosophy of Andy Warhol (From A to B & Back Again)* (New York: Harcourt Brace Jovanovich, 1975), 136.

3
Dear Jacques Derrida
(Ray Johnson)

It may sound blasphemous, but I've never been interested in the concept of mail art in relationship to Ray Johnson, in the sense of a relay of postal exchanges between Johnson and other parties. All that matters is the insistent, audacious gesture of initiating the possibility of an exchange (generally unsolicited, and often unrequited), radiating out from Johnson and projecting a world of new relations. It's hard to say how Johnson's work will change as the circulation of pieces of paper invested with meaning and emotion is superseded by digital gestures of reciprocation that produce entirely different archives, social networks, and chemical reactions in the bodies of sender and receiver. To dispel the notion of mail-art as "fathered" by Johnson ("father of nothing"), William S. Wilson, his early supporter and most sensitive interpreter wrote: "During the Civil War, envelopes became vehicles carrying political slogans. At the same time, in France, many painters were already sketching on envelopes, sometimes watercoloring images. If these activities are deemed mail-art, then that title is retroactive, and helps to make a point about the way the history of art works. A movement in art is not founded on a ready-made foundation: a structure builds and rebuilds its foundations as it develops."[10]

Johnson so successfully created his own context through his work that I associate him with the real and insinuated network of his making more than with any of his actual contemporaries.

10. William S. Wilson, *Retrospections on West 23rd Street* (New York: Printed Matter, 2006).

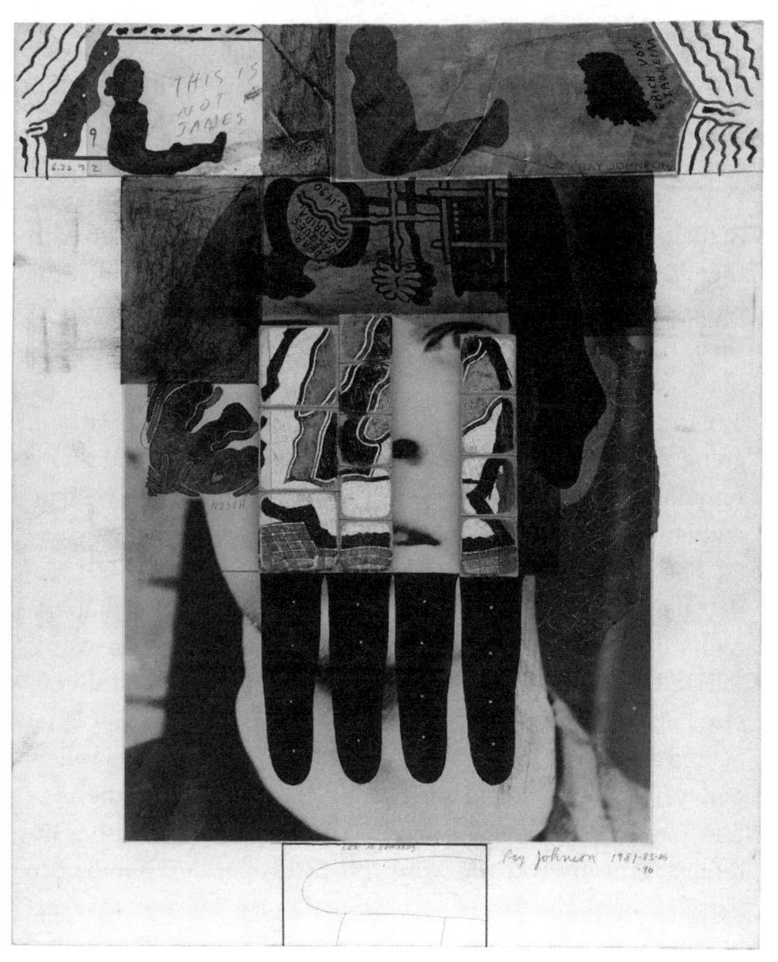

Ray Johnson, *Untitled (Dear Jacques Derrida)*, 1981–92.

The net he cast—in redefining the public sphere, and projecting a counter-world—is so wide, that centuries of future scholarship and even algorithmic study will be unable to pin it down. I was surprised to learn of his interest in the philosopher Jacques Derrida, though in Johnson's hands, of course, the desire to be in dialogue with Derrida is camp. Scholar Clive Phillpot recalls that Johnson liked Derrida's book *The Post Card*, in which the philosopher innovates new forms of correspondence such as this: "The emission of sense or of seed can be rejected (postmark, stamp, and return to sender). Imagine the day, as I have already, that we will be able to send sperm by post card, without going through a check drawn on some sperm bank, and that it remains living enough for the artificial insemination to yield fecundation, and even desire."[11]

The collage addressed to Derrida is full of graphic and verbal cues that cannot be united, but sit side by side in compartmentalized friction. In the upper right hand corner, the words "THIS IS NOT A JAMES" accompany what looks like a silhouetted armless doll sitting on a cartoon stage, a form that is repeated once more, though slightly more eroded, beside a yellow and a black splotch and the name of the director of the 1924 film *Greed*, Erich von Stroheim. An organic shape with a little heart throbs over the word "NUSCH", perhaps alluding to Nusch Eluard, the surrealist artist and muse. If I were to resort to conventional terms such as figure and ground, the ground of this work is a photographic self-portrait by Johnson, oft-reproduced, manipulated, Xeroxed, and mailed, which has been caressed with sandpaper to create a haze of fine white looping

11. Jacques Derrida, *The Post Card. From Socrates to Freud and Beyond*, trans. Alan Bass (Chicago: University of Chicago Press, 1987), 24.

lines over its surface. An upside down silhouette of a hand, and a game-like arrangement of tesserae adorn and obscure the face, like a mask. The words "DEAR JACQUES DERRIDA" are turned 200 degrees from what I (falsely) assume to be the standard orientation of the collage, since this is a work to be held in the hand, to be looked at from multiple points of view. ◆

This text was originally published in October *179 (Winter 2022).*

Another Function of Speech. On Werner Schroeter

naive poem.
Basic tone.
   Passion. etc.   by means of imagination
Language.
  Feeling Passion Imagination   Feeling Passion
    Imagination Feeling.
  By means of imagination.
Effect.
—FRIEDRICH HÖLDERLIN, *FEELING SPEAKS IN A POEM . . .*[1]

Once characterized as "a total critique of our consciousness," Werner Schroeter's work achieves its willful coherence through incessant cutting.[2] Montage in tremolo. Image and soundtrack, body and voice, gesture and language stray apart, occasionally reconcile, but otherwise waver and digress, sustaining discrepancy as the through-line of lived experience.

The face is a film. Schroeter recapitulates the lessons he learned from Carl T. Dreyer's *Passion of Joan of Arc* and Warhol's *Blowjob,* fixating on the play of facial expression as the seam between inner and outer space. In *The Death of Maria Malibran* and *Flocons d'or,* Schroeter stages cramped annunciation scenes between two faces held in such tremulous proximity that one can sense the eyelashes of one bat the cheek of another. Foucault, in conversation with the director, recounts

1. Friedrich Hölderlin, "Feeling speaks in a poem . . ." (1799), in *Essays and Letters*, ed. & trans. Jeremy Adler and Charlie Louth (London & New York: Penguin Classics, 2009), 65.

2. Willfried Wiegand, "Sinnlose Rituale: Filme von Werner Schroeter in Frankfurt," *Frankfurter Allgemeine Zeitung* (November 22, 1969).

"bodies, faces, lips and eyes. You let them perform a kind of evidence of passion."[3] Lips moving in pantomime emit detached words: the gradual production of thoughts whilst speaking.

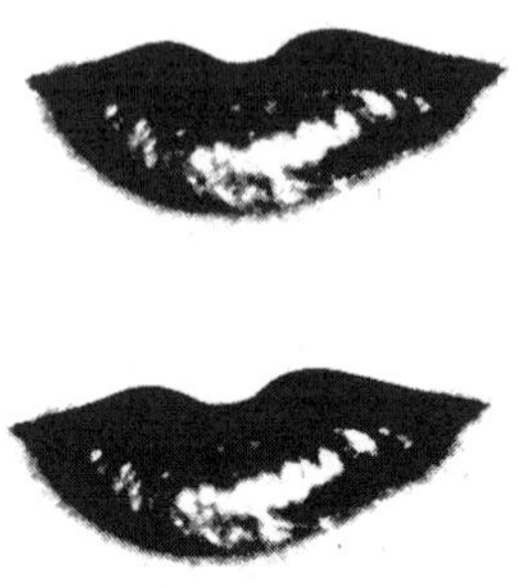

Lines from Lautréamont, Patricia Highsmith, William S. Burroughs, and the late fragments of Hölderlin flutter like errata onto operatic climaxes taped off the radio, intercut with tracks from LP's found in the garbage. In the words of critic Frieda Grafe, the films of Schroeter "invent nothing new, but alter what is given."[4]

Song floods the frame with emotion the way a dance track blaring from the window of a passing car can puncture "reality" when you're absent-mindedly walking down the street. The refrain- or chant-like recurrence of musics, texts, images, and gestures lends Schroeter's films an apparently intuitive, but deliberately composed polyphonic structure, akin to a lieder-cycle in which people can live. A woman caught in a

3. Gérard Courant, "Werner Schroeter and Michel Foucault in Conversation" (1981), in Patrice Maniglier and Dork Zabunyan, *Foucault at the Movies*, trans. Clare O'Farrell (New York: Columbia University Press, 2013), 180.

4. Frieda Grafe, "Schauplatz für Sprache: Neurasia," *Filmkritik*, no. 3 (1970).

rainstorm reads aloud from Freud's "Mourning and Melancholia" under a dripping rosebush. There is Candy Darling, hardly even in drag, staring like a sphinx towards the unattainable horizon, the same point beyond the audience to which opera divas train their gaze. Kazuo Ohno, a flower in his hair, prances along a canal in a loincloth, and throws himself against what looks like a penitentiary wall to the sound of Maria Callas singing Puccini's aria, "Oh Mio Babbino Caro." The lamentation of a corpse transported by a cortege on a country road becomes a jubilation in death as Tina Turner sings "Save the Last Dance for Me." In tandem with these competing styles of radical will, "the viewer is meant to fill in the various omissions built into every level of the film, whether in the music, dramaturgy, or narrative."[5] Foucault, again, explains what Schroeter is doing: "The problem exactly is to create something that happens between ideas and to make it impossible to give it a name. So at every instant, the aim is to try to provide a coloration, a shape, and an intensity to something that never says what it is." To create, "unnameable individualities, beings, relationships, and qualities within oneself and with others."[6]

Beside the many films (and subsequent plays and operas) Schroeter directed, there are films he was not able to realize, including those he initiated and then deviated from, arriving instead somewhere entirely unforeseen. His unmade films include: a diptych titled *Gender: Ways into Reality*, and *Gender: Ways out of Reality*; a film about the poet Thomas Chatterton;

5. Austrian Film Museum, recording of exchange between Schroeter and audience following his screening of *The Death of Maria Malibran* at the Film Museum, November 19, 1975.

6. Courant, "Werner Schroeter and Michel Foucault in Conversation," in *op. cit.*, 182.

an adaptation of James Baldwin's *Giovanni's Room*; an adaptation of Jean Genet's *Querelle*; a film about Vaslav Nijinsky; and "a structuralist work based on Andy Warhol's portraits of Marilyn Monroe, with music by Elvis Presley, featuring Allen Ginsberg."[7]

Schroeter's early films enact preposterous kinships and misaligned fates—on the level of narrative as much as in the collision of New German Cinema with American underground aesthetics. Home-made, hand-made, and spontaneous, they preserve the intimate rites of a small group of friends—people with names like Magdalena Montezuma, Eduardo Manet, Carla Aulaulu, or Anna Spaghetti—*counter*-acting their post-war German identity formations. Schroeter plays aspirations towards beauty (the obligatory orchids pressed against the temples of every actress in *Flocons d'or*) against the offal of culture (repurposing the irradicable remnants of Nazi architecture as set pieces throughout his films) to express the reality of living under what he calls "romantic capitalism."[8] "Incongruity," observed the anthropologist Esther Newton, "is the subject matter of camp, theatricality its style, and humor its strategy."[9] Still, I hesitate to call Schroeter camp, for fear of taking away his difficulty, and because "what will be 'camp art,' no queen will own."[10] To my mind, Schroeter's closest kin in film is the American auteur prodigy Edward Owens, who made all four of his

---

7. Schroeter in *Dietrich Kuhlbrodt Im Gespräch Mit Werner Schröter* (documentary, Austria, 24 min, 2010); available on the DVD, *Eika Katappa & Der Tod der Maria Malibran* (Munich: Filmmuseum München, 2014).

8. Austrian Film Museum, recording of exchange between Schroeter and audience following the screening of *The Death of Maria Malibran* at the Film Museum, November 19, 1975.

9. Esther Newton, *Mother Camp* (Chicago: University of Chicago Press, 1979), 106.

10. Newton quoting one her informants who rejects the normalization of camp, *id.*

surviving films in the late 1960's, when he was not yet twenty. It is likely that Schroeter would have seen Owens' *Tomorrow's Promise* at the 1967 Knokke-le-Zoute avant-garde film festival, on whose fringes the young German director screened his own films. Owens' devotional films emphasize the dissociation between image and sound, and intercut portraits of his intimates with personal emblems, aborted narratives, and verité to distill a lifetime's yearnings. A strangely palpitating quality is achieved through the interjection of black film frames whose visual silences threaten to delete the memory of what has just been seen.

Schroeter's meditation on the voice as a cinematic body began in the late 1960's, at the very moment when a number of visual artists experimented with the "dry" implications of non-diegetic sound in film and video. More politically consequential was the simultaneous elaboration of the open-lip sync (only possible thanks to the mass availability of 45 rpm records since the previous decade) as a new form of popular performance art that marked the transition from a private act of the self projected into images, to a self catapulted, via borrowed voice and gesture, into fully embodied non-normativity. The performers in Schroeter's films, argues Grafe, "point to practices rather than to some separable 'meaning.' They follow, in reverse, the path that in western cultures inevitably leads from expression to idea, from representation to a premeditated concept."[11] Achieving what she calls an "agitation of language" by dislocating the causality of image from sound to create aching film-images that speak music and sing literature—Schroeter

11. Grafe, *art. cit.*

articulates a theory of history through "bad" lip syncing, like the misregistration of Warhol's screen and brush. Open amateur mouths emit silences or song delays that burst into arias they may be incapable of singing, but not of feeling. This rupture is elaborated by Schroeter into a new terrain for the viewer, where "the auditory plane is eternal—it is past, present, and future. The visual plane is the present, and memory."[12] ◆

12. *Dietrich Kuhlbrodt Im Gespräch Mit Werner Schröter, op. cit.*

This text, previously unpublished, grew out of a public conversation between Nick Mauss and curator Kathy Halbreich that took place at the Swiss Institute in New York on December 6, 2021, on the occasion of the exhibition Rosemary Mayer: Ways of Attaching *(September 9, 2021– January 9, 2022), curated by Laura McLean Ferris.*

Remaking Ghosts.
On Rosemary Mayer

I don't go looking to make a discovery. But certain figures have a way of appearing unannounced, and reappearing—even interfering—while I'm already on my way elsewhere. Asleep in a footnote, pinned to the background, a name suddenly everywhere, until the din of recurrence reaches a frequency so startling, I wake up to the fact of an unshakeable presence, making new circuitry.

I was led to Rosemary Mayer through the poetry of her sister Bernadette and of her friend Hannah Weiner, my interest in second wave feminist art, gestures of evocation, the history of textiles, and the expanded practices of New York painting of the 1970s. All these wayward threads I tried to hold were twined in the revelation of Mayer's expansive work and thought, which described a previously unlocalizable nexus of poetry, conceptual art, decoration, feminism, mannerism, and historiography. But Mayer had appeared to me before I even knew what she meant. For at least two years, the time- and sun-faded image of her bewildering *Galla Placidia* (1973), hovering on the cover of Alan Sondheim's 1977 anthology *Individuals: Post-Movement Art in America*,[1] migrated from my studio desk to piles on the

1. *Individuals: Post-Movement Art in America*, ed. Alan Sondheim (New York: E.P. Dutton & Co., 1977).

floor, to a shelf and back to the windowsill, as if signaling by its restlessness that I still didn't know what it was, where to locate it, or how to see it.

Seated low to the ground in a child-sized chair, I studied a sequence of saturated vintage slides projected onto the wall at close range while glancing around the periphery of the darkened space to take in whatever else I could make out. In her brother Max's East Harlem studio, the art historian Marie Warsh had shown me drawings of words and archaic vessels by her late aunt, Rosemary Mayer, and was now guiding me through images of her sculptures and sight-specific outdoor works in a manner that veered between the affectionate familiarity of the beloved niece and the analytical remove of the art historian surveying a life's work. The jewel-toned slides zeroed in on carefully knotted ribbons, cords, weather balloons painted with all-caps names, and festive, short-lived events framed by aerial decorations, fleeting signposts, drifting markers, groups of clouds or figures made from crumpled translucent paper. I had come to ask Marie and Max if I could include Mayer's work in an exhibition I was conceiving for Kunsthalle Basel, titled *Bizarre Silks, Private Imaginings and Narrative Facts, etc.*[2] What began as a request for an existing work branched into conversations about the deliberate process of re-situating a "forgotten" feminist artist and the status of nonextant works in her legacy, ultimately leading to an unexpected collaboration with the estate to re-perform vanished works by Mayer into the present. It's rare to watch an artist resurface to

2. *Bizarre Silks, Private Imaginings and Narrative Facts, etc.*, at Kunsthalle Basel (February 7–September 20, 2020).

public consciousness in real time, and that labor of making visible again is all too easily swept away as the artist's work attains the appearance of a constant resonance. In this case, Marie and Max's devotion to Mayer's art and writing, through which they continue to rethink the mission of an artist's estate and the ways in which it makes itself available to new publics; the support of artists James Walsh and Amanda Friedman in researching and presenting Mayer's work; and a 2016 exhibition organized by Maika Pollack (in cooperation with the estate) at SOUTHFIRST, Brooklyn, created the framework for my own confrontation with this work.[3]

The singular constructions for which Mayer became known in the 1970s defy the categories of painting and sculpture, and insist—via acts of naming—on the acknowledgement and reinvention of a repressed feminist history. Titled after historical figures of whom no images remain, these textile invocations of female presences recall the cascades of drapery in quattrocento painting: "... all the layers of clothing that cover this person ..." as Mayer noted in a lecture on her work; inventions of garment-like facture, hanging in tensile suspension as if a moment of unspeakable drama had been stilled in time, others brush the floor like the hem of a dress. The fashion historian Anne Hollander speaks of a "visionary cloth made into garments which have no discernible shape, no seams and no identifiable woven texture" when describing the mesmerizing renderings of fabric in classical Western art, "the swathed pictorial yardage used by so many painters ... for the purpose of theatricalizing portraiture, allegory and heroic or religious subject matter.

3. *Rosemary Mayer: Conceptual Works & Early Fabric Sculptures, 1969–1973*, presented at SOUTHFIRST, Brooklyn (October 21–December 11, 2016).

Such drapery is emphatically not to be considered as clothing since it is used to dress figures (as it may dress scenes) only for the sake of increasing their possibilities as elements in the composition."[4] This textile excess, Hollander suggests, increases the "possibilities" of figures by transforming, or extending the limits of the body, delivering it to formlessness. Spyros Papapetros goes further in arguing that the "inorganic piece of fabric is the most alive and palpable feature of representation—a transient body, whose rustling movement activates the synaesthetic interface between two remote worlds."[5] Mayer's work proliferates in transitions, where drawings beget event-like constructions, which in turn become drawings again or generate parallel incantatory language that may be transcribed into illuminated books. ". . . yellow-orange under lavender," begins her description of *Galla Placidia*, "lavender on yellow-green, ochre under lavender, purple on blue-green. Bowed wood, gauze and satin enveloped in colored overlays. Lavender on green, green on lavender, projecting outward. Color in space as transparent films, one over, under the next. Layers behind."[6] The work catalyzes an ekphrasis to describe its operations of near-iridescence derived from the palette of Rosso Fiorentino and the bleeding color layers of Morris Louis. Later on, Mayer writes more generally about the encounter with a work of art—its ideal mode of address—as "pointing at you the way painted angels in An-

---

4. Anne Hollander, "The Clothed Image: Picture and Performance," *New Literary History*, vol. 2, no. 3 (Spring 1971), 483.

5. Spyros Papapetros, *On the Animation of the Inorganic: Art, Architecture, and the Extension of Life* (Chicago: University of Chicago Press. 2012), 46.

6. Rosemary Mayer, "Two Years: March 1973 to January 1975," in *Individuals, op. cit.* 96.

nunciations extend an arm, pointing an imperative."[7] In keeping with these emphatic non-verbal communications between worlds, Mayer's list of inspirations alludes to the figurative language of religious iconography, art history, and epic poetry as coexistent with the unexalted states and substances of everyday life: "Novocaine . . . Studying, Church statues . . . Dante, Dinners, Drawings, Ingres, Brooms, Yogurt" and "Sheets, Stains, Aspirin."[8]

Every artist works with history. What one does with it, how one approaches it, or how one orients oneself within it makes the difference. Mayer reroutes a monolithic relation to history towards the layering of temporalities that are perishable, momentary, even irrational. "No one has ever seen a ghost," she writes. "You prefer not to remember. It's easy. They're visible only for seconds and even then they change. They live in the fall of a sleeve or a skirt, the shapes in a coat laid over a chair. When the light changes they're different or gone."[9] Specific durations are measured and held as they detach from the names by which we are meant to understand them: the blooming of certain flowers, the appearance of constellations in the sky, and occurrences of birthdays appear in Mayer's work as palimpsests of systems that mark events and cycles in human or celestial timescales. As I looked over Mayer's work in the archive I sensed

7. *Ibid.*, 98.

8. See Mayer's work, *Everything that's influenced my work/me* (c. 1978); reproduced in *Rosemary Mayer: Ways of Attaching*, ed. Eva Birkenstock, Laura McLean-Ferris, Robert Leckie, Stephanie Weber, exh. cat. (Munich: Lenbachhaus Kunstbau; Aachen: Ludwig Forum; Bristol: Spike Island; New York: Swiss Institute & Cologne: Verlag der Buchhandlung Walther und Franz König, 2022), 13–14.

9. Rosemary Mayer, "A Moon Tent," *White Walls*, no. 8 (Summer 1983), 80.

the pervasive implications of embodiment and performance throughout drawings, discrete constructions, and in the public installations conceived as "temporary monuments." I understood that the work will always be different, variable, adjusted, requiring an investment of attention and sensitivity in order for it to attain its vividness in each instance. Mayer described a later series of destroyed works as follows:

Since mid-1980s, I have been making the "ghosts," fragile structures made from wood through and over which different papers are draped. In these works I'm looking for an edge between abstraction and figuration, using the paper and wood to suggest and subvert both. The wood rods for each ghost are painted with several different metallic powders in an attempt to dematerialize the structure by making it changeable in its subjection to changing light. Ribbons mark connection points between rods, hopefully emphasizing the fragility of the whole structure but, because they are decorative, undercutting fragility with elaboration, possible elegance.[10]

While sharing a family resemblance with the fabric works of the 1970s, the images I saw of the *Ghosts* appeared more extreme in their instantaneous, reduced humility. And they seemed to hold no mysteries, beguiling instead with their emphatic stance and dime-store materiality, which guaranteed that these diaphanous presences would not last beyond the short life-span of each exhibition. Like all of Mayer's art, these figures pose

10. *Ibid.*, 81.

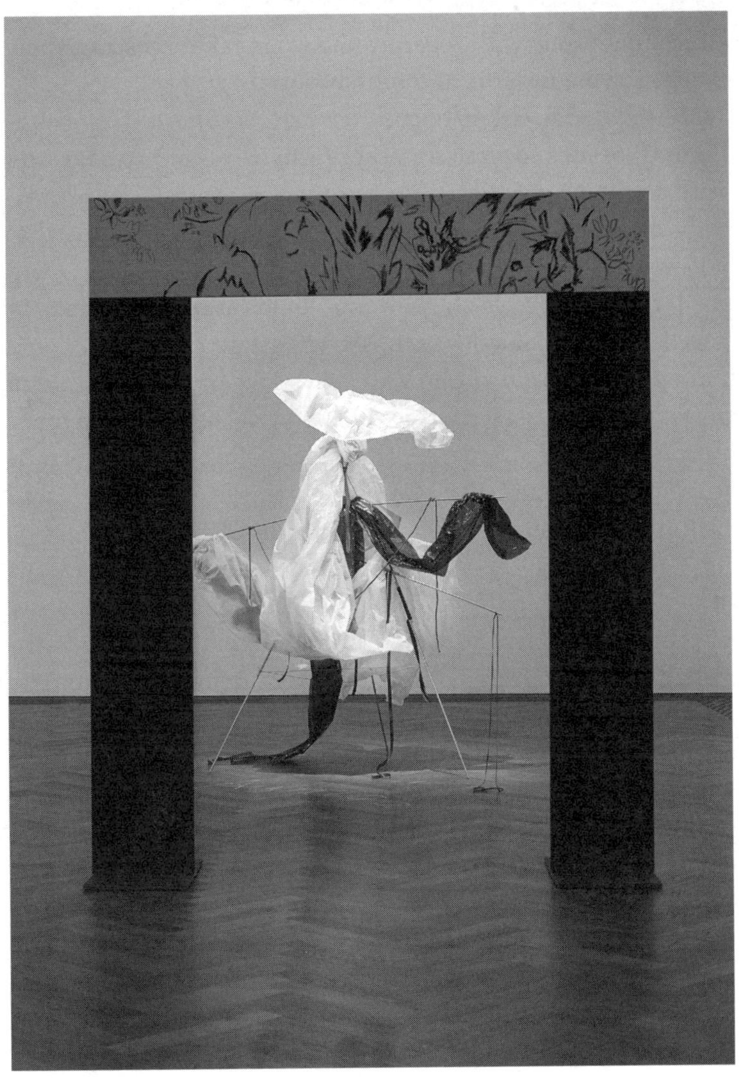

Installation view of *Bizarre Silks, Private Imaginings, and Narrative Facts, etc.*, Kunsthalle Basel, 2020. With Nick Mauss, *Thresholds*, 2020; and Rosemary Mayer, "reenactment" by Nick Mauss in collaboration with the Estate of Rosemary Mayer, *February Ghosts (Monoceros, Auriga, and Orion)*, 1981/2020.

ethical questions with regard to how one takes up space: how much, in what fashion, and for how long?

I hesitated to ask if I could remake the *Ghosts*. Not everything translates in time. In other instances I had remade and reiterated texts, textiles, rooms, costumes, scores—out of curiosity, as a way to understand from the inside something that no longer exists, or can't be exhibited, but must be seen—and yet I was not certain these works could be reconstructed. In parallel to my dialogues with Mayer's estate I had been living through the question of how an artwork changes in relation to new audiences, as a performer in the revival of Yvonne Rainer's 1965 *Parts of Some Sextets*.[11] The dance hadn't been performed in over 50 years, and, like Mayer's *Ghosts*, was essentially lost to history until Emily Coates and Rainer embarked on its restaging. Over several weeks we inhabited the process of its reconstruction, building the hour-long dance from documentation of the first performances, half of the original score (the other half had disappeared), and notes from Rainer's archive. The spaces opened up by such partial evidence (and by the erosion of memory) allowed for this new iteration of the dance to escape the trap of fidelity or any notion of an "original," while maintaining the overall structure and force of the work.

As a full-body preoccupation, this practice suggested the possibility that the *Ghosts* might also be approached as a score—that is, with rigor, sensitivity, and as a highly interpreted performance. What would it mean to present some version of them that was not an archival display of their documentation, but an enactment of their continued presence? Mayer's

11. See note 12, page 127.

estate responded with curiosity when I finally asked if they would consider re-presenting the *Ghosts* in Basel, seizing it as an experimental form of study, and an opportunity to create a dossier of information around these fleeting works that might be useful in the future. Mayer had made *Ghosts* often enough, and with enough variation, that they could be read as a set of flexible instructions. Part of their power lies in their realizability, in the fact that anyone might make something so emphatic out of next to nothing.

A procedure had to be invented. We studied the remnants of previous *Ghosts*: gold-painted dowels, colored foils, and ribbons, some of which Marie recalled were the same materials Mayer used to wrap gifts, or decorate tables for her elaborate dinners. Along with existing documentation we deduced a manner of construction and sourced the materials we needed. Chains of questions cropped up: how to name these *Ghosts*, how to differentiate them from those made by Mayer, how to signal to an audience encountering Mayer's work for the first time that these works emerged from a conceptual and performative procedure rather than a traditional mode of single authorship, how to address my role in performing them again now? The sessions during which we practiced making *Ghosts* in my studio became "rehearsals," and we deliberated over the implications of terms like "re-makes" or "exhibition copies," choosing instead to refer to the *Ghosts* to be exhibited in Basel as "reenactments," to underscore their relation to history and temporal transience, as well as to distinguish this procedure from the concerns of appropriation or post-appropriation artists. The challenge was to maintain irregularity, variability, improvisation, and instantaneity, and more importantly, what

Harmony Hammond described as Mayer's knack for "using cheap materials to perform opulence." Mayer's working notes for the *Ghosts* listed:

> *presence & absence*
> *paper—impermanence*
> *engagement not an issue—chance & trash*
> *transparency*
>
> *returning, dissolving*
> *impermanence of individuals of things/of appearances*
> *attempts to suggest*
> *attempts to catch appearances*
> *beauty and trash*
>
> *glass people*
>
> *Trial ghost with a cellophane heart*
> *Pix of shopping bag ladies*
>
> *Draping & structure acquire meaning*

I thought of the methodology developed by Aby Warburg in his study of the "Costumes of the Intermedia of 1589," which relied on tailor's expense ledgers, etchings, and written testimony as primary documents in the reconstruction of a specific style of costumed procession performed in sixteenth century Florence. In his fastidious analysis of the impact of these "intermedia" in the minds of its spectators Warburg argues: "There is only one way to make the descriptions [of costumed performances], which appear to us today at first sight as dry or strange lists, manifest as truly vivid memory pictures: namely by trying to consider them in connection with contemporaneous works of art . . ."[12] Warburg's formula for the production of "memory pictures" (*Erinnerungsbilder*) through the synthesis of archival documents and works of art fit with Mayer's own way of working, as well as my own. One important marker that distinguished the singularity of each presentation of *Ghosts* during Mayer's lifetime was the word written on the floor beneath it, "naming" each ghost after seasons, or subdivisions of the day according to hours of prayer, or constellations, or flowers. This echoes Mayer's insistence on the impermanence of her own work against the cyclical nature of lived and invented durations, occasions for celebration or coming together. To mark the new *Ghosts'* position in time and space, Marie Warsh had the idea to look for constellations that were visible in the night sky above Basel during the run of the exhibition. After a night of giving form to four ghosts in the Kunsthalle galleries, I wrote each of the names of these "February Ghosts" on the parquet floor beneath them in oilstick cursive: Monoceros, Gemini, Auriga, Orion.

"There are other rules," Mayer wrote, "there are other methods." While her work can be contextualized historically with that of her peers—Ree Morton, Sylvia Sleigh, Adrian Piper, Harmony Hammond, Howardena Pindell, or Tina Girouard—its relative independence (due to its false "newness", or rather, our belated consciousness) should provoke more far-reaching

12. Aby Warburg, "I costumi teatrali per gli Intermezzi del 1589. I disegni di Bernardo Buontalenti e il libro di conti di Emilio de' Cavalieri" (1895), in *Gesammelte Schriften* (Berlin: Akademie Verlag, 1998) 260. Our translation.

conversations with other contemporaries, including Sam Gilliam, Lili Dujourie, Michael Buthe, Diane Simpson, or Bas Jan Ader. In exhibiting Mayer's work in Basel I wanted to avert narratives of recuperation and mystification, to maintain the initial shock of the work by contextualizing it with jarringly distinct works by historical and contemporary makers. I had begun to see her everywhere, "in the fall of a sleeve," on a visit to Piero della Francesca's *Madonna del Parto*. Life and history are reconfigured in the encounter with a significant person or event, to make room for them. In Mayer's words: "What can I tell you about ghosts? A human figure is the densest sign. *Ghosts* are fronts, codes for nets of reference spread as wide as words." ◆

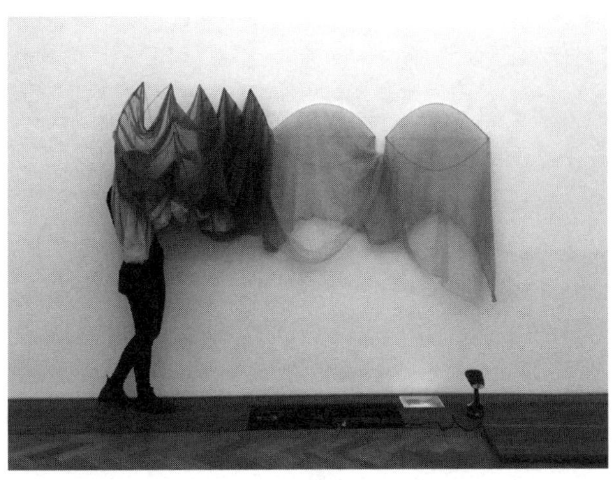

This essay was originally published in French in Perspective, no. 2023–2 (2023), the journal published by the Institut national d'histoire de l'art (INHA) in Paris.

In Anticipation
of a Body

I owe my introduction to working with costumes—beginning with the intimate, tactile encounter in the archive, where uncountable styles, temporalities, and techniques are compressed—to curator Célia Bernasconi, who invited me to collaborate with her on the 2015 exhibition *Designing Dreams, A Celebration of Léon Bakst*,[1] for which I conceived the exhibition scenography in every detail as an artistic intervention. Bernasconi understood implicitly that a contemporary perspective on Bakst's oeuvre could only be opened in the process of new production and a rethinking of the total work of art. The museum exhibitions I had staged previously involved breaking works "of art" out of conventional narratives and associations by period or medium to propose new genealogies, but my first experiences with textile objects exposed me to another dimension of affective charge, distinct from the more direct legibility of painting or sculpture, or the "historicist assumption that

1. *Designing Dreams, A Celebration of Léon Bakst*, curated by Célia Bernasconi and John Ellis Bowlt, at Villa Sauber, Nouveau Musée National de Monaco (October 23, 2016–January 15, 2017).

every event and every object has its proper location within objective and linear time."[2] Indicating the body as undeniably close, yet absent, costumes narrate their own multiple histories through the imagined time and place they evoke, as well as the real names of various performers stitched into their linings. This bonding of designers, artists, makers and performers in a single object complicates questions of authorship and presentation. But if, as Anne Hollander observed, "no surviving costume itself can convey its proper effect in context,"[3] then this distanced condition poses the challenge to imagine how different approaches to display can vivify what is not there, and to directly address the viewer through the simple fact that every one of them has worn, imagined, or made a costume for their own body or for another.

In the process of assembling stage designs, photographs, maquettes, costumes, textile designs, and drawings related to Bakst, I began to apprehend his lifework as a form of expanded painting—or rather, as the organic trajectory of a career from painting through theater to fashion, whose arc circumvented the categorical separations otherwise so staunchly border-policed. The exhibition scenography itself would need to communicate the all-enveloping impression his work left on the public imaginary, to show that his designs not only changed the sensorium of the stage, but also how spectators dressed, desired, and perceived. I resorted to the original techniques of the material itself—to the costume fabrics that had been directly

2. Alexander Nagel and Christopher S. Wood, *Anachronic Renaissance* (New York: Zone Books, 2010), 13.

3. Anne Hollander, "The Clothed Image: Picture and Performance," *New Literary History*, vol. 2, no. 3 (Spring 1971), 485.

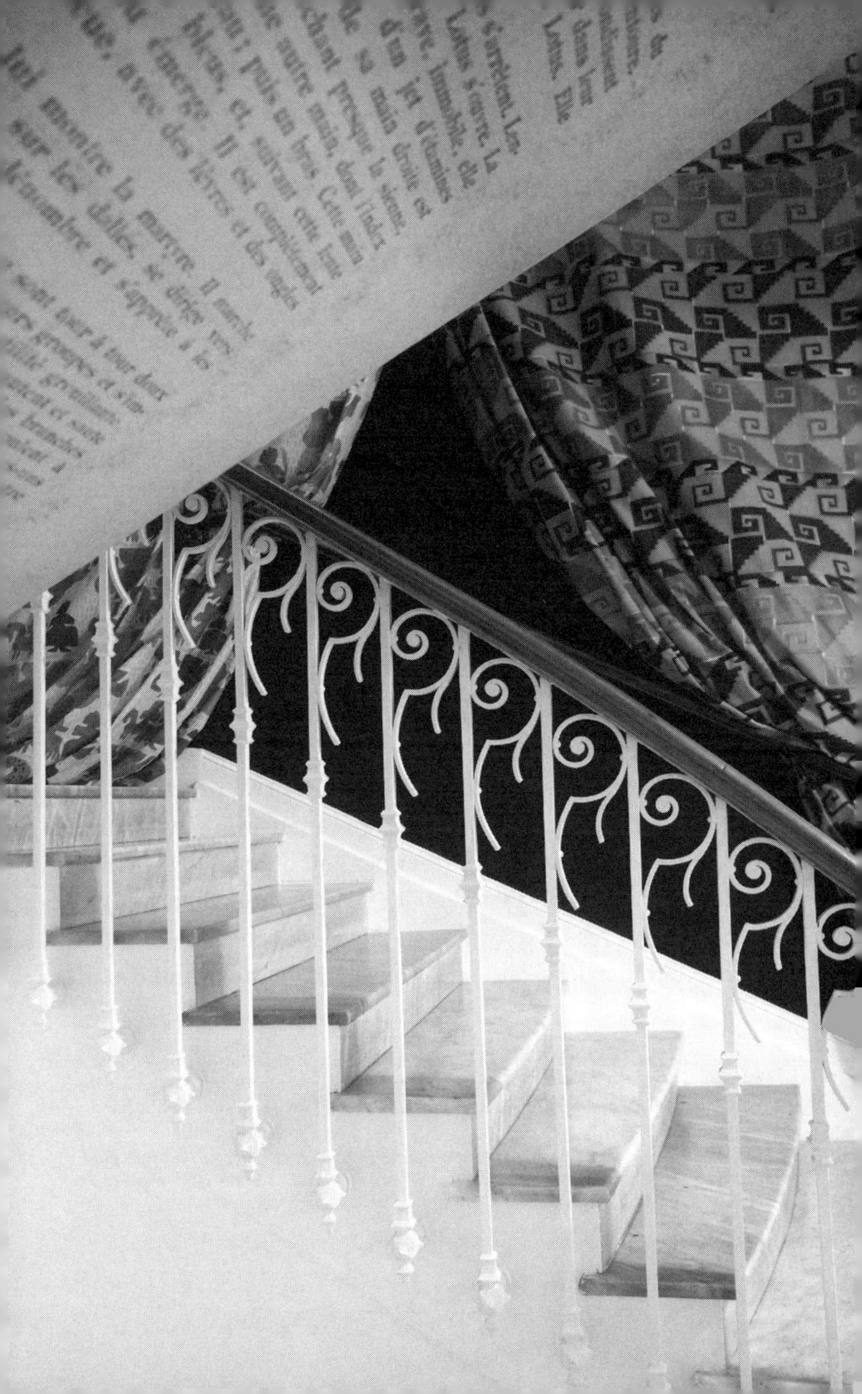

painted or airbrushed (rather than printed or woven) and the contemporaneous souvenir programs and magazines colored by pochoir—leading me to entirely hand-paint and stencil the scenography, which included re-making the late fabric designs Bakst produced for the New York company Clingen and Selig (who issued them as prints on silk for dress and furnishing in the 1920s, and of which only scraps remain in museum collections).[4] The resulting hand-painted *métrages* were hung in the entrance to the exhibition in a manner evocative of both modern department store fabric displays and Bakst's paradigmatic vision of ornamental excess for the 1910 ballet *Scheherazade*.

I located another nexus of modern art, fashion, and performance in the work of Florine Stettheimer, whose 1921 painting *Spring Sale at Bendel's* transposed the frenzied orgy scene from *Scheherazade* to the hystericized arena of conspicuous consumption, rendering in caricatural precision the battles among competing customers for last season's fashions in a velvet-draped department store warren of folding screens and mirrors. *Spring Sale at Bendel's* is a play, perhaps, on the traditional motif of "the hunt" as much as a self-ironizing depiction of the context in which Stettheimer and other artists exhibited their paintings side-by-side with seasonal merchandise in department stores.[5] Expanding to poems of radical vulnerability, decorated interiors, and sugary designs for stage and costume,

4. The covers of each copy of *Designing Dreams: A Celebration of Léon Bakst*, ed. Célia Bernasconi, John Ellis Bowlt, Nick Mauss, exh. cat. (Monaco: Nouveau Musée National de Monaco and Milan: Mousse Publishing, 2017) were also stenciled by hand. [Editors' note]

5. Heather Hole, "Florine Stettheimer, the Department Store, and the Spaces of Display, New York 1916–1926," *Panorama: Journal of the Association of Historians of American Art* 3, no. 2 (Fall 2017).

Stettheimer's art sits at odds with a conception of modernism shored up against decoration and theatricality; a modernity that was invented, in the words of Jacques Rancière, to "prevent a clear understanding of the transformations of art and its relationships with the other spheres of collective experience."[6] On the occasion of the 2014 Stettheimer survey at the Lenbachhaus in Munich,[7] I created reverse-glass mirrored paintings set into the museum's walls to suggest devices of transition and multiple points of view. Like oversize revolving doors or monumental dressing mirrors these surfaces activated a space where the viewer could negotiate oblique reflections of the exhibition and of their own poses entangled in the act of looking. "Performance implies a temporal act," writes Hollander:

Mental pictures composed of the body in its clothing are recreated at will in mirrors, which become pictures for the purpose. The concept of dress as an element in social role-playing is obvious and as common in sociological and psychological study as is the notion of theatrical dressing for particular dramatic roles. By pursuing further the study of actual clothing as if it were theatrical costume, one then passes beyond the basic notions of role into the realm of visual style, which has an organic life of its own in dress as it does in all its other manifestations in art."[8]

6. Jacques Rancière, *The Politics of Aesthetics. The Distribution of the Sensible*, trans. Gabriel Rockhill (New York & London: Continuum, 2004), 26.

7. *Florine Stettheimer*, curated by Karin Althaus, Matthias Mühling, and Susanne Böller, Lenbachhaus Kunstbau, Munich (September 27, 2014–January 4, 2015). See also the text, "Quivers in Time and Place. On Florine Stettheimer," pages 81–84.

8. Hollander, *art. cit.*, 477.

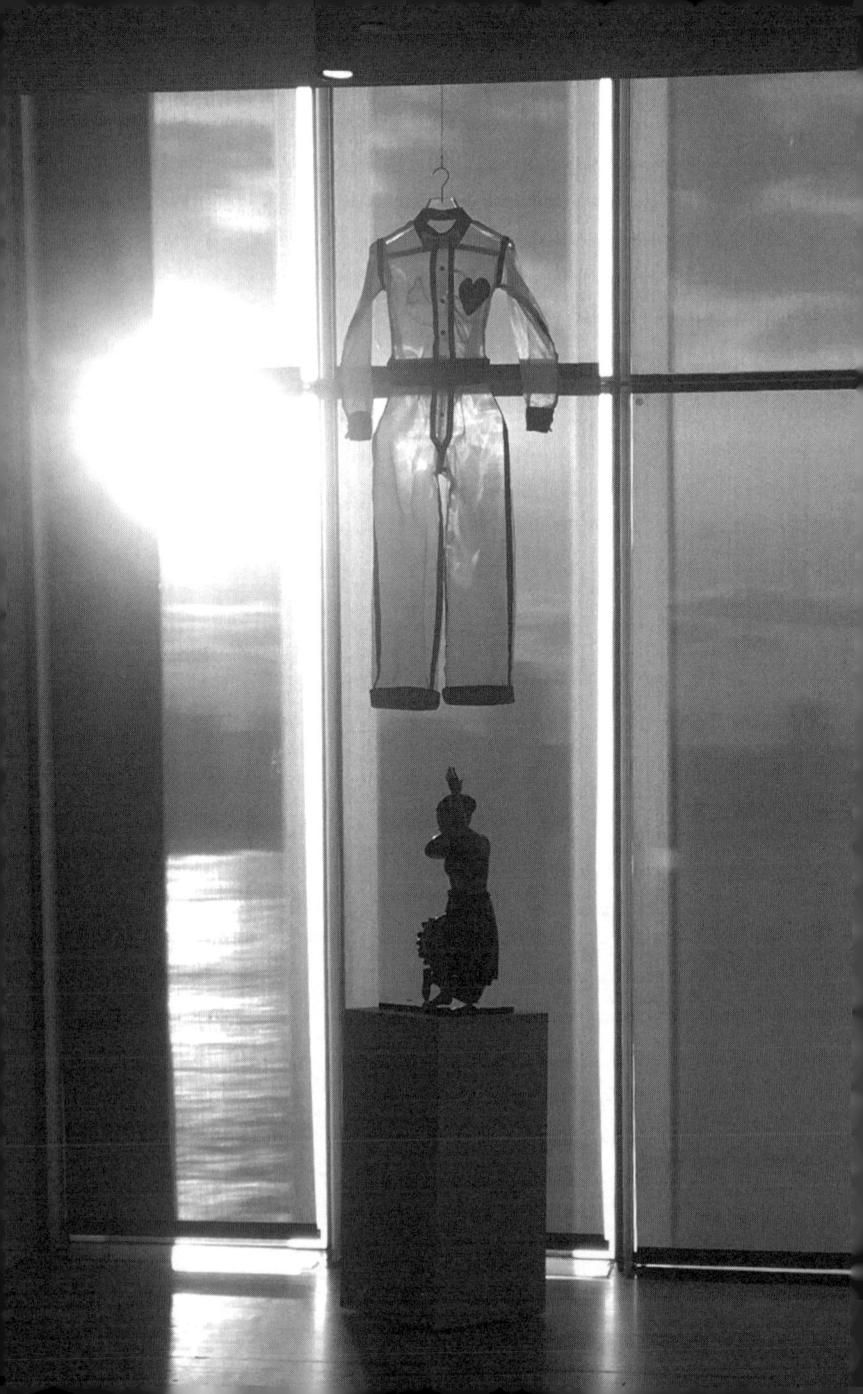

I had worked in window display for department stores as an art student—an anachronistic job that took me into nearly extinct New York City neighborhoods specializing in buttons, ribbons, artificial flowers, leather, and plastics, and that involved orchestrating tableaux in the shallow stage-like boxes behind plate-glass windows at night. Only later did I understand that this work was itself a complex art form related to theater, trailing a circuitous lineage of artists and designers, inseparable from the development of mid-twentieth-century vanguard art in the US. Like the posed and styled fashion photograph, the meticulously arranged window presented a general public with a literal showcase of the newest tendencies in art as enmeshed with the newest fashions, often responding in real-time to exhibitions, films, theatrical productions, or national politics. The phenomenon of these displays behind glass had served as perhaps the main conduit for Surrealism's entry into American popular consciousness, but also as a testing-ground for young artists, who presented their work in this stage-like space as a prelude to the ultimate validation of a gallery exhibition. As an indirect public discourse at street-level, Friedrich Kiesler declared that "the store window is a silent loud speaker," in his 1929 manual, *Contemporary Art Applied to the Store and its Display*.[9] And as a new condition of vision, the transparent and reflective glass that intervenes between daily life and the display of a culture's varied products and projections manifested explicitly in the work of artists including Marcel Duchamp and Joseph Cornell. Most relevant to my own formation was the little-discussed fact that "doing windows" (along with millinery,

9. Friedrich Kiesler, *Contemporary Art Applied to the Store and its Display* (New York: Brentano, 1929), 9.

fashion design, work in theater and ballet décor, and fashion photography) had been the tacit professional domain of queer men throughout the twentieth century and into the Cold War, the era in which US homophobia became expressed in explicitly anti-gay laws. Indeed, a queer history of modern art could be told through a careful reading of these public enactments of commodity fetishes, their various orchestrators, and the ways in which they uniquely maneuvered and dramatized the dense interplay of fashion, "high" art and camp.

The queer New York painter of mid-century social satire, Paul Cadmus, designed the sets and costumes for the populist American ballet *Filling Station* (1937), set in a gas station animated by dancing archetypes of extractive capitalism. Emphasizing the modernity of the production, Cadmus rendered the coveralls of Mac, the filling station attendant and main protagonist of the ballet, in completely transparent material—an innovation only recently made possible thanks to the invention of nylon in 1935. The promise of transparency as related to contemporary vision and embodiment can be traced throughout the pre-World War II avant-garde, from the artists already mentioned (including Stettheimer, who festooned her studio/apartment and the stage décor for Virgil Thomson and Gertrude Stein's 1933 opera *Four Saint in Three Acts* in masses of cellophane) to Francis Picabia's painted *transparences*, Pawel Tchelitchew's transparent torsos, or Naum Gabo and Antoine Pevsner's transparent sets and costumes fashioned out of rhodoid (another new transparent material) for the 1921 ballet *La Chatte*. Through fairy-tale ingenuity, Cadmus created a costume that was both "nude" and "clothed," and guaranteed that the dancers who filled Mac's role would be elevated to the status of sex symbols. In fact, photographs exist of dancer Jacques d'Amboise completely nude and exposed in Cadmus' transparent costume in addition to the "official" photographs in which d'Amboise's genitals have been air-brushed out. Relying on Cadmus' original drawings for the costume, alongside images by the fashion and ballet photographer George Platt Lynes, I recreated Mac's coveralls for my exhibition *Transmissions* at the Whitney Museum in 2018,[10] suspending the transparent costume over a 1916–18 bronze sculpture by the émigré artist Elie Nadelman of a "dancing figure" in a chiton (placed on a rotating pedestal), in front of a window overlooking the Hudson River and the remnants of a pier demolished in 1979, which until then had been frequented as a site for queer cruising. Dismissing the conventions of museological display in favor of the incongruous contrasts by which window displays seduce, I confronted two images of dress and dance—an art deco re-imagining of antiquity, and a preposterous futurism—against the backdrop of what the city had become.

The evocative potential of fashion, that "schoolroom for an awareness of the historicity of style" that "also confuses chronology,"[11] can expand art's histories to include dynamics of pose, modelling, recirculation, and temporal distortion. In place of a monolithic, linear "history of autonomous aestheticized objects,"[12] art history is rendered as a complex terrain expanded through other practices. My interest in medial transpositions that fray the contours of specific disciplines—the reciprocal

10. *Transmissions*, Whitney Museum of American Art, New York (March 16–May 14, 2018). See also the text, "Gesturing Personae," pages 117–4.

11. Wood and Nagel, *Anachronic Renaissance, op. cit.*, 89.

12. Griselda Pollock, *Vision & Difference: Femininity, Feminism, and the Histories of Art* (New York: Routledge, 1988), 25.

transfer between painting and scenography into fashion; window displays commenting on opera to sell clothes; the quotation of art and dance history in fashion photography—ultimately implies the mediation of fashion *as* a crucial dimension of art history. The *Théâtre de la Mode*, an exceptional exhibition from 1946, spans the eighteenth-century practice of *poupées de mode* (portable dolls wearing fashion samples) and post-World War II cultural diplomacy in the form of a monumental tribute to painting, fashion, and scenography. Devised as a travelling exhibition reaching across Europe and the US, it was the product of a collaboration between Parisian couturiers, stage designers and artists.[13] The *Théâtre de la Mode* remains an unlikely document of Transatlantic modernism that fits no single category: it is at once a time-capsule of 1946 couture collections, an exhibition of inter-war scenographic painting, a symbol of collective defiance, and an interdisplinary artwork. In 2022, on the occasion of Célia Bernasconi's survey of Christian Bérard, *Excentrique Bébé*,[14] I had the opportunity to devise a new display for a selection of mannequins from the *Théâtre*. Working with a sartorial atelier, I translated a pattern of crudely hand-drawn stars into a seamless fabric backdrop perforated with laser-cut, star-shaped openings, dramatically back-lit as a tattered expanse on which the floating mannequins modeled 1946 fashions for the present.

---

13. About the *Théâtre de la Mode*, see "The Painter of Inner Life. On Christian Bérard," pages 217–21.

14. *Christian Bérard, Excentrique Bébé*, curated by Célia Bernasconi at Villa Paloma, Nouveau Musée National de Monaco (July 9–October 16, 2022).

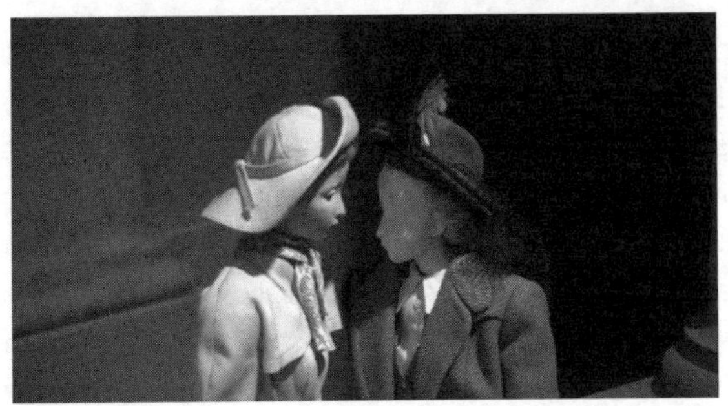

In 2020 I staged *Bizarre Silks, Private Imaginings and Narrative Facts, etc.* at Kunsthalle Basel, an exhibition of works by historic and contemporary artists and unnamed makers.[15] The exhibition was titled after its central juxtaposition of Edward Owens' exquisite filmic portrait of his mother, *Private Imaginings and Narrative Facts* (1966), and vitrines displaying seventeenth- and eighteenth-century textiles of a type called "bizarre silks," originally made into sumptuous gowns, and later, when the eccentric patterning had fallen out of fashion, reconstructed into religious vestments, and finally, cut apart centuries later to be sold piecemeal to collectors and archives.[16] In adjoining rooms of the exhibition, I included works by Rosemary Mayer, whose textile constructions from the 1970s were named after forgotten historical female figures in an adamantly feminist insistence on counteracting their erasure. Made from readily available, inexpensive materials, Mayer's *Ghosts* were assembled to create instantaneous and fleeting traces of embodiment.

15. *Bizarre Silks, Private Imaginings and Narrative Facts, etc.*, at Kunsthalle Basel (February 7–September 20, 2020).

16. About bizarre silks, see the text, *"Interwoven Globe: The Worldwide Textile Trade 1500–1800* and *Decorum: Carpets and Tapestries by Artists,"* page 59.

After detailed study of the materials and techniques involved in making the *Ghosts*, I embarked (with Mayer's estate and the artist Amanda Friedman) on several "rehearsals" in my studio to achieve the variable, improvised, and apparently casual sensibility of these apparitions—literally "performing" Mayer's works according to the protocols she had established for these figures of instability. The process of giving form to the *Ghosts* required a simultaneous recollection and forgetting of rudimentary struggles with techniques of making: learning to tie knots, assembling a tent, helping a child get dressed, wrapping a gift, decorating a table. At the same time, the process conjured sophisticated actions such as "draping," or making an effigy.[17] At Kunsthalle Basel the *Ghost* "reenactments" were shown together with video documentation of a performance for late-night television by the artist and window-dresser Victor Hugo Rojas, whose 1970s tableaux for Halston's boutiques showed mannequins misbehaving, giving birth, and engaging in acts of destruction. In the recording by artist Anton Perich, Rojas performs an elaborate travesty of art and fashion to a disco soundtrack, slicing a knife through his own likeness by Andy Warhol, "dressing" himself in toilet paper, shaving cream and baby powder and irreverently quoting Schiaparelli. Appearing incommensurable at first, Rojas' and Mayer's (and by proxy, my) acts of refashioning were performances of presence, against disappearance. ◆

17. See also the essay, "Remaking Ghosts. On Rosemary Mayer," pages 265–76.

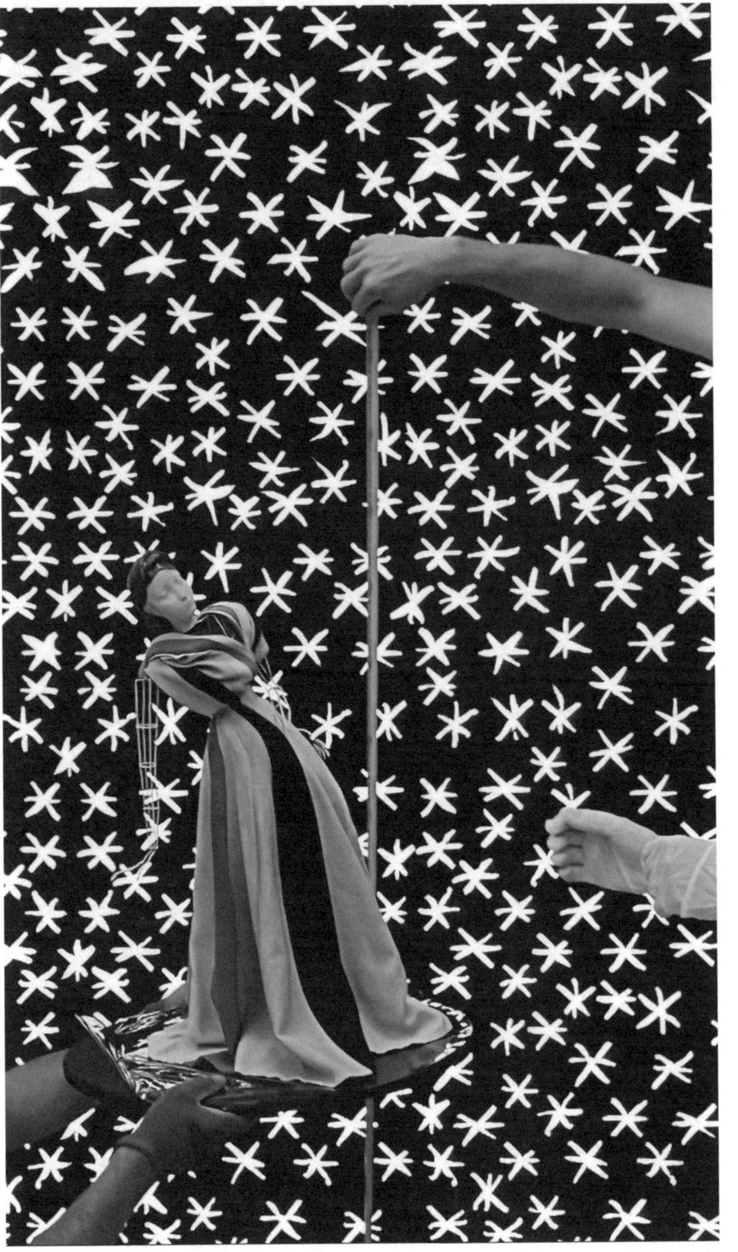

AUTHOR'S ACKNOWLEDGEMENTS

Thank you to everyone who invited me to write (or speak), and
to the brilliant editors who sharpened my ideas: Tim Griffin,
Elisabeth Schambelan, Scott Rothkopf, Michelle Kuo, Lucy Ives,
Caroline Busta, Barbara Schroeder, Karen Kelly, Ana Janevski,
Martha Joseph, David Joselit, Adam Lehner, Hilton Als, Claire
Gilman, Matthias Mühling, Karin Althaus, Baptiste Pinteaux,
Émilie Hammen, Marine Kisiel, Matthieu Leglise, Marie Caillat,
Negar Azimi, Michael Vazquez, Kyle Croft, Thomas Beard, Élisabeth
Lebovici, Célia Bernasconi, and Elisabeth Sussman, as well as
Emanuela Campoli and Gil Presti for championing my work.

My thanks to Lynne Cooke for her inspiring and category-
defying work, and for her beautiful introduction to this volume.

I am indebted to Ken Okiishi—always my first
and fiercest reader—for giving everything, and for
coaxing my voice to the page again and again.

Thank you to 303 Gallery and Galerie Chantal Crousel, and to Phil
and Shelley Fox Aarons for their years of support and friendship.

And to every artist, couturier/e, curator, filmmaker, director,
choreographer, and author whose work still hasn't let go of me.

Above all, thank you to Antonia Carrara and Benjamin Thorel
for lovingly giving form to this collection and to everything
they do. I can't begin to name the ideas and books they have
exposed me to, and the precise spirit of generosity, devotion,
and humor that defines their experimental proposition.
After 8 Books is a persistent and necessary divagation
in our world, a model without a blueprint or goal.

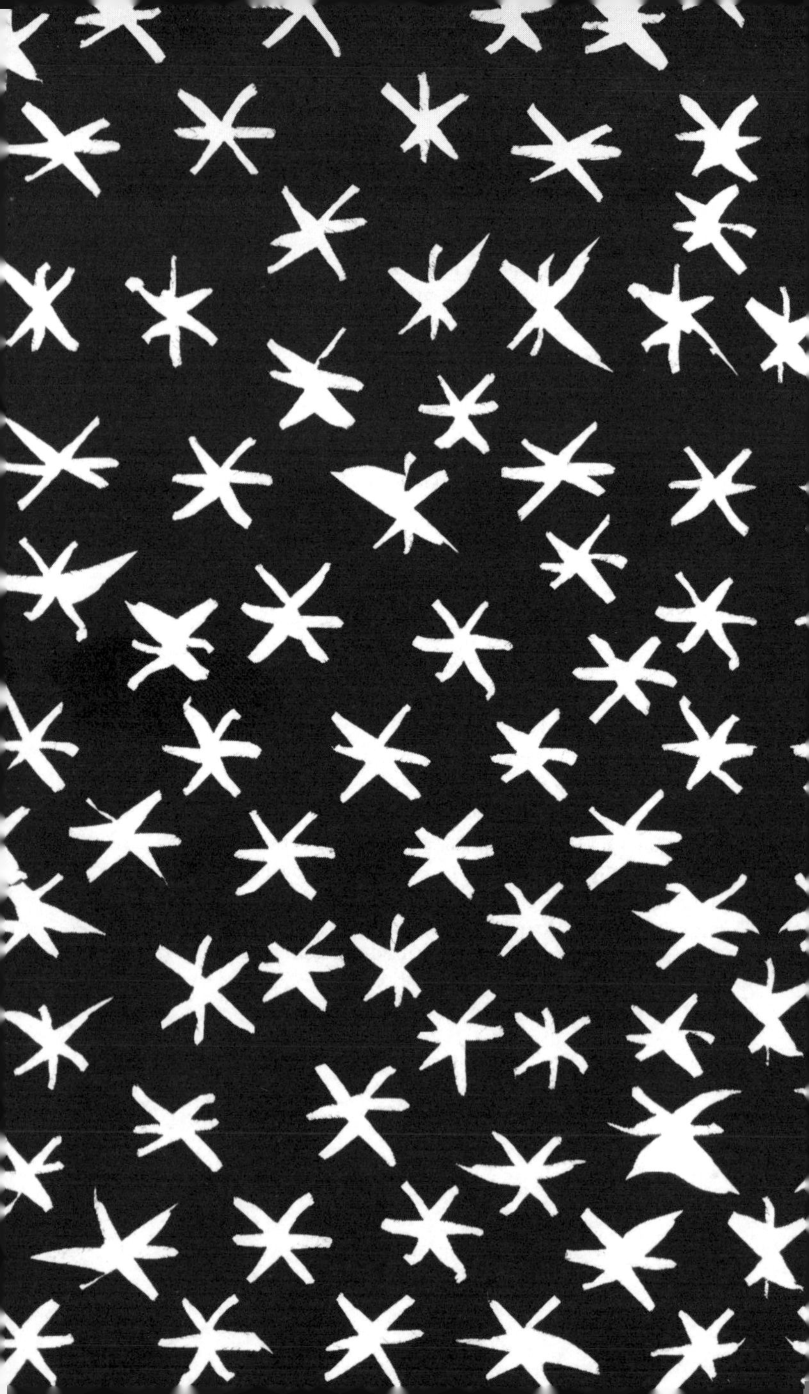